In *Islam and Resistance in Afghanistan*, Olivier Roy convincingly argues that the forces opposing Marxist rule of the country, though advocating a return to the basic tenets of Islam, are not all reactionary or backward-looking. Indeed, he contends that an Islamic revolution, advocating a modernisation of Afghan society, took place under the eyes of the Russian occupation forces, whose efforts to contain it served mainly to consolidate it.

In this new edition, the author expands his penetrating study of the history, ideology and structures of the Afghan resistance movement to mid-1989. He examines the evolution of the military and political situation inside Afghanistan during the last years of the Soviet presence and discusses relations between the Afghan resistance and the Islamic fundamentalist movements. The situation created by the Soviet withdrawal from the country is also explored and in a new conclusion Professor Roy assesses to what extent the war has altered the traditional fabric of Afghan society.

Professor Olivier Roy is a researcher at the Centre National de la Recherche Scientifique.

Some reviews of the first edition:

"This is the most instructive study of the Afghan response to Marxist rule and Soviet intervention published to date. It is based on Roy's several lengthy visits throughout Afghanistan between 1980 and 1985 . . . this is preeminently a study of Afghan society, religion and politics in an elemental struggle for cultural and national survival."   *South Asia*

"This superb book . . . has instantly become the standard reference work on the subject."   *Religion in Communist Lands*

Cambridge Middle East Library

Islam and resistance in Afghanistan

Cambridge Middle East Library

Islam and resistance in Afghanistan

OLIVIER ROY

CENTRE NATIONAL DE LA RECHERCHE SCIENTIFIQUE

Second edition

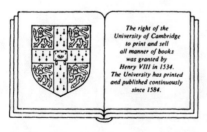

The right of the
University of Cambridge
to print and sell
all manner of books
was granted by
Henry VIII in 1534.
The University has printed
and published continuously
since 1584.

CAMBRIDGE UNIVERSITY PRESS

CAMBRIDGE

NEW YORK   PORT CHESTER

MELBOURNE   SYDNEY

Published by the Press Syndicate of the University of Cambridge
The Pitt Building, Trumpington Street, Cambridge CB2 1RP
40 West 20th Street, New York, NY 10011, USA
10 Stamford Road, Oakleigh, Melbourne 3166, Australia

Originally published in French as *L'Afghanistan: Islam et modernité politique* by
Éditions du Seuil, Paris, and © Éditions du Seuil, 1985

First published in English by Cambridge University Press as *Islam and resistance in
Afghanistan*. English translation © Cambridge University Press 1986, 1990
Translation by First Edition, Gwydir St, Cambridge
Reprinted 1988
Second edition published 1990

British Library cataloguing in publication data

Roy, Olivier, *1949–*
   Islam and resistance in Afghanistan. – 2nd ed. – (Cambridge
   Middle East library ; 8).
   1. Afghanistan. Politics. Role of Muslims
   1. Title
   332.10882971

Library of Congress cataloguing in publication data

Roy, Olivier, 1949–
   [Afghanistan. English]
   Islam and resistance in Afghanistan / Olivier Roy. – 2nd ed.
      p.   cm. – (Cambridge Middle East library)
   Translation of: L'Afghanistan.
   Includes bibliographical references
   ISBN 0 521 39308 6 – ISBN 0 521 39700 6 (pbk)
      1. Islam and politics – Afghanistan.   2. Islam – Afghanistan.
   3. Afghanistan – History – Soviet occupation, 1979–1989.   1. Title.
   II. Series.
   BP63.A54R6813   1990
   322'.1'09581–dc20   90-1709   CIP

ISBN 0 521 39308 6 hardback
ISBN 0 521 39700 6 paperback

Transferred to digital printing 2001

Contents

Acknowledgements

My information on the Afghan resistance has been gleaned during six journeys made between 1980 and 1985. I have greatly profited from information brought back by Jean-José Puig and others who have made similar journeys. I am also indebted to the two information centres in Europe: CEREDAF in Paris, founded by the AFRANE Association, and the Bibliotheca Afghanica at Liestal in Switzerland.

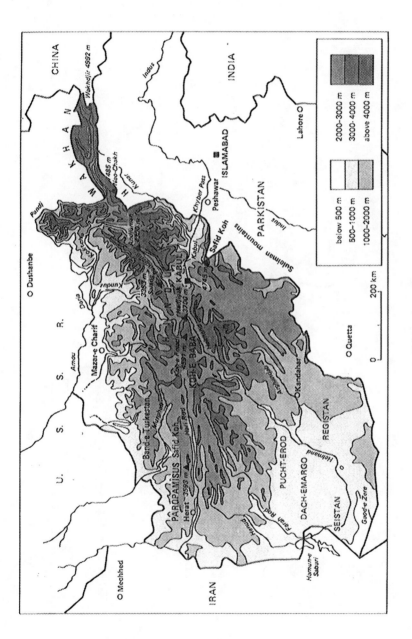

1 Afghanistan

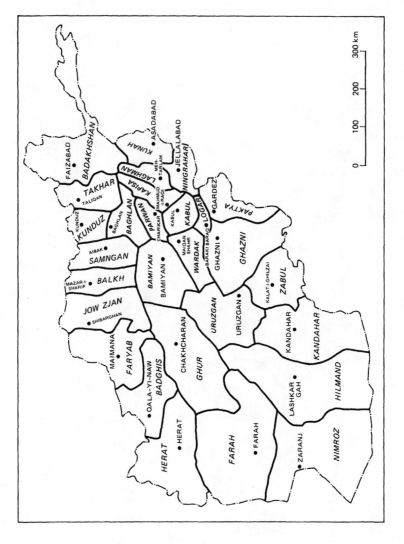

2 The provinces after 1964

Introduction

What interests us in an account of the Afghanistan resistance movement? Has this movement already receded into the past, its history to be written as an obituary? Such resignation in the face of a defeat which has not yet occurred presupposes a specific view of history: that nothing can stand in the way of the Soviet system and that when it has steamrollered its way across a country steeped in the age-old traditions of Islam, something fundamentally new will be born, obliterating the past. This is the posthumous triumph of Marxism over those very people who oppose it, yet accept that its ultimate victory is assured.

Even though the resistance movement cannot hope for a clear-cut military victory, no-one can deny that guerilla wars are political wars and that in the end the slow wearing away of a colonial power may still be decisive. Whatever the outcome of this war, the Soviet system is evolving, as is the contemporary world of Islam. The Afghan resistance movement lies at the intersection of these two histories. Far from being a mere spontaneous revolt, it has its roots in the popular Muslim uprisings of the past and also in the current of Islamic reformism, which runs from Shah Waliullah to the contemporary so-called fundamentalists. This story, as yet untold, will increase our understanding of the link between Islam and the popular movements. Finally, whether the armed resistance is successful or not, the lines of force which it embodies will necessarily be present in the Afghanistan of the future, whether that Afghanistan is free or is under Soviet control.

The various liberation movements have struck a chord in the West because they appeared to echo a universal concern with the workers of the world or the liberation of the Third World. Western intellectuals, who started by vehemently supporting movements which they saw as embodying the onward march of history, soon settled for more ethical protests in the name of human rights, and, by so doing, often ignored historical development and even the concrete reality of the events they condemned. This shift of focus is evident when we compare the support for the Palestinians, the most recent embodiment of a universal value, with the affair of the "boat people", who, as passive victims, were almost overlooked. However, the Afghan resistance movement is very much a historical phenomenon. A people of victims and martyrs they may be, but they are also a people with a long history who have grasped the meaning of their struggle.

To many people, the Afghan resistance movement seems to be a survival from the past, a struggle in pursuit of narrow sectional interests. The mullah and the warrior are two stereotypes which the media present in their accounts of the war. Tribalism is seen as a survival from a folk past, hence sub-political; fundamentalism is defined as fanaticism, and thus as politically retrograde. It is precisely the link between these two sets of ideas that this book sets out to question, because what is at stake is not only the question of the Afghan resistance but the whole issue of politics in Muslim countries – the rebirth of tribalism, of the *asabiyya*, in the heart of modern states such as Syria and the Lebanon,[1] the spread of Islamic revivalism in all its forms, ranging from the Iranian revolution to the preaching in the mosque in Regent's Park. The emergence of nation-states founded on secular ideologies may once have seemed to be the route which societies must necessarily take if they were to undergo modernisation, rejecting tribalism as a form of primitivism and confining religion to the inner world of the individual. But the movements of the last few years show that matters are not so simple. The Iranian revolution has taken the state as its political unit and has developed policies of regional expansion by means of warfare and the patronage of Shi'ite minorities in the Lebanon and Afghanistan (a status which those same minorities have been unwilling to accept). On the other hand, in the states called modern because they are secular, sectional interests based on geography, religion or race have developed, and their proponents are ever ready to appropriate state institutions to their own ends – a development which clearly calls into question the whole idea of the development of the universal nation-state. The Palestinians and the Kurds alone seem to be striving to give expression to a national identity. Even in the "progress-ive" movements we find traces of the old *asabiyya*: aristocracies in decline in the case of the Iranian Tudeh (dominated by the Qadjar princes) or the Baluchi *sardar* of the National Liberation Front; tribal rivalries at work in the Afghan Khalq and Parcham; or the identification of the community with a political party.

This rapid survey of the politics of the Middle East (to limit ourselves to the Muslim world) shows that the definition of what constitutes modernity is not as clear-cut as it might once have seemed, and so we are led to question commonly accepted ideas. There is no need to invert the usual pattern in order to redefine modernity as traditionalism; rather, we should reflect on the concepts of the "revival of religion", "fundamentalism", "the development of political society" and of "civil society". Since the structure of society in Afghanistan has not been undermined by colonialism, it provides us with an excellent opportunity of testing the validity of these concepts. But before embarking on a more detailed study we should define the terms we shall be using.

Obscurantism, the Middle Ages, fascism, clericalism . . . the most arrant nonsense has been written on the subject of the religious revival in the Muslim world. The West has long been haunted by the spectre of Islam. The different phenomena that are usually lumped together under the heading of "fundamentalism" are many and varied and should be regarded as quite distinct; in fact, only one of these movements (Islamism) is totally new. We should see the revival of Islam not in terms of our own recent history, which typically views the modern state as the end-product of a process of secularisation within society, but in the light of the historical and social context of the Muslim world.

By traditionalism we mean the desire to freeze society so that it conforms to the memory of what it once was: it is society as described by our grandfathers. In this vision history and tradition are merged; the historical development of society is effaced in favour of an imaginary timeless realm under attack from pernicious modernity. Traditionalism can never provide the basis for any coherent political programme; it is riddled with nostalgia and its politics naturally incline towards all that is conservative. At the same time it is quite capable of profiting from economic development, and the nostalgia is concerned more with morals than social justice. It embraces social customs: the veiling of women, filial obedience, and respect for hierarchies. The social stratum which is the vehicle of this ideology is the landed gentry, and in Afghanistan the *khan*, who still feels ill at ease in the town.

Fundamentalism is quite different: for fundamentalism it is of paramount importance to get back to the scriptures, clearing away the obfuscation of tradition. It always seeks to return to some former state; it is characterised by the practice of re-reading texts, and a search for origins. The enemy is not modernity but tradition or rather, in the context of Islam, everything which is not the Tradition of the Prophet (the *sunnat*). This is true reform. In itself fundamentalism sits uneasily within the political spectrum, for the "return to first things" may take many different forms. First, there is the return to strict religious practice, found most frequently in emigré circles. A return to the carrying out of the injunctions of the scriptures (the study of the Qur'an and the *hadith*) is the fundamentalism of the *madrasa*; while a return to the religious law, to the practice of the *shari'at*, is the fundamentalism of the *'ulama*. The

3

return to the scriptures brings with it the birth of a new tradition and the establishment of a new system of exegesis which obscures the text as much as it illuminates it. Thus, this search for origins has not the same meaning for an *'alim*, who interprets what he reads in the light of a tradition of scholastic commentary, as for a young intellectual who seeks exemplars from the like and times of the Prophet upon which to model his life. Not only does the definition of fundamentalism vary greatly (a return, yes, but a return to what?), but the political implications of fundamentalism will also differ according to the cultural context. In a country like Afghanistan, where everyday life revolves around Islamic religious practices and where common law in the non-tribal zones is impregnated by the *shari'at*, fundamentalism is not very different from traditionalism. On the other hand, where fundamentalism appears in urban environments or in countries where the social structure has been disrupted by modernisation, as in Iran, it opposes the status quo and evolves towards political Islamism. I have previously compared fundamentalism to sixteenth-century protestantism;[2] there is the same complexity in the way in which the Reformation influenced the social movements of the period so that it became a vehicle for the German aristocracy, as there is in millenarian peasant revolts or bourgeois republics which fabricate modern democracy. It is important to avoid automatically identifying the religious attitude with its political expression. Within the body of the *'ulama* we encounter a certain reserve towards fundamentalism. All that can be said is that in Afghanistan fundamentalism, defined as a desire to get back to *shari'at* as the sole authority, is the natural attitude of the educated clergy, the *'ulama*, whereas the mullah of the villages, who have not mastered the whole corpus of the law, are traditionalists and not fundamentalists.

This leads us on to the question of clericalism: can we not see fundamentalism as an expression of the political ambitions of the clergy and scholars, that is to say those who have an expert knowledge of the sacred texts and exercise control over their exegesis? This line of thought leads to the paradox that those who stand to gain by a return to the sacred texts are precisely those whose existence is nowhere envisaged within those very same texts: there is no such thing as an established clergy in the Qur'an, no rock on which to build the church. The clergy as an institution dates only from the Middle Ages. The *fiqh*, the concrete application of the *shari'at* to society, is the product of a thousand years of commentary, a process of reading and re-reading. The text itself has been lost, and the *fiqh* is usually taught by means of summaries of commentaries on other commentaries.

Sunni Islam has no organised clergy. The clergy are not a social body

4

with a clearly defined set of interests. It is not mere chance that it is Sh'ite Iran which has seen the dominance of the clergy, whereas nowhere in the Sunni world has the *'ulama* gained power. Even in Wahhabite Saudi Arabia the attitude of the *'ulama* to politics is more secular than one might think, since they are willing to acknowledge that there is such a thing as a legitimate de facto political power, something which the Sh'ite clergy are unwilling to accept. The fact that there is an officially constituted branch of the Islamic religion in the USSR is an indication of this. Yet, if fundamentalism is defined as being a return to the Holy Scriptures of Islam, this poses the problem of the relation between the corpus of Holy Writ and its exegesis. There is little in common between a Qadhafi, for whom the only sacred text is the Qur'an, and a classical *'alim* for whom fundamental texts (such as the Qur'an and *hadith*) could not possibly exist without the commentaries and their interpreters (the *'ulama*). This explains why the fundamentalism of the *'alim* is essentially juridical and not political.

The fundamentalism of the *'ulama* conceives society as being governed by law: social space is regulated by objective norms, which are as independent of the whims of the prince as is the doctrine of positive law in the West (that is to say neither more so nor less). The West's criticism of the *shari'at* (its harshness, its primitive quality) should not blind us to the fact that it is, nevertheless, a system of law. There is no such thing as totalitarianism (the reduction of civil to political society) in Islamic countries, in so far as in Islam the development and interpretation of law does not depend on the state. By definition, a return to the *shari'at* can be neither fascist nor totalitarian (which does not mean that it is therefore democratic). Western criticism of the *shari'at* brings into play different cultural values. We will not involve ourselves in this debate (which is often sterile and in which each of the parties is frequently guilty of hypocrisy), but will merely note that it rests upon a consensus which recognises that the concept of society governed by law involves the further concept of a code of law, personal freedom and limits to despotic powers. Furthermore, and particularly in the countryside, the legal order established by the *shari'at* is seen as a protection against economic injustice. Even if, in reality, it fails to fulfil this role (for example, because of corruption), what is important is that it provides a spiritual resource for the peasant when faced with injustice and, in the final analysis, if driven to revolt he will find in it the blueprint for a political organisation compatible with his cultural universe.

Some commentators see fundamentalism as the negation of the tradition of spirituality which is so typical of Islam, as if it were true to say that the letter kills the spirit.[3] There is, however, a complication here, in that the study of Islam by Europeans has traditionally focused on Morocco, Algeria and Tunisia, in which countries the great figures of nationalist fundamentalism, such as 'Abdul Krim and Ben Badis, were very much opposed to Maraboutism, which they condemned for its heresy and its collaboration with the colonial powers. It is possible to find forms of Maraboutism in the tribal areas of Afghanistan, but the form of Sufism which predominates in that country is fundamentalist by tradition, just as it is in the Indian subcontinent, a point to which we shall return. In the same way the great anti-colonial movements have nearly always resulted from a tribal uprising, accompanied by the emergence of a charismatic leader, originating from a Sufist background. In this respect Afghanistan is different from North Africa, in that here Sufism, fundamentalism, millenarianism and the anti-colonial struggle go hand-in-hand. Thus it is clear that fundamentalism embraces the whole spectrum of attitudes, ranging from tradition to political opposition.

On the other hand, a new phenomenon came into being in the thirties, both in Egypt and in the Indian subcontinent: the movement known as the Muslim Brotherhood.[4] Forty years later, many students of Muslim religious movements have come to the conclusion that it is no longer possible to interpret the politics of the Islamic world by restricting themselves to concepts such as fundamentalism and traditionalism; for which reason the term "Islamism" was coined.[5] What is meant by this and in what way is it new? First, with regard to the social origins of the militants: far from having emerged from the clergy or traditional circles, they are to be found within the modern institutions of society (colleges, faculties of science, and in general in the urban environment). Next, there is the political connection: the Islamists speak of Islamist ideology rather than of religion in the strict sense of the term. The great challenge that faces them is to create from Islam a political model capable of competing with the great ideologies of the Western world. In the forefront of their thinking is the problem of the state (the "Islamic republic"). They have worked out a theory concerning the nature of the political party, and their political militancy goes hand-in-hand with a sense of history. Instead of wishing, like the *'ulama*, to manage civil society, their ambition is to reconstruct society, starting with the state. It is, therefore, not surprising that relations between the Islamists and the *'ulama* are marked with a mutual mistrust. Islamism is not a form of clericalism, for the simple reason that, except in Iran, its members are not drawn from the ranks of the clergy.

In one sense, the fundamentalism of the Islamists is more radical than that of the *'ulama*: what they seek is not a return to the *shari'at*, which is a means not an end, but the total reconstruction of political relations on the lines of the first Muslim community. No longer state and law but utopia, the millennium and revolution. In this context, the return to first things makes it possible not only to circumvent the accretion of tradition, but the social stratum which manipulates that tradition, namely, the clergy. Although their hoped-for reconstruction of society is based upon a mythical model, it nevertheless provides a pre-eminent role for a new kind of "cleric" – the intellectual. For the difference between the intellectual and the religious scholar is that the former takes the state as his ultimate point of reference. Whether or not he finds himself in militant opposition to the status quo, his political dialogue is conducted with the state, for his education (the school), his position in the political process, and his place in society (he is frequently a civil servant) all presuppose that there is such a thing as the state. The *'alim*, on the other hand, is indifferent to the state, for he belongs to a stratum of society which does not depend on the state for its continued existence. The intellectual justification for his existence, the Muslim *umma*, represents a corpus of writings which is quite independent of the secular state. In the Muslim world, civil society is a society ordered by religious law and it is the state which, in the final analysis, may appear narrow and "fanatical". This is the fanaticism of "might is right" and the refusal to accept that the individual has certain inalienable rights; the fanaticism of the *asabiyya* which can only maintain itself in power by opposing all other social forces. The particularism of the state explains why it can be personified: the theme of the "good ruler" or the good guide is of great importance in the Muslim world. Though tyranny is possible, there is no place for totalitarianism, and the Islamists have been made aware of this in the face of the cohesion of the *asabiyya* and of a civil society administered by the *'ulama*. At least, this is how things stand in Afghanistan, where there is a constellation of closely knit groups (the *qawm*) and a society founded upon religious law. The two social systems (Syria and Libya) which have seen the emergence of dictators are those in which only *asabiyya* comes between the individual and the state. In Iran the clergy have taken upon themselves the task of asserting Islamic rights, this being due to the particular nature of the Shi'ite clergy. In this case there is no distinction between the *shari'at* and Islamist ideology, which fact, as can never be sufficiently emphasised, has only served to undermine the *shari'at*. As evidence of this, consider the eccentric system of legislation at present in force in Iran, which borrows its external symbolism from the *shari'at* but is, at heart, secular; further evidence of this is provided by the confusion between the clergy and the revolutionary party. As ever, Iran appears as the exception and not as the prototype of the "Islamic republic".

Since the Islamists have no intrinsic means of exerting political leverage on secular society, the way forward must lie in their links with the *'ulama*. The only alternative tactic for exercising influence in secular society is that of attempting to make political capital out of people's everyday grievances, which, as experiments carried out by the local communist parties have shown, only pays short-term dividends. In fact, Afghanistan provides a rare and instructive example of cooperation between *'ulama* and Islamists, probably because the Afghan Islamists were not cut off from traditional society. To be more explicit, among Afghan Islamists one finds neither a hatred of the West nor the anti-semitism which is so characteristic of those groups in Egypt which go under the same name. This, no doubt, is one of the advantages of not having been subjected to the colonial experience, but it is also due to the profound mistrust the Afghan rebels feel for the PLO, which is seen by them as being pro-Soviet.

Value judgements on Islamism need to be revised, and its modernity must once more be emphasised. To say this is not to adopt a partisan stance as far as Islamism is concerned, nor to accept that it has all the answers to the crises which afflict Muslim societies today; but rather to affirm that its goals, like its social origins, are certainly contemporary. Its outdated views on social customs need not engage us unduly. The most controversial question, the role of women, involves a cultural element which goes far beyond Islamism, and even Islam itself; while extreme puritanism often comes to the fore during revolutionary periods. The fact that such attitudes are commonplace in Muslim countries leads to the conclusion not only that the problem is often posed out of context, but that the virulent polemics one hears so frequently in the West concerning the treatment of Muslim women conceals a deeper preoccupation. In any case, we should make a distinction between two quite different things: the position of Muslim women in traditional society, which cannot be blamed on Islamism, and the way in which Islamism is attempting to ensure that urban, educated – and therefore emancipated – women should come to accept the dictates of Islam.[6]

I am in no doubt that the key to understanding modern developments is first to grasp the importance of the transition to political society. But the perspective within which we should view this transition is clearly not purely religious, nor even ideological. Afghanistan illustrates well the problems of the transition to political society, particularly with regard to the question of tribalism, the state and more universal implications.

In Muslim countries, with the exception of a few states (such as Egypt, Iran and Morocco) which have an indigenous tradition that strongly emphasises the role of the state, loyalties are divided between the more localised community (*asabiyya – qawm* in Afghanistan) and the *umma*, the Muslim community. The "Arab nationalism" of Baathist ideology is but one variant of this. The development of modern states exhibits the same tension, and this fact explains the many short-lived unions which have been arranged between different states (here Libya holds the record, but Syria is another case in point). It also helps us to understand why the state apparatus has often been captured by one communal group or another, whether religious or tribal. Afghanistan provides a particularly rich field of study for the transition. First, in the period when the state came into existence through the formation of a tribal federation (1747–1978), secondly, the moment of the communist *coup d'état* of 1978, and finally the resistance. Each of these breaks with the past was carried out in the name of a universal ideology (nationalism, Marxism, fundamentalism, mingled with Islamism), but the forms they took are evidence of the persistence of communal groups. Let it be stated here quite clearly that there is no possibility of a stable Marxist regime emerging from the present conflict. If the resistance is defeated Afghanistan will be a Soviet province, without any firm basis in law. As far as the resistance is concerned, matters are more complicated. The future of the resistance depends on the outcome of the rivalry between the traditional divisions of society and the development of state structures such as political parties, a rudimentary army and the beginnings of a unified administration.

It is interesting to compare the Afghan resistance with the Rif war (1921–6), the only comparable movement, although the former differs in that it involved Sufi brotherhoods. The question has been raised whether the Rif war was the "last colonial campaign" or the first revolutionary war.[7] In the same way, one might ask whether the Afghan resistance is the last war waged by the *basmachi*, traditionalist rebels fighting a rearguard action against Soviet expansion, or the first stirrings of an Islamic revival within the Soviet Empire, which will go on to invent new forms of organisation that are, at one and the same time, both modern and rooted in tradition. The members of the Afghan resistance are no longer *basmachi*, just as the Russians are no longer Bolsheviks. The war in Afghanistan certainly marks a turning point in the history of Central Asia; it can be illuminated by the past, but we should acknowledge innovations even though, as with 'Abdul Krim, it is the connection with traditional society which is most apparent.

This reality will be the object of the present study, which will focus on structures rather than events. In a country where the pace of life is slow, where dates and names are often confused, and where dust is something more than a figure of speech, we often lack the most elementary facts. Nevertheless, certain things are becoming clear, so that it is now possible not only to shed light on the origins of the Afghan resistance, but also to set in a broader context the historical forces which are at work far beyond the frontiers of Afghanistan.

Chapter One

State and society in Afghanistan

The spontaneous uprisings against the communist regime which broke out in 1978 and 1979 were directed as much against the state itself as against the Marxist government. The imposition of communism on the country may be seen as a new and even more radical phase of the penetration of the countryside by the state bureaucracy. These two dimensions, opposition to the state and the rejection of Marxism, are closely interlinked. Yet the attitude of the countryside towards the state has always been more ambivalent than might at first appear: the Afghan state was born in the tribal lands; the symbols of authority which it exercises are not foreign to peasant experience and many of the leaders of the resistance movements visualised a state – for them an Islamic state. At the same time the recent history of Afghanistan is one of revolts against the central power and of resistance to the penetration of the countryside by state bureaucracy.

To oppose state and society is always somewhat artificial. Yet in Afghanistan this separation is rooted in everyday experience. It is apparent in rural villages, where the administrative buildings are set apart from the people's dwellings. It may be seen in the clothes worn and the general behaviour of individuals performing their roles in society. And it makes itself felt in the patterns of everyday speech.[1] For the peasant the state is alien, and the relationship between the peasantry and the state official is characterised by a profound and mutual contempt. In fact, there is only one real town, Kabul, the capital, where, of course, the distinction between state and society is blurred. But there are really two Afghanistans: first there is the town (*shahr*), the place of innovation (*bid'at*); this is the natural environment of the civil servant, the teacher, the soldier and the communist, all "intellectuals" and "bare-heads" (*sar-luchak*), held to be unbelievers and arrogant; and secondly the province (*atraf*), the home of religion, tradition (*sunnat*) and values which stand the test of time.

The game of politics is played out against each of these two backdrops. In the town, politics (*siyasat*) is followed attentively by students and the middle classes, whose very existence is bound up with the state, whereas it holds little interest for the peasant who only gets news of what is happening in the town when he fiddles with the knobs on his radio in search of music. The "double-dealing of kings" (*padshahgardi*) only affects him when it threatens to disturb the pattern of his daily life in some way. In the countryside the drama of politics revolves around the struggle for local pre-eminence carried on by the *khans*. They strive to enlarge their patronage, to be deferred to as judges in local disputes and thus increase their wealth and extend their family connections.[2] In tribal zones this struggle is sometimes violent, but it is carried on behind closed doors; whatever the outcome it never has any effect on the traditional social structure.

There is constant interaction between these two social worlds. The form it usually takes is the gradual wearing away of rural society by the growth of state institutions and the tapping of state resources for the private use of groups within the community. Or it may take the more turbulent form of a cultural revolution instigated from above, as was the case with King Amanullah from 1924 to 1928, and under the *Khalq* regime in 1978 and 1979), accompanied by a general uprising in the countryside in the name of *jihad* (as in 1928 and 1979). In these times of crisis ideological divisions transcend the narrower village and tribal groupings, which nevertheless still make themselves felt in the forms of political organisation (including that of the communist party).

What distinguishes the two camps – neither of which can be described as stable or homogeneous – cannot really be defined in sociological terms; it is their relation to the realm of politics that counts. The stereotype which equates the town with progress and the countryside with tradition has little basis in reality. In both town and country there is a wide range of diversity; they are both constantly changing though there is a core of continuity. Urban society has changed a great deal since the time when it consisted almost entirely of a royal court and a bazaar; now, besides the aristocracy, there is a new state bourgeoisie of officials, students and soldiers whose very existence depends on the institutions of the state, though it must be added that real power within these institutions eludes them.[3] Another stratum of the middle class which has been of importance since the thirties comprises those who make their living by trade. In the countryside a complex pattern of different ethnic groups, whose identity is not clearly defined, is the basis for subtle inequalities of status and different relationships with the state. They range from the dominant ethnic group, the Pashtun, to isolated groups such as the artisans in tribal zones, who have only a negative identity, for they are placed even lower than the lowest rung of the ladder of ethnic groups.[4] Since the end of the last century, migrations, evictions and modifications occurring in the social structure itself have thrown the country into turmoil, especially in the north. The introduction of a market economy, the increase in population and the intervention of the state have all accentuated divisions within society and created the conditions for the emergence of a class of well-to-do property owners and entrepreneurs living around the towns; radios and lorries mean that news now travels faster. We should also distinguish between the tribal and the non-tribal zones, even if the line between the two is often blurred. Every Afghan is linked to the past by a line of ancestors traced back through his father. He is also conscious of belonging to a larger entity which takes the form of a more or less endogeneous community (the *qawm*), whether its sociological basis is tribe, clan, professional group (*qawm* of the mullahs or of Barbars), caste (the *bari* of Nuristan), religious group (the *sayyad*), ethnic group (*munjani*), village community or simply an extended family. We will reserve the term 'tribe' (*qabila*) for the *qawms* having traditional rights and customs, a system within Islam of autonomous values (honour, vengeance, etc.), and a complex of specific institutions. These are essentially the Pashtun zones of the east where we find the *pashtunwali* (which is at one and the same time both a code and an ideology) and the institution of the *jirga*, the assemblies of all the men in the tribe.[5] Moreover, the great tribes (Mohmand, Jadran, Jaji, etc.) have territorial bases. For the Pashtun of the west, essentially the Durrani, the case is more complex. There is certainly a tribal memory, in the sense that belonging to the tribe and the clan is something of which people are well aware and quite happy to talk about. Their allegiance is directed towards the great families, such as the royal family, or, in the case of the Popolzay tribe, the Karzay; they also respect the tribal mythology of the great *jirga* and the principle of egalitarianism. However, Durrani tribal institutions are nothing like as strong as those of the tribes of the eastern part of the country, or those of the Ghilzay. On the other hand the influence of the *'ulama* is stronger amongst the Durrani. Is it possible, then, to speak of a process of detribalisation? In fact, it seems that the Durrani have never been as conscious of their tribal affinities as people in the east;[6] having always had a closer relationship with the structures of the state (Safavides, then the Amir of Kabul), they have, in a very short time, developed a kind of aristocracy reinforced by gifts of land made by the monarchy (this is the system of *jagir*). Yet the Durrani form an integral part of the Pashtun tribal world, and are looked upon as its cradle.

Although there has never been such a thing as an Afghan nation, there is certainly an Afghan state whose history can be traced. In this respect the locus of power may be pinpointed. But it is more difficult to document in political terms the ways in which society has attempted to evade, to infiltrate or even to radically oppose the state, in so far as the latter has not suddenly emerged as an abstract entity, but is historically rooted in a specific sector of society: the tribal confederation. We shall, therefore, now trace the history of the state back to its origins and consider the interrelationship between state and society.

The origins of the Afghan state

The tribal confederation

The Afghan state was established in the eighteenth century, when a tribal confederation developed into a dynastic state. In 1747 Ahmad Shah, of the Saddozay clan of the Popolzay tribe, led an Abdali confederation, now known as the Durrani, in the conquest of the area between Persia and the river Indus.[7] The Saddozay dynasty was to be followed in 1818 by another Durrani dynasty, the Muhammadzay clan of the Barakzay tribe, which held power until 1978. The confederation (*ulus*) was held together by the common aim of conquering neighbouring areas with a view to pillaging or exacting tribute. The political and military forms of this period were characteristic of tribal warfare. War was a short-lived affair and decided upon by the council of clan chiefs (a limited *jirga*); the troops that went into battle were selected from the total number of warriors under arms (*lashkar*). The framework was that of traditional society, but the *lashkar* usually had a supreme and temporary leader whose room for manoeuvre was limited, for he was always suspected of favouring his own clan. He was first and foremost a warrior chief,[8] with whom his followers entered into a contract. His right to lead was based upon the fact that he had been enthroned by a great tribal *jirga* (an assembly of all the warriors). The great *jirga* was the founding myth of the Afghan state and was to be re-enacted in periods of crisis (as for the enthronement of Nadir Khan in 1929). There was no spirit of patriotism, but a profound sense of cultural identity. One's allegiance belonged to the restricted group and the tribal code (*pashtunwali*), not to the Pashtun community or to the state; to join the enemy in order the better to affirm the tribal values (vengeance or self-assertion) was not seen as constituting treachery. "To exercise *pashtu*" (to identify oneself with values) was more important in the context of the tribe than "to be a Pashtun" (to be identified with an ethnic community or a nation).[9]

From the Amir to the state

The relationship between the tribal confederation and the centralised state is not to be compared with the relationship one finds in Morocco between *dar as-siba* and *dar al-makhzan*, that is to say between a tribal zone which is autonomous and a zone which is controlled by the central power. The Afghan tribes (especially the Durrani, but also the Ghilzay) see the central power as their representative; it manages on their behalf the conquests that they have made together in order that the material benefits or the glory may be later shared out. The tribes see the state as existing on the periphery, responsible for administering land whose boundaries are constantly fluctuating on account of conquests carried out by the tribal confederations, in respect of which the state is no more than the means of continuity. As far as their own territory is concerned, the presence of the state would seem to be redundant and totally unnecessary. The historical mission of the Afghan state may be summarised as an attempt to reverse this relationship in order to pass from the periphery to the centre. But the state was never to escape the implications of the original principle which gave it legitimacy and, even when it became most Westernised, it was to remain tribal and Pashtun.

The history of the Afghan state (*dawlat*) from 1747 to the present is bound up with the search on the part of the state bureaucracy (*hukumat*) for autonomy from the tribes. The state bureaucracy has escaped the influence of tribalism in the sense that individual tribes no longer retain specific responsibilities, but it is still subject to the patronage of the *qawm*. The summit of power in the state still belongs to the Muhammadzay establishment. The development of state institutions has brought into being new social strata (intelligentsia, army, a state bourgeoisie), a product of the government education system which has experienced considerable growth since 1950. (The number of students has grown from 450 in 1945 to 7,000 in 1975, 90 per cent of whom are destined to become employees of the state.)[10] These new social strata are not easily absorbed by traditional society, but at the same time they wield little influence within the state to which they owe their professional and ideological existence, for the state is, as it were, the reason for their existence. In the process which has seen state bureaucracy extend to the whole of the country (both tribal and non-tribal zones), the state has made use of three modes of persuasion in order to gain legitimacy: tribalism, Islam and nationalism.

When the Durrani dynasty was founded in 1747, a specific and autonomous locus of power was established. The state that was created was a prize to be competed for in accordance with certain relatively precise rules. One clan was certain to provide the sovereign (Saddozay until 1818 and Muhammadzay until 1978), then matrimonial alliances between families were created, from which there sprang up a complex pattern of factions intriguing against each other. This brought tribes other than the Durrani into the picture, usually through the mothers of the pretenders to the throne. The responsibilities of state were shared out amongst the great Durrani families (this was to remain true until 1973, at least as far as the army was concerned). There was no shortage of pretenders, who usually sprang from the immediate family (brothers and cousins),[11] since Muslim law does not recognise the right of primogeniture. The choice was made either by consensus (the *jirga*) or by having recourse to arms. The conflicts were often symbolic and, because all the pretenders were members of the Durrani, the decision was taken by the non-Durrani Pashtun tribes. The original tribalism was reinforced by matrimonial alliances, in which only the wives which had come from distinguished families had any political influence. Thus an establishment came into being based upon Durrani aristocracy and the great families which had become linked with it. This establishment was cut off from its tribal origins in the sociological sense: neither the tribal code, nor the attachment to tribal zones, nor the Pashtun language retained any relevance. But the mythological reference to the tribal past which legalised their position still had a large part to play, as did the influence of groups under their patronage and genealogies. It is in this sense that we may speak of a tribal state.[12]

From the very first right up to the present, the state has been the driving force behind modernisation, provided support for new ideas and legitimised them. Until the reign of Abdurrahman (1880–1901), the institutions of state were indistinguishable from the court, though even by the time of Dost Muhammad (1835–63) the need for an army which was something more than a simple *lashkar* had become apparent.[13] The reforms carried out by Abdurrahman were not based on any reformist ideology. His conception of modernisation was purely pragmatic: to rationalise the institutions of the state to make them more efficient, without thereby affecting traditional society. New techniques were adopted and key sectors were reformed, but in a piecemeal fashion. Nevertheless, this started a slow process of modernisation which filtered through the body of society; but this process was a by-product and not an end in itself. Increasing state power meant starting with the army; for that it was necessary to increase the supply of weapons and money, to create a manufacturing industry and to rationalize the fiscal system. Overnight, the state began to intervene in the economy and divide the country into neat blocks for administrative and military purposes. At the same time, the Amir, in order to curtail the influence of tribalism, for the first time focused attention upon the legal function of Islam: as Amir by divine right and defender of the faith he imposed the *shari'at* in order the better to enforce state laws.[14] He attempted to integrate the clergy with the secular institutions of state by control of the *madrasa*, the *waqf*, and of their wages, even going so far as to intervene in the theological domain.[15]

The introduction of these purely pragmatic reforms was carried out within the framework of the traditional exercise of power in medieval Islam: the de facto power of the Amir, who had come out top in the contest within the tribe, was legalised by the consensus of the tribes and by the ceremony of enthronement carried out *a posteriori* by the 'ulama. In his turn the Amir was charged with the responsibility of ensuring public well-being (*maslahat*) and with the task of defending the religion. Within this framework the technical reforms carried out by Abdurrahman did not arouse any opposition. It was not just the introduction of piecemeal modernisation within state institutions which was to bring society face-to-face with modernity. In Afghanistan, as elsewhere, it is not modernisation (the introduction of new technological methods or the rationalisation of some state institutions) which brings problems, but modernity, the hypothesis which holds that modernisation must necessarily involve a "cultural revolution", a transformation of the way of thinking and the adoption of new social paradigms.

A new policy was adopted under Amanullah (1919–29): faced with the fact that modernisation had met with certain insurmountable obstacles, the state attempted to reshape and reintegrate civil society. The arguments used, borrowed from the European Enlightenment and from the *salafiyya* (a reformist movement), in favour of education and progress, but spiced with a certain anti-clericalism, were authoritarian in nature and tended towards state control. In Afghanistan, the main lines of thought of modernist elites were laid down as early as 1911, with Tarzi in the newspaper *Seraj-ul Akhbar* (1911–19), and were to remain unchanged by later groups including the communists, for whom the main obstacle in the way of progress was the alienation and the illiteracy of the peasants. A complete revolution of outlook, controlled at a distance by the central power, was the condition of progress. The question of education became the recurring theme in progressive rhetoric.[16] From 1924, the consensus between state and society, which rested largely upon a mutual indifference, was broken. The result of the slow process which resulted in the separation of the institutions of the state from society was the creation of a new political space, an urban space whose denizens were moved by values imported from a West which was more imagined than real.[17] It was then, and only then, that a "tradition" came into being in response to the ever widening gulf between the people and those who held the reigns of power. In one sense, traditional society, far from existing in its own right, now became the pole of opposition to the state. Conversely, it became the shadowy projection of all the state was not, for, in order to arrive at a definition of itself, the state was forced to invent a changeless, frozen world which had remained the same for centuries, incapable of coming to full consciousness of itself without "enlightenment". Here we see the significance of such metaphors as dawn, light, torch (*seraj*), which became current at the end of the nineteenth century as a challenge to a seemingly obscurantist rural world. The status of the intellectual rose at the expense of that of the religious scholar. A good example of the views of the intelligentsia, whether liberal, Marxist or even radical Islamist, is to be found in the *Kabul Times* of 29 August 1970 (the constitutional and royalist period): "What our peasants really need is for all those quaint ideas to be flushed out of their brains . . ."[18]

The concept of the nation proves elusive

The state of the Amir of Kabul was given stability by foreign imperialism. Afghanistan became a nation-state because it was a buffer-state. The state was only able to impose its will upon the tribes and occupy its own territory thanks to the financial subsidies and weapons which were freely provided by the English between 1880 and 1919. The establishment of the frontier was carried out more or less single-handedly by the British, in agreement with the Russians. The English forced the Afghans to accept the Treaty of Gandamak (May 1879) and the frontier formed by the Durand line (1893), the Russians dictated the settlement of 1888 (Amou-Darya) and that of 1895 (Pamir); all of these were underpinned by the St Petersburg Anglo-Russian agreements of 1907. The frontiers thus defined were purely strategic and did not correspond to any ethnic or historical boundary. As an English analyst noted:

What was meant by the term scientific frontier in this connection? . . . . it would have been impossible to demarcate on the north-west of our Indian Empire a frontier which would satisfy ethnological, political and military requirements . . . What was meant by a scientific frontier was the best strategical boundary which could be used as a line of defence against invasion from the direction of Central Asia.[19]

How do the Afghans themselves see their territory? As Elphinstone commented in 1809, "these people have no name for their country".[20] There are two possible interpretations: the first, a territorial and dynastic view, identified Afghanistan with the area ruled by the Amir of Kabul (thus a reference to the tribal origin). The other, seeing things from a religious perspective, identified the country with the area which had remained Muslim, surrounded as it was by the kingdoms of the infidels (Britain and Russia) or the heretics (the Persians); this was the *millat*, the "nation" in the sense given the term in Ottoman law, that is to say a religious community. The *millat* is a geographical sub-region of the *umma*. This is how the great majority of the Afghan peasants have always understood the idea of the nation. Until 1924 (the date of the abolition of the Ottoman Caliphate and the first series of reforms by Amanullah), the means by which the Amir legitimised the authority of the state was to rouse the people in defence of the Muslim *millat* threatened by the infidels. But in 1924, with Afghanistan recognised by the European Nations and the Caliphate abolished, such ideas became outmoded; the state thereafter attempted to promote a spirit of nationalism which would be purely Afghan. The national flag and the celebration of a national day had already appeared during the reign of Abdurrahman,[21] and these were followed in the succeeding reign (Habibullah, 1901–19), by a national anthem.[22] The constitution of 1923 defined Afghanistan as a nation in which every resident had the right of citizenship whatever his religion (no reference was made to the Muslim *millat*).[23] The rupture with Islamic forms of legitimation was also marked by the quest for a pre-Islamic "Indo-Aryan" past (hence the importance of archaeology), and the invention of a folklore comprising a number of incongruous elements (the "national" sport was supposedly a Turkish game known as *bozkashi*; the "national" dance, called *atan*, was provincial, and came from Paktya). History was rewritten as if the political unit "Afghanistan" had existed from the earliest times. The school was, of course, the principal vehicle of this nationalist ideology.

But the state always oscillated between the concepts of an abstract nation, defined on the basis of its own sovereignty, and the historical reference to a Pashtun nation defined as an ethnic group which had not yet achieved its nationhood (the only possible outcome for the other ethnic groups was to become Pashtun). While the first of these two definitions had no implications for any of the groups within the nation, the second worked to the advantage of those Pashtun who were not Durrani (and therefore did not belong to the tribal aristocracy). They now found in Pashtun nationalism an ideology which gave them an opportunity to improve their social lot and the means of wresting the monopoly of power from the establishment. This group gained recruits especially amongst the young educated elite (particularly those who came from the Ghilzay) who had recently moved to the towns and were rapidly losing their tribal customs. It was amongst these that the Khalq tendency of the communist party took root, the last phase of an extreme Pashtun nationalism which, however, had only minority support, even within the linguistic community of the Pashtun. After the Soviet invasion, the resistance gathered strength and the idea of the *millat* was revived.

The expansion of state bureaucracy

We turn now to the policy of extending the state bureaucracy from the reign of Abdurrahman up to the date of the communist coup; it is this policy that the Babrak regime and the Russians hope to reinstate. The Khalq regime of 1978 attempted to bring all social relations within the ambience of the state. They considered society to be no more than an aggregate of individuals incapable of controlling their own destiny and bereft of all social ties now that feudalism, as they defined it, had been abolished. Up to then the state had come to terms with civil society, and had even recognised that it had a positive value.

Even though the state was born out of conquest, it did not impose itself by brute force. On the one hand it used the traditional networks of power in order to connect up with society and to transform the way those networks operated. On the other, it manipulated legitimising symbols which were recognised as such by the peasants.

Since the state did not have at its disposal enough officials to be able to spread out from the capital and divide the countryside up neatly into administrative areas, it was obliged to delegate some of its functions to people of standing in the local community, who thus became inter-mediaries between the state and the people; by this means their power was enhanced for they had become, in the eyes of the state, the representatives of their community. These people of standing were not necessarily *khan* (or *bay*), whose power, based on their wealth and the power of the *qawm*, was both greater and more informal. They were more likely to be *malik* or *arbab*, terms sometimes translated as village chiefs; they represented, in fact, a local *qawm* (there could be several *maliks* per village) and were elected by heads of families. They received a remuneration from the families they served, and sometimes a payment from the state, and in return they acted as registrars, dealing with census returns, conscription and the collection of taxes; they also assisted those within their administrative area in their dealings with the authorities. The position of the *maliks* was somewhat ambiguous, for they represented the state to the community and the community to the state; in the years immediately prior to the coup, they tended to use this ambiguity to strengthen their personal position. But they were considered by the peasants to be one of them. On the other hand, as far as the administration of justice was concerned, the state had embarked upon a course of systematically removing from the village assemblies all their authority, and the *qazi* who were not appointed by the government were deprived of the right of making judgements.[24]

Over the years, the symbols used by the state to legitimate its authority have varied. The original symbol, that of tribal legitimacy, was, of course, only valid in tribal zones, especially those of the Durrani, and there it retained its force. It was in the name of tribal solidarity that Abdurrahman asked the Durrani to people north-western Afghanistan[25], and Amanullah made an appeal from Qandahar in order to regain his throne in 1928. It was in the name of tribal solidarity that Nadir Khan retook Kabul from Bacha-yi Saqqao in 1929 (see p. 67). In these cases, legitimacy was conferred by the ritual of enthronement carried out by the great *jirga*, the founding myth of the Afghan state. A second legitimating symbol consisted simply in the actual possession of power, since, for the peasant, such power is automatic, and is held to exist as soon as it manifests itself; power is recognised simply because it exists and because no-one is attempting to gainsay it. The existence of the state was, therefore, not at issue; what was at issue was its right to encroach upon the country. With the exception of the tribal zones and Hazarajat, Afghanistan has always been subject to a central power, whose legitimacy, ever since the Muslim conquest, has been symbolised by the minting of money and the *khutba* (the Friday sermon) in the name of the sovereign; the constitution of 1923, article 7, ratified these two outward signs. It mattered little which individual became the incarnation of this de facto power (a question asked after the communist coup was: "Is Taraki the new king?"). The existence of the state is not what is at stake for the peasant, whose chief concern is to resist the encroachment of state bureaucracy, which will endure whichever regime or sovereign is in power.

The third source of legitimacy is Islam. The need to have a strong central power to defend the community of believers against infidels is recognised by everyone and always becomes more important in periods of crisis, receding into the background in the absence of external threat. Of course, this source of legitimacy only comes into play if the sovereign is seen to be Muslim. The final ground of legitimacy is provided by the nation itself, although this only has significance for the detribalised Pashtun, since the others are more receptive to the tribal myth; non-Pashtun exclude themselves from this conception of the nation (an Afghan will never define himself as an Afghan if he is not a Pashtun as well).

The elusive society

The exclusiveness of the state

The fact that the state exists outside and apart from civil society has, as we have already said, its basis in everyday experience. The machinery of government stands out clearly from other forms of social life in both a literal and a metaphorical sense: it draws attention to itself by a form of symbolism which is quite distinct – the location of its buildings, the clothes worn by its officials, its turns of phrase. Everything to do with administration is isolated from village life, and as far as possible is ignored by the community. This, of course, does not mean that the villagers are unwilling to accept that certain government requirements (imposition of taxes, conscriptions and so on) do indeed have to be met. In the countryside, state bureaucracy has a precise location, which is referred to as *hukumat* (which, at the same time, means "state bureaucracy", "government", "administrative building"), or more vaguely *ta'mir* (the building). This place is set apart from the village, though sometimes a purely functional bazaar is joined to it. Here you will find the school and all the local state employees, supported by a few dozen soldiers. Civil servants do not wear a turban, but the astrakan cap. Their physical bearing is somewhat different also; these officials dress like Europeans, and thus the postures made possible by the width of traditional clothes are quite foreign to them; even their gait is different.[26] Whether the official speaks Pashtu or Persian, it is always a language which smacks of officialdom, quite different from the local dialects. In particular, educated civil servants enjoy using neologisms borrowed directly from English or French (*dimocrasi, displin, riform, libral, kulcher*) and thought by them to express concepts which cannot be said in any other way in the cultural context. But, at the same time, the physical separation of the official from the places where village people congregate (the mosque or the village guest room (*hujra*)) means that he needs an intermediary in order to communicate with peasant society. This intermediary, the *malik*, is thus in a position to decide what information he will convey to the administration.

Having emphasised the fundamental state of alienation that separates the two, we must add that traditional society has many ways of dealing with state bureaucracy. The more aggressive mode of action, which we shall consider later, consists in penetrating the ranks of the bureaucracy. But this offensive also takes the more benign form of simple corruption. Corruption, if it is done at a reasonable price and kept within acceptable limits, is not wrong as far as the peasant is concerned: it makes it possible for him to resist regimentation, and to avoid dealing with issues which he does not understand and whose purpose is, in any case, beyond him (for example, agricultural production quotas, or pest control campaigns). Corruption makes the official powerless and ensures that bureaucratic machinery can only function in a vacuum. Another more passive form of resistance consists in erecting a systematic screen to keep the official from contact with the life of the village. The administration often sends officials on a mission to the villages. The villagers always suspect that the mission has an ulterior motive and they attempt to convince the official to leave as soon as possible. Ethnologists have related how a harmless pair of officials from the Ministry of Agriculture, who had come to see how locust control was faring, were astonished to find themselves being given a lump sum by the village people, on the condition that they should never ever set foot there again.[27] In this sense, the proverbial hospitality of the Afghans is also a form of defensive screen. The guest, assigned to a precise place (the *hujra*) which he dares not leave without offending his host, is enmeshed in a formalism in which the ceremony of greetings and the ritual of the meal leaves little place for the exercise of authority or even simple investigation; those ethnologists and tourists who have the misfortune to be mistaken for civil servants know something about this. The foreigner finds himself confronted by an endless series of evasions, procrastinations and side-stepping of the issue. The person who is responsible is always somewhere else, the horses are in the mountains and the truth is in the depths of the well.

But what is there to hide? Does village society have a real existence, an autonomous life which establishes it as an entity in its own right, bracing itself to resist the unwelcome arrival in its midst of state bureaucracy? This is at the heart of the question concerning the relations between state and civil society. First, an individual's desire to avoid the attentions of the state does not necessarily mean that he lives outside the state. Peasant society does not mount guard at the frontiers against an invader, for it has no frontiers. Secondly, there is no such thing as a totally self-sufficient economy, and thus it is impossible to describe the introduction of the market economy as a violation; the community does not have its own territory to guarantee its separateness. Finally, and above all, there is no locus of power within civil society which can be the object of a strategy of control. The locus of power, the administrative post and the *malik* co-opted into the ranks of officialdom, are, as it were, invented and defined by the state. This, then, is the arena in which the fight between society and state is waged, and in which the latter is the more vulnerable because its people and its buildings are highly visible targets. In guerilla warfare the insurgents know what to take and whom to kill; the inverse is less often true.

Power in Afghan peasant society resides neither in a specific locality nor in a person, but in an elusive network, which needs constant maintenance and reconstruction. It is a network which depends upon patronage, where one's degree of prestige is proportionate to the largesse distributed. Power is granted by consensus and is not necessarily given to a man for life; this is not a world of vassals, of allegiance entered into by oath. Afghan society is not feudal. It resembles more the constant disequilibrium which characterises social relations in the *potlatch* than the stable architecture of the feudal system. A *khan* depends for his power on the consensus of his *qawm*, except when his authority has been superseded by a state nominee, which has been the case amongst the Durrani since the eighteenth century through the institution of the *jagir* (the *iqta'* of classical Islam). Although this has never been the general rule, it has become more frequent in recent decades, when economic wealth has made it possible for the rich to gain the favour of the administration. The *khan* must always show, by his generosity and his availability to those who need him, that he is the only person worthy of fulfilling this function: "there is no *khan* without *dastakhan*" (without "a tablecloth", that is, without keeping open table).[28] Elphinstone has expressed this idea well: "Power consists in the number of a man's relations".[29] And if the son inherits prestige from his father, he must maintain his status according to certain informal but demanding rules: he must provide food for others, arbitrate in their disputes and be unflinching in the defence of the interests of his *qawm* in the clash with the state.[30] In fact, the state has been forced to transform the village communities into abstract entities – units within the system of administration which can thus be managed with the help of their *malik*.[31] More precisely, this is one of two possible options: either the community is made into an abstraction, and the state imposes order upon the patchwork of *qawm*, assisted by the fact that it alone is able to transcend tribal fragmentation (which has been the policy of the kings and the Soviet Union); or the village community is crushed, and the government deals directly with individuals with no group-consciousness (the policy of Amanullah, the Khalq, and perhaps the radical Islamists). Traditionally the state has always treated the village communities as a unit: taxes are levied collectively for such things as the maintenance of roads passing near the village, or the construction of the school; when there are rebellions or crimes which remain unsolved, fines are imposed on the community. By making the *qawm* into an entity which it can only approach through the mediation of the *malik*, the state has strengthened the authority of the latter, who now has at his disposal other weapons than the traditional consensus: he can help people to avoid military service, and he can act on their behalf when they have taxes or fines to pay.

The insubstantial state

At the very moment when the state institutions were attempting to establish themselves, to rationalise and integrate the village communities, they themselves became the object of a strategy on the part of the *qawm* which involved not so much the assertion of power but the infiltration of those same institutions. Only two groups in the country aim for power: the notables within the establishment, who would leave intact the general social structure, and the intelligentsia, who would not. For the other groups, the aim is to insert the *qawm* into the state institutions at a level which befits their own importance, from the minor local official to the minister. This operation is intended not only to produce material benefits (posts for the young, sinecures, exemption from the payment of taxes and from conscription), but especially to ensure that the local power game carries on as it has always done, and that the traditional rules of the game of politics will determine the way in which the state functions. Judging by the recent history of Afghanistan, the *qawm*'s strategy has been a success: the state of Zahir Shah and of Daoud (1933–73, 1973–8) was tribal in the way that it was run, even and especially during the period which saw the establishment of a constitutional monarchy.

While it is true that the state institutions have a certain bureaucratic stability, the state itself seems to have no other goal than that of perpetuating itself. One interesting example is provided by the constitutional episode of 1963–73. The elections of 1965 and 1969 were free and yet the constitutional period was a failure; many observers attribute this to the fact that political parties were not made legal. But this absence of parties was a consequence not a cause of the weakness of the political class,[32] for it took some time for parties to come into existence even clandestinely (1965 for the PDPA, the communist party). The political class had become depoliticised. The deputies from the provinces came as representatives of their local *qawm* to obtain subsidies and privileges, for the state was seen by them merely as a powerful and external agent at whose expense they should profit as much as possible. The establishment was disunited because it lacked any coherent political goals; instead each clan sought political dominance. The ruling class had no conception of a unified state. The selection of political appointees clearly reflected the divisions within a society where primary allegiance was to the family and patronage was still a major factor: ultimate loyalties were not centred upon the state. No attempt was made to transcend the immediate group, or rather, if such an ideal determined the rhetoric used (the nation, state, Islam or class struggle for the Marxist opposition), it had no influence on individual behaviour, nor even on the strategy pursued by a group. This explains, for example, why the struggles between various cliques within the communist party often made it appear to the onlooker that they harboured a death-wish. The state was no more than a stake in a larger game and the strategy of a *qawm* consisted in establishing an advantageous relationship with the institutions of the state.

This failure to reach out towards a broader social unity resulted in an ideological vacuum; political terms borrowed from the West circulated from one group to another, losing their precision as they did so. The word "revolution" could mean not only the communist coup but also any uprising in the countryside. The networks based on patronage and personal links remained firm, as if the most serious political disagreements did not exist: for instance, the communist Parcham (nicknamed "royal communist party") was linked to the royalist establishment.

The atmosphere in parliament (elected with an abstention rate of 90 per cent) was anarchic: a quorum was never reached, there was a constant din, and simple-minded and fanciful speeches were the order of the day.[33] Typically, a great number of villages had refused to have a secret ballot and a polling booth. The state was viewed much as the court was in former times by the deputies: each came there to seek for favours. On the stage of the political theatre, it was truly a comedy which was being played out. Even the word "theatre" is hardly a metaphor: the debates were broadcast on the radio, and in the schools pupils applauded, booed, or imitated the speeches in the playgrounds. The experiment in democracy was all form and no substance. Western democracy is only meaningful under certain circumstances: the identification of civil society with the state, and the evolution of a political entity which is something other than political theatre. The battles fought out in the sphere of politics must be a way of resolving tensions for the benefit of society and not a theatrical presentation of imported concepts, which tend to hide the fact that what is going on is a struggle for power within a restricted group. The alienation of the political class from real politics, especially when that class has its social origins in the countryside (which was, indeed, the case for the two parliaments), was another piece of evidence pointing to the separation between society and state. The intelligentsia fiercely combated this democratic parliament from which it was excluded and which set up in opposition two old accomplices: rural society and the tribal establishment. As a result of their demonstrations communist and Islamist students were instrumental in the dismissal of the liberal Yusuf cabinet in 1965 – an event which aroused the profoundest indifference in the countryside, not to mention the court.

Can it be said that a rural community exists in its own right?

The *qawm* is a network, the village a territory, and even though the two are often one and the same (for very frequently, but not necessarily, the village corresponds to a *qawm*), their mode of functioning in relation to politics is very different. As a network, the *qawm*, since it has no precise geographical location, cannot be taken over by the state; on the other hand, the *qawm*, as a solidarity grouping, is able to penetrate to the very heart of the state.

The existence of peasant communities in Afghanistan presents a problem, and the response of writers when faced with this problem is either to deny outright that they exist, or to apologise for them.[34] I do not intend to become involved here in the finer points of this debate. It is, however, necessary to distinguish two things: the village community and the power networks. It should be stressed that the solidarity grouping does not exist only in a precise geographical space; the essence of rural society is to be found in a cultural whole which cannot be reduced to the "village community". The social practices which exemplify group solidarity in the villages and on which writers like to base their definition of "village communities" may seem banal: they include the existence of "common land" for pasturage, people working for the common good in the digging out of irrigation channels, internal settlement of quarrels, and the fact that people can rely upon one another to help in times of crisis. There is nothing here which suggests a basis for an alternative centre of power. In addition, local society finds ways of regulating its own activities to deal with situations which are somewhat out of the ordinary: for example, when, as often happens in summer in the centre of the country, temporary bazaars are held, the two principal communities (Durrani and Ghilzay) each elect, with the blessing of the administrative authorities, a *malik* who is responsible for keeping order.[35] It is only in the zones where tribalism is still strong that villages have institutions endowed by long custom with a specific authority, which exercise pressure towards conformity:[36] only in these cases is it possible to speak of an autonomous village community. But the existance of group solidarity does not mean that there is an alternative centre of power in opposition to the state, since such groupings are easily absorbed within the state structure. The essence of Afghan civil society is not to be found in the autonomy of the village community, but in those elements which, at the very heart of civil society, have as their point of reference a state, which as yet exists only as an ideal and is quite different from the actual one.

Afghan rural society is a society regulated by law. There is a body of law, the *shari'at*; formally appointed judges, the *qazi*; and legal authority is vested in Islam. It is not important whether this legal system functions in reality. During the period of the old constitution when the legal system was in competition with the power game being pursued by the *khan* and was being taken over by the state, references to Islam, in the main, were merely symbolic. But it was precisely this symbolism which helped to resist the onward march of state institutions by the creation of a space within which real autonomy was possible, in that the appeal to a broad unifying principle implicit in the use of the term *"umma"* was backed up by another idea having the same force, at least for the Persian-speaking zones. This was the direct link created with the culture of classical Persia, which was nothing if not a culture centred upon the idea of the *state*, but a state of much greater antiquity than the modern Afghan state. (The Persian spoken in Afghanistan – a more literary language than the dialect spoken in Iran – was known as *dari*, "the language of the court".) Paradoxically, the whole cultural emphasis of the Pashtun state of the Mosahiban (the family of Nadir Khan and his brothers), in power from 1929 onwards, like that of the communists, has been to encourage a culture which can best be described as "popular" (the oral literature of the Pashtun, codified by a "Pashtun Academy" was set up in 1935); while the resistance of Persian-speakers to this attempt to make the whole country conform to Pashtun culture has been carried out in the name of a more sophisticated culture, spread abroad in scholarly books such as the *Panj-kitab*. Neither peasants nor scholars view the role of the present state as the manifestation of the ideal of a united society; the only function that they are willing to allow it, besides the maintenance of public order, is to be a symbol of a unity conceded long ago, as demonstrated by the *shari'at*, and classical culture. If it sets about imposing its own norms, then the state is considered to be no more than the instrument of sectional interests.

To understand this, it is necessary to realise that the space between the village community and the state is occupied by another social network, that of the scholars: the *'ulama*, *qazi*, scribes and poets of the villages. This network has its own educational institutions: Qur'anic schools and *madrasa*. It would be wrong to think that these institutions provide a purely religious and legal education. The Afghan clergy is imbued with a knowledge of the Persian humanities; many of the religious leaders have come from the mystical Sufi movement, and combine a sense of the importance of legal formalism with a spiritual and literary dimension. Until about 1950 all the clergy and most of the officials came from the social network of the *madrasa*. In the next chapter we shall consider in some detail the curriculum and intellectual background of the Afghan *'ulama*, but in brief it has to do with Muslim universalism. Somewhere around 1950, the state was establishing not only a network of government schools, but also a faculty of state theology: judges were appointed strictly from the ranks of the graduates of this institution. The network of non-government *madrasa* has not been abolished, but it has been much reduced in importance, both socially and politically. Government institutions are now staffed by intellectuals, whose thinking, whether

27

they be Islamists or communists, is state-centred, while the *'ulama* are concerned only with knowledge, and the question of power is peripheral. Thus, the opposition is not between rural particularism and the universality of the state, but between the religious scholar and the intellectual,[37] both of whom claim to be the vehicles of knowledge which can unify society. Now, it happens that the links between the *qawm* and its individual members are much looser in the case of the scholar than in the case of the peasant, even when the intellectual's social origins are in the countryside. The function of the scholar, as far as the peasant is concerned, is to represent a principle of universal worth: if he were too closely linked with any particular community his standing would be in jeopardy, whereas, by definition, the *khan* only exists within the context of a specific *qawm*.

As we have said, the rivalry of the *khans* is carried on behind closed doors: it does not upset the order imposed by the state – indeed it may even serve to reinforce it. On the other hand, the *'alim* provides a principle of unity which the state can only use when it is confronted by the non-Muslim world. In normal times, the state finds it necessary to attempt to reduce the power of the clergy, and the influence of Islamic doctrines, in order to prevent people questioning its right to exist; it hopes, of course, by this means to suggest that it alone has access to a modern, secular creed which can act as a basis for social unity. In seeking to orientate himself the peasant oscillates between these two landmarks of rural life: the *khan* and the *'alim*, the *hujra* and the mosque. The first assumes importance in tribal zones and the second in non-tribal areas; but Islam always reasserts itself in times of crisis.

To understand rural society it is important to see it not as a so-called village community but as a space within which law and institutions exist, even though these norms are, to a great extent, imaginary. Consider the political vocabulary used by the peasants: *siyasat*, politics, suggests the town and the state (*dawlat*); *zolm* means the arrogance of power, de facto power, tyranny, epitomized both by officials representing the state and by the local *khan*. The term *sunnat*, "tradition", recalls the example provided by the Prophet: this is an ethical model and not a state of society. It is impossible to speak of "traditional society" in its usual sense for the *sunnat* is not the opposite of "modern" society; modernity has the sense of innovation, and thus irreligion. This of course does not prevent the peasant from enjoying the products of the modern world, such as radios, since for him they do not have such connotations.

Islam conveys an ideal of social justice, but it does not, in itself, have a blueprint for a state to rival the state which actually exists. It does not promise a utopia that involves upsetting society, for the peasant is not revolutionary, neither does it present a political programme of the kind espoused by the Islamists, because the peasant regards the reform of personal behaviour as being more important than the transformation of social structures. He sees "true" Islam as enjoining upon its followers a number of very specific rules, obedience to which ensures economic and social justice (for example there is the condemnation of usury). It is an ethical vision, for at the same time the arrogance of power (*zolm*) and corruption are seen as natural. It little matters that very few people who exercise power act justly. What is important is that the peasant should be able to judge, and, even when he is defeated, refuse to approve of injustice.

Thus, when the peasant appeals for justice it is on ethical grounds. He has little knowledge of the intricacies of the *shari'at* and they do not interest him; for him it is sufficient that a concern with justice should characterise the "Muslim". On the other hand, the *'alim* is inclined to see the *shari'at* in a formalistic, almost casuistic, fashion. The fact that civil society in Afghanistan is something more than a mere aggregate of rural communities, whose status is unclear, is also due to a particular characteristic of Muslim law. Its validity does not depend on the existence of any given state since it is grounded in the absolute, and it has proved capable of developing its own hermeneutic tradition, including the education of those upon whom that tradition depends, outside the institutions of the state. This is why the differentiation between civil society and the state is very marked in those Muslim countries which have not been colonised.

The idea of Islam as a countervailing authority to the despotism of the state is not of recent origin, but it gained in importance after 1924 when the state embarked upon a process of secularisation, accompanied by the growth of state bureaucracy. The removal of the *'ulama* to the fringes of social life meant that they became isolated from the centres of power, and thus of corruption, which, in turn, gave them an aura of integrity which would certainly not have been theirs if they had been given official posts. On every occasion, even when the state is acting with the best intentions, its edicts are seen as tyrannical, because they remove from the peasant overall responsibility for the conduct of his affairs. The intellectual explains the peasant's unwillingness to accept reforms as a consequence of his alienation, while the peasant actually feels alienated because the state is intent upon relating him to the process of production.[38]

The essence of civil society is to be sought, therefore, not in the village community, but in a wider context which transcends the fragmented *qawm*; because of the social problems of its human agents, and educational networks, this essence is firmly rooted in traditional society. There can be no doubt that Islam is fundamental.

Chapter Two

Islam in Afghanistan

Apart from a few thousand Hindus and Sikhs and a few hundred Jews, all Afghans are Muslims. Eighty per cent of these are Sunni of the Hanafite rite, and the rest are Shi'a of the Jaffarite rite, with a small Isma'ili minority of one to two hundred thousand people. In a country like Afghanistan, where the concept of the nation has developed but recently, where the state is seen as external to society and where people's allegiance is directed primarily towards their local community, the only thing which all Afghans have in common is Islam.

Afghan peasant life is permeated by religion. It provides the intellectual horizon, the system of values and the code of behaviour, even though occasionally this may involve a clash with other codes of conduct, such as the tribal system; it provides the only source of legitimation based upon universal values. Nevertheless, the social basis of this religion varies according to whether the context within which it exists is tribal or non-tribal, rural or urban, and in the same way the link between ideology and religion varies according to whether a group is secularised or fundamentalist, traditionalist or reformist. Thus one finds different forms of religious expression, each with its own dynamic and symbolism. In this context, we should distinguish between the village mullah, the 'alim (doctor of law), the sayyad (reputed to be a descendant of the Prophet), the pir (a charismatic figure sometimes to be found at the head of a Sufi brotherhood) and finally the Islamist intellectual. Amongst the different forms of religious expression, we should distinguish between popular devotion, the legal orthodoxy of the 'ulama, the mysticism of the Sufis and the political Islam of the Islamists. Recent developments have seen a gradual erosion of the influence of the 'ulama, which has been going on since the last century, though this has suddenly been reversed because of the present war. There has also been a schism in Sufism between the orthodox orders in the non-tribal zones and the non-clerical orders in the south. Other developments have been the decline in the influence of the sayyad and the charismatic leaders, and a crisis in the relationship between shari'at and custom in the tribal zones. Finally, the Islamist movement, led by young intellectuals, has greatly increased its power and influence.

Popular religion

It would be a mistake to make a stark contrast between the religion of the people, the legalistic Islam of the *'ulama*, and the political Islam of the Islamists, if only for the reason that the last two categories also form part of what, for want of a better word, we call "popular religion". It is not so much a difference of content that we are concerned with here as a difference of approach. Included in the concept of "popular religion" are such things as the way in which religion structures everyday life, the way it constitutes a language, a meaningful experience, a cultural identity. The way it stabilises a relationship with the sacred world is quite different from that offered by "official" theology – although in Afghanistan it would be very difficult to identify an "official" Islam as opposed to an unorthodox Islam.

By "popular" I do not mean a religion which has its origins in the people as opposed to the scholars (*'ulama*) and the Islamist intellectuals, but rather one which derives from a world-view common to all these social categories, which provides the basis for the more intellectual constructions of the *'ulama* (the Muslim law) and the intellectuals (Islamist ideology).

Islam in the village

The mosque is the centre of the village; it is also the only suitable place for communal gatherings, although the larger villages will also have tea rooms, and the *khan*'s residence has its guest room (*hujra*). The mosque is, of course, used for the performance of religious rituals; collective prayer (*jama'a*) is regarded as having greater spiritual value than personal prayer – an example is the Friday gathering, when the whole village comes together at midday. But the mosque is also the place where men can meet to discuss various matters and swap news; it is the place where the venerable elders come to discuss problems and resolve conflicts. It is also here that strangers passing through the village are accommodated, when there is no man in the village rich enough to provide hospitality.

Religion structures space and time. The space of the village is centred upon the mosque, but there is also a world-space, with its concentric circles of the *umma*, of other religions and finally of unbelievers. The rhythm of the day contains the five prayers, and the meals which have something of a sacrament about them; the rhythm of the year has its feasts which culminate in Ramadan; the rhythm of the language has time-hallowed forms of address and expressions of courtesy which invoke the name of God. Anyone attempting to rid his speech and expressive gestures of all reference to the Deity would be unable to convey his meaning to others. The mullah is, first and foremost, the mullah of a particular village and not of the clergy;[1] he is not a member of an institutionalised body and has scarcely any links with his superiors (the *'ulama*). He is not appointed by them, neither does he depend upon them for his income. When it becomes necessary to appoint a new mullah the village will come to a collective decision, choosing someone on the grounds of his piety and for his wisdom and one who, frequently, comes from a family which traditionally provides the mullah; this is particularly the case in tribal zones, where the mullah may almost be said to belong to a professional caste.

The mullah is often poor and his "job" is a way of supplementing what he earns growing crops – an activity which continues to take up part of his time. In Afghanistan there is no longer any *waqf* in the form of land or property owned by the mosque; the only *waqf* in the village is the mosque itself and its outlying buildings, which are not enough to provide an income for the mullah's needs. Sometimes he becomes a kind of employee of the village, paid yearly in kind (this is the case in tribal zones),[2] and in these instances he is considered to be a craftsman specialising in religious ritual in the same way as the barber and the carpenter each have their own specialisations. He will then be paid once a year on a contractual basis; or he may be provided with money from the Islamic taxes (*'ushr* and *zakat*) as well as a payment for the work he has performed.[3] Nevertheless the people give as they are able; there is no pressure upon them to do so and the gifts never reach the upper limit provided for by Islamic law. Naturally, the rich play a greater part than others in supporting the mullah, but it is unusual for him to depend directly on the *khan* for his upkeep.

The social status of the mullah, then, varies considerably: it is low in the tribal zones, because of his exclusion from the tribal community and his inclusion in professional groups which are looked down upon (except by the Durrani); it is higher elsewhere according to his knowledge and the traditional esteem granted to his family. The mullah has a monopoly on all religious activities such as prayers at the time of baptism, circumcision, marriage and burial, childrens' catechism, and the conduct of the Qur'anic school. In the small villages the mullah is frequently the only educated person. Even though he may never have any political power, he acts as a mediator in disputes. Sometimes he provides services which may best be described as on the fringe of religion, or even as quite straightforward magic: dispensing medicine, the use of talismen, or exorcism. The rivals of the mullah in this field are the quacks, the doctors and other workers of magic, but in another direction he is also in competition with the teachers at the government school and all the newly educated members of the population, who do not have much respect for him.

From casual conversation you might get the impression that anti-clericism is rife amongst the people, but this would be somewhat misleading. It may take the form of upgrading the mullah's role while remaining sceptical about the ability of the one who fulfils that role: in jokes, the mullah appears as ignorant, lazy and greedy. But this reaction has nothing to do with free thought. The level of education of the mullah varies a great deal: he is able to read and write (but there are a few who are illiterate), he knows by heart the prayers and the quotations from the Qur'an in Arabic (but he rarely uses that language), and he also has some knowledge of the rudiments of Muslim law and classical literature.

Religion: is it a normative system or an ethic?

Islam provides a system of norms, a code regulating human relations, in a word a social morality. But by insisting too much on this aspect, one is apt to forget its spiritual dimension, which manifests itself in behaviour and which opens up a transcendental sphere, for inner meditation, and access to the universal beyond the everyday rules of community life. The approach of Western anthropologists, like the utilitarian understanding of Islam which one finds in the writings of certain Muslim modernists,[4] and the way in which some of the *'ulama* insist on a purely legalistic interpretation of the religion, go too far towards reducing Islam to a system of rules.

As we have seen, the idea of tradition conveys to the peasant not something static, but the aspiration to live his life in accordance with an ethical model: by imitation of the Prophet (*sunnat*), and in his behaviour, gestures and dress.[5] It does not matter very much that this tradition is more imaginary than real, that there has been constant change or that the ethical standard is often scorned by the very person who claims to live by it. The rhetoric of tradition in no way rules out a certain pragmatism in everyday life. This rhetoric gives meaning to the world, provides the peasant with a means of expression, and access to the universal. In Islam, truth is something that you arrive at less by interpretation than by imitation. This fact inevitably means that the development of political thought is inhibited but it also strengthens personal morality. Thus, one finds moral conformism (unquestioning obedience to the norms) as well as the practice of spiritual exercises in pursuit of piety – the interactions of social norms as well as the creation by the individual of an inward space for meditation – a practice which some may accept and others refuse.

Religion also provides access to a universal through its use of language: the words used by those taking oaths, words which signify shared values, words which refer to a world common to one or more speakers. Even though the right to speak reflects the hierarchical relations within society, and this, in effect, means that scholars are a privileged elite, the peasant may say what he thinks before the *qazi*. There are certain principles held in common and he is able to speak without any intermediary. However, when he finds himself face to face with a government official, he may feel insignificant and ill-at-ease and remain silent, involved as he is in a set of procedures which are foreign to him and whose overall purpose escapes him. In such a situation he usually gets the *malik* to act as a go-between. Far from being imprisoned within the narrow confines of a religion shot through with a sense of fatalism, the peasant finds in this same religion a useful tool of analysis, a means of comparing one thing with another and of making sense of his own personal universe.

Religion also puts the peasant into contact with the universal, because it provides access to a transcendental sphere through which he is able to speak of the world in general, of humanity (*bashariyyat*), of good and evil. Now dialogue with the stranger is made possible, whereas if Islam were nothing more than a set of rules the other would be incomprehensible to him. It is this mixture of formalism (and thus of latent sectarianism) and profound humanism which outsiders find baffling when they come into contact with Muslim peasants. Behind the mistrust of the stranger, behind the fear of moral contamination and the evil eye, behind the age-old tradition of hospitality which travellers find so engaging and yet which, even as it welcomes them, manages to neutralise any potential threat, behind all this formalism of human relations, there is a desire to understand and engage, on the deepest level, in a dialogue made possible because of a shared humanity. This is a conception more firmly rooted in the believer than in the unbeliever, for whom irreligion is but the latest fashion imported from the West. In Afghanistan atheism signifies the adoption of Western ways, and thus it constitutes a form of alienation; so, it is not mere chance that of the two forms of communism in Afghanistan one, the Khalq, is driven by a suicidal and destructive lust for violence, the other, the Parcham, is slavishly pro-Soviet.

Islam, traditional law and the tribal code

Throughout Afghanistan, Islam is far from being a single system of norms. While state law (*qanun*) is alien to the country communities, customs (*riwaj*, *'adat*) and superstition, often of pre-Islamic origin, exist everywhere. Furthermore, a certain number of institutions, such as the counsel of the venerable elders, and *mirab* (see appendix 2), have developed without any direct link with the *shari'at*. In particular, a complex but precise system of common law has gradually evolved in the countryside. But, as far as the non-tribal zones are concerned, the general framework of penal law and of common law is still provided by the *shari'at*.[6] And even though reference to the *shari'at* is often purely rhetorical, no positive system has come to take its place.

The situation in the tribal zones is quite different: here there is a positive system, comprising the tribal code (*pashtunwali*) and the assembly (*jirga*). *Pashtunwali* is at one and the same time an ideology and a body of common law[7] which has evolved its own sanctions and institutions. Political power in the tribes is secular in origin (that is to say not dependant upon religion) and, on the level of law, the tribal code and the *shari'at* are clearly opposed. We have already seen that the status of the mullah is low in the tribal zones. Even if his native tongue is Pashtu, he would never say that he was a Pashtun. The son of a *khan* would never engage in religious studies (at least in the twentieth century, for the situation seems to have been different in earlier times).[8] To be a Pashtun is to be integrated into a tribal structure. Priests are outside the tribal system, either below it, or above it. The village mullah is placed below, above are those people who have *barakat*, the *myan*, *sayyad*, *pir* and charismatic leaders. Thus, the mullah is in the same category as the artisan: since the family from which he comes is usually considered to be outside the tribal group – the position of mullah is often handed down from father to son – he is dependant upon his own particular group. In the zones where the tradition of tribalism is still strong, such as Kunar and Paktya, he does not take part in the *jirga*, though elsewhere (for instance, in Wardak) he attends but as a "technical counsellor". If he attempts to go beyond his function as a person entrusted with the task of managing rituals, an anti-clerical reaction will always follow: "the mullahs to the mosque". Later, we shall consider the status of charismatic leaders. But in each case the representatives of religion exist outside the tribal structure, a fact which has had important consequences with regard to the way in which Islam found political expression during the war and to the influence exercised by the political parties which make up the resistance movement.

The tribal code and Muslim law are in opposition. Adultery (*zina*) should, according to the *shari'at*, require four witnesses if it is to be proven; for the *pashtunwali*, hearsay (*peghor*) is sufficient, for what is at stake is honour (one's self-image) and not morality (defined by the *shari'at* as what is permitted as opposed to what is not). Women in the tribes are not allowed to inherit property, for that would contradict the principle of strict patrilineage, which is the very basis of the tribal system; while the Qur'an grants to women half the share of the male. The dowry, a sign of prestige, frequently exceeds the limits set by the *shari'at*, while, on the other hand, the repudiation of a wife by her husband, something which, according to the Qur'an, presents no difficulties, is practically impossible in the tribes, for that would be an insult to the wife's family. Vengeance (*badal*) is commended within the tribal code, while the *shari'at* attempts to limit the occasions on which it can take place. The *wesh*, the usual way in which land is redistributed, is contested by the mullahs on the grounds that landed property is something intangible.[9] It would be possible to provide many more examples to illustrate that it is not a question of reinterpreting the *shari'at* to satisfy particular interests, but of two positive systems which are quite frankly opposed to each other, because they each present a different image of social order. The *pashtunwali* has as its goal the maintaining within the tribe of an equilibrium which is always under threat – as to the definition of the tribe, this is arrived at by a consensus of opinion. A Pashtun defines himself in opposition to everything which is not Pashtun. The *shari'at*, on the other hand, attempts to transcend specific groups such as tribes, *qawm* and other *asabiyya* in the universality of the *umma*.

The tribal code is more democratic but more restrictive; it does not attempt to transcend the particularity of the group, but makes appeal to the consensus of the tribal community. As far as political life in Afghanistan is concerned, the tribal code tends to isolate the Pashtun community, while the *shari'at*, which does not recognise that ethnic groups have any ultimate reality, envisages a more universal social order. For this reason the work of the *'ulama* is seen as a threat to the identity of the tribe, in so far as they wish to replace the *pashtunwali* by the *shari'at* and to minimise the role of the *khan*, whose power rests entirely upon secular foundations. The village mullahs are often closer to the tribal community than the *'ulama*, and are careful not to interfere in these matters; the charismatic leaders are quite willing to make use of the tribal code so that they may act as mediators.[10] In due course we shall observe how the idea of *jihad* suddenly becomes prominent in times of crisis in tribal zones and how this brings with it a restoration of the power of the *'ulama*. Although the various forms that Islam takes in the countryside have nothing to do with the degree of intensity which the individual brings to his private devotion – and certainly these form an important aspect of life in the tribal zones – they explain to a large extent the differences between the north and the south which have become apparent during the war, differences which cannot be explained on ethnic or religious grounds, but which spring from the different relationship that exists between Islam and politics in these two zones.

Holy men and barakat

Barakat is a form of holiness which brings blessing to all who come into contact with it and which emanates from certain people, places or objects;[11] it is an inherent power which may be transmitted. Sacred objects may be talismen, pages of the Koran, relics; sacred places: may be the *ziyarat*, the tomb of a *pir*. Certain individuals may have *barakat*: the *sayyad*, who, whatever his personal merits, continues to possess and transmit a part of the aura of the Prophet; and the *pir*, the spiritual master, sometimes incorrectly translated as "saint", though in Islam there is no parallel to the Christian theory of mediation, and the *pir* sanctifies others not by his personal intercession, but by contact. The *pir* is most often associated with a Sufi order.

The tombs of the *pir* become places of pilgrimage; a guardian (*muwajer*), living from the offerings of the faithful, looks after the *ziyarat*. Pilgrimages are very much a family affair; many *ziyarat* have a reputation based on their ability to cure specific illnesses: that of Ofyan, in Koh-i-Daman, for instance, was renowned for its power to cure rabies. The attitude of the orthodox clergy towards these manifestations of popular religious sentiment is one of reservation, which is more marked amongst the more highly educated clergy. On the other hand, the village mullahs share wholeheartedly in these practices, and the Afghan clergy show no signs of being opposed to the *pir* in principle.

The concept of the holy man is a broad one, ranging from the *malang*, a vagabond, to the highly respected *pir* who has become an *'alim* of a great *madrasa*. Here, too, there is no clear frontier between popular Islam and other more sophisticated forms. The *malang* or *qalandar* are vagabond preachers, half-crazed and half-naked; they are story-tellers who sell charms and they come originally from outside Afghanistan – often from India; they hang around the *ziyarat* and go freely from mosque to mosque, living on the fringe of a society which does not concern itself over much with the question of its borders.

The *sayyad* are reputed to be descended from Muhammad and the *khwaja* from Caliph Omar. In their social life they benefit from a kind of symbolic circus value, without being necessarily men of religion. They have no political role save that given them by their position in the social structure and their personal qualities. Thus, in tribal zones, the *sayyad* is, by definition, set apart from the other segments of society. Even if his mother-tongue is Pashtu, he will not be thought of as a Pashtun: his *qawm* is *sayyad*, that is to say "Arab". This position of neutrality vis-à-vis the agnatic rivalries implicit in the tribal structure makes him, by definition, the mediator.[12] Many *sayyad* have been able to take advantage of their position to obtain local political influence, and it is for this reason that people, especially the more educated amongst them, exhibit a certain ambivalence towards them, particularly when their ignorance of religious matters is too obvious.

The charismatic mullah is a figure who provides an insight into the social milieu of the tribe when it is undergoing upheaval and suffering from disunity; he emerges at times of crisis, when the ideology of the *jihad* transcends tribal divisions. At such times a figure often comes from outside the world of the tribe to unify the various factions: a *sayyad*, a *pir* or simply a mullah, such as the Somali "mad mullah" of the British raj.[13]

The *pir* are spiritual masters surrounded by their disciples (*murid*). Each region of Afghanistan has its own local *pir*, and when he dies a *ziyarat* will be erected on his tomb. Hermit, healer, or simply "a holy man" in the sense that this term is used in the countryside, his prestige may be limited to his own village or it may reach throughout Afghanistan. Most frequently *pir* are linked to a Sufi order. The dividing line between the *'alim* and the *pir* is indistinct, especially in the north: many of the local *'ulama*, completely orthodox in background and theology, are revered as *pir*, and in the course of time establish a reputation as healers. In Afghanistan, the *'ulama* have never persecuted the *pir*, except, of course, when the latter adhered to extremely unorthodox forms of Islam (like the *rushani* in the sixteenth century). With the *pir* we have reached the institutionalisation of *barakat*. It is no longer a question of "popular religion", but of Sufi orders whose role in the history of Afghan Islam and in the resistance has been very significant.

Sufism

Sufism, which, in essence, is embodied in three orders (*naqshbandiyya, qadiriyya, cheshtiyya*), flourishes in Afghan society and is especially influential in the middle classes of the larger villages and the suburbs of the towns. The great centres of Sufism are Kabul and Herat, but the whole of the north of the country and the region of Kandahar have been very much influenced by Sufism. While Sufism may have experienced an overall decline amongst the intelligentsia of Kabul, it has retained a number of zealous but discrete devotees amongst the intellectuals educated in the classical school and also amongst the scholars of towns such as Herat, which still retain something of the older culture. Many *'ulama* are attached to a Sufi order.

Sufism makes a contrast between two forms of revelation: the former is exoteric (*zahir*) and the latter esoteric (*batin*). To reach the truth through the latter path, it is necessary to receive a spiritual initiation from a master (*pir* or *murshid*). Each pupil (*murid*) must follow the pathway (*tariqat*) in order to attain a knowledge of the divinity, a knowledge which is not discursive but intuitive. The love of God is the merging of the self with the divine infinite; the "orthodox" school (*tariqat-e shari'ati*) maintains that there is a separation between creature and Creator (*wahdat al-shuhud*), the unorthodox school states that there is an essential unity between the two (*wahdat al-wujud*). To reach this stage, the *murid* carries out spiritual exercises, the form of which varies with the different orders. Generally this consists of continuous intoning of one of the names of God (*zikr*), which may be recited either out loud (*qadiriyya*) or silently (*naqshbandiyya*). The authentic Sufis have an intense spiritual life, but one that is not ostentatious. They generally meet in small groups in an out of the way place (*khanaqah*), often linked to a *madrasa*, where they practise recitation under the direction of the *pir*. The Sufi keeps to a strict daily programme of mental discipline, which, although it does not cut him off from social life, nevertheless ensures that he stands aside from it.[14] The link between Persian literature and Sufism is very strong, and particularly so in the case of authors such as Ansari, Jami of Herat and Rumi of Balkh, all highly regarded in Afghanistan. Nevertheless, Sufism was introduced into Afghanistan, as elsewhere, in two very different forms. It is necessary to enlarge upon this point, for Sufism has played an important role in the Afghan resistance, while in the fundamentalist movements (Wahhabism in particular) of the Arab world it has often been decried.

Orthodox Sufism

Orthodox Sufism does not set out to rival formal religion, but offers the believer the opportunity to strengthen his spiritual life, while at the same time scrupulously respecting dogma and the *shari'at*. The *pir* is in this context an *'alim* as much as an initiator. Even if the tradition of his family plays a great part in his decision to seek membership of the *tariqat*, the *murid* is always a member in his own right, undergoes a spiritual initiation and owes a personal allegiance to the *pir*. The members of the *tariqat* regularly attend the meetings of the *zikr*, under the guidance of the master. The religious novice is not cut off from social life; on the contrary, the *tariqat* sometimes strengthens the feeling of solidarity which exists within professional bodies (the corporations or *senf*) by overlaying it with another form of solidarity – that of co-religionists.[15]

The brotherhood constitutes a sort of club for spiritual exercises. This form of Sufism, which originated in the reforms of Shaykh Ahmad Sirhindi (Mujaddid Alf-e Thani) and of Shah Waliullah,[16] is not in any way in conflict with the more formal Islam of the *'ulama*. Most *pir* are perfectly orthodox *'ulama* and carry out, at one and the same time, both exoteric (*fiqh, shari'at*) and esoteric teaching. The relationship between *pir* and *murid* exists in tandem with that of *'alim* and *talib*. To clearly establish their orthodox status, these brotherhoods call themselves *tariqat-e shari'ati*, "a brotherhood which adheres to the teachings of the *shari'at*". Naturally, the *pir* is something more than an *'alim*: he is considered to be endowed with *barakat*, the succession is hereditary and the corporate *murid* may even constitute a *qawm* whose political influence in the area may be considerable. We shall find evidence of this in the networks which form the substratum of the various groups within the resistance.

The orthodox brotherhoods are, above all, *naqshbandi*, but there are also some *cheshti* and some *qadiri*. These have become established in the north and recruit members from the traditionalist and cultured bourgeoisie, from small craftsmen and officials as well as peasants living around the great cultural centres such as Herat, Kabul, Maymana and Mazar-i Sharif. There are also some examples in the provinces amongst the Aymaq, and in some parts of the south, such as Kandahar and Zabul.

"Marabout" Sufism

"Maraboutism" is the collective allegiance of a clan or a tribe to a family of "saints" reputed to be endowed with hereditary *barakat*, which family may act as a channel to sanctify the community. In this case there is no personal commitment, and there are certainly no instances of individuals receiving initiation or involving themselves in meditation. There is a clear distinction between the community and the family of the saint, who alone is supposed to give himself up to the practice of *zikr*, but who, in practice, usually limits himself to manifesting to the community at large his possession of *barakat* by healing the sick, or pronouncing blessings. The disciples call themselves *mukhlis* rather than *murid*, the term implying a less firm relationship with the *pir*. The principal act of devotion of the *mukhlis* consists in an annual visit to the *pir*, to whom they bring presents, in exchange for the *pir's* protection and hospitality, in a relationship of interdependence. The spiritual relationship is replaced by a veneration which can only be described as superstitious. The clan or the tribe is represented in their dealing with the *pir* by the great families and not by the mullahs or by the *'ulama*. In Maraboutism the *pir* is never an *'alim*, and Sufism is strongly marked by anti-clericalism. This is one way in which the tribes may reconcile their need for religion with their desire to assert the specific character of their tribe with regard to the *shari'at* which does not accept common law. In the tribes, Sufism is the expression of secularised politics, while in the north of the country it is the contrary – the affirmation of a strict orthodoxy. Among the tribes, it is rare to find a mullah who belongs to the *tariqat*.

This type of Sufism has, then, established itself in Pashtun tribal zones. The brotherhood which has most members is the *qadiriyya*, which, in the tribal zones, has the Gaylani family at its head. The *naqshbandi* groups, which have been established in the same areas, may belong to either category. To distinguish between these, it is necessary to know if the *pir* is an *'alim* or not; if not he is called *ruhani* and the brotherhood is always a Marabout one. In the south, the distinction between *ruhani* and *'alim* is very clear-cut (whereas the two words have the same meaning in the form of Persian spoken in Iran), and there are very few people who belong to both at the same time. In the north there is no *pir* who is not also *'alim*. The nomads, who are very often linked to a *pir*, always adhere to the Marabout sect, which is only to be expected where the tribal structures are strong. I should mention in passing the interesting and little-known instance of gangs of lawless youths, in Kabul (*koka*) and Kandahar (*payluch*), who have their own hierarchy and initiatory tests. There is no vestige of Sufism in these groups, but it is possible that they may have been influenced by it.[17]

The pir *travellers from Aymaq lands*

All attempts at definition must be somewhat arbitrary and the sharp contrast made above between orthodox and Maraboutic brotherhoods should, in reality, be seen as two poles between which there exist innumerable permutations. In particular, Aymaq territory (in Ghor province) has witnessed a great growth in the teaching of a Sufi doctrine which combines aspects of each of the two types mentioned above. The *pir* are *'ulama* and are not at all opposed to the orthodox clergy of which they are members. But their members come mainly from certain subgroups within the tribes. Based at Purchaman (Farah province) and being a *naqshbandi*, the *pir* (the last of whom, Baha'uddin Jan, was killed under Taraki) delegated *khalifa* (representatives) throughout Aymaq territory to preach to the *murid* and to collect the donations of the faithful. Membership of this movement was, in general, collective: but the *qawm* of the *sayyad* of Khwaje-Hashtomin (Faryab) belongs as a body to the *tariqat*. Far from being in opposition to orthodox Islam, these groups joined the Islamist parties (see p.112) when the resistance movement came into being. It seems that the phenomenon of the travelling *pir* exists throughout all the northern marches of the Hindu-Kush.

The brotherhoods which go to make up Sufism

The qadiriyya

The tomb of the founder of the order, 'Abdul Qadir Gaylani (sixth century AD) is at Baghdad. His descendants were closely linked to the Ottoman regime, which granted them the title of *naqib ul-ashraf*, and it was to Baghdad that the *mukhlis* from many different countries came to visit them. In the sixteenth century, the order was established in India and it was through this route that it reached the Ghilzay Pashtun, in particular the Sulaymankheyl and the Khugiani. The order has a great number of different branches led by descendants of the original founder. Hazrat Naqib Saheb, father of the present Afghan *pir*, left Iraq in the twenties and established himself at Chaharbagh, in Nangrahar, to exercise closer control over the local order. At his death in 1947, his son, Sayyad Ahmad Gaylani, known as Effendi Jan, succeeded him. Very soon the family had formed close links with the rôyalist establishment (Ahmad Gaylani married a Muhammadzay in 1952) and invested the money which it received from donations in activities which were wholly secular: Ahmad Gaylani was the Peugeot representative at Kabul. While the *pir* made concessions to the external symbols of religion (allowing the water which he had used to wash his hands to be distributed to the sick), he permitted the order to become secularised and it was transformed into a network of dependents. Nevertheless, the prestige of the Gaylani family is still as high as it always was amongst the Ghilzay (in particular with the nomads) and the Wardaki. The Gaylani family provides a perfect example of Maraboutic Sufism. But the *qadiri* in the north and the west, except, of course, those who emigrated from Ghilzay, are not linked to the present Gaylani family and lead a far more genuine religious life: they are associated with other branches, such as the *silsila* of Abdurrahman Ibn Auf at Shindand.

The naqshbandiyya

The *naqshbandiyya* was founded at Bukhara by Baha'uddin Naqshband (1318–89). This is the order with the most members in Afghanistan, where there are several branches and two different influences can be felt. The western and northern branches are linked to the birthplace of the order, Central Asia, and include the branch known as "Khwaje Ahrar";[18] the branches in the east and in Kandahar are directly linked to the

Mujaddidi family, descendants of the reformer of the order, Shaykh Ahmad Sirhindi.[19] This family, which came from India, established itself at Kabul at the end of the nineteenth century; a branch of the family went to live in Herat, but never had the political influence that the Kabul family had. In the capital the Mujaddidi founded a *madrasa* and a *khanaqah* at Shor Bazar, from whence stemmed the title of the head of the family, *hazrat-e shor bazar*. The *naqshbandi* of Kabul have followed the Mujaddidi family in accepting orthodoxy; in the tribal zones of Ghilzay, the tribes have adopted Maraboutic ideas; the *naqshbandi* of the north and the west are "orthodox" and do not follow the Mujaddidi family. We shall find these divisions within the resistance.

Unlike the Gaylani, the Mujaddidi have played an important political role. As purely orthodox *'ulama*, they first supported the pan-Islamism of King Amanullah, but later they opposed his reforms. The two strands in the political campaign waged by the three sons of the first Hazrat of Shor Bazar were anti-imperialism and anti-modernism. They were involved in the revolt at Khost in 1924, where a *murid*, 'Abdul Ghani, roused the Sulaymankheyl in the neighbourhood of Mulla-i Lang. In 1928, after the arrest of the Hazrat, his brother Fazl Umar, known as Shir Agha, stirred up the Ghilzay tribes in support of Nadir Khan, after having supported Bacha-yi Saqqao (see p. 67).[20] At the beginning the alliance between the new dynasty of the Musahiban (Nadir, his brothers and his son Zahir) and the family was very tightly knit: Fazl 'Umar was Minister of Justice, and the third brother, Sadeq, was ambassador in Cairo; in 1936, the King granted them the domain of Qala yi Jawan. Through the Osman family, they now had matrimonial links with royalty. Relations became tense again after Daoud's ministry in 1953; members of the family moved to Egypt and there established close links with members of the Muslim Brotherhood, such as Sebghatullah, the present leader, and Harun, who was later arrested by Nasir. Sebghatullah came back to Kabul to teach, joined the Islamist opposition and was arrested and exiled to Denmark in 1959. From the death of Fazl 'Umar in 1956, the new *pir* was Muhammad Ibrahim ("Shir Padshah"). He was executed with all the males of his family in January 1979 by Taraki; Sebghatullah Mujaddidi, who was himself not a *pir*, then succeeded him.

Thus, contradictory influences are at work within the Mujaddidi family. They are linked to the royalist establishment but view the westernisation of the country's customs and legislation with distaste; they are wealthy, but stand outside the capitalist forms of development; they occupy official posts, but they form part of the political opposition; they are conservative, but are also linked to certain radical currents (political Islamism) within Islam.

Yet, as I have said, the Mujaddidi family is far from typical of the Afghan *naqshbandi*. Herat, Purchaman and Karukh are very active *naqshbandi* centres. In the regions, the *naqshbandi* network is identified with that of the *madrasa* and the *'ulama*: thus, the Hazrat of Karukh, whose authority stretches from Herat to Maymana and whose title is Sharafatuddin, is a *Shaykh ul-islam*, and therefore an *'alim*. His authority is bound to be obeyed by his subordinates, as for example, when the Hazrat of 1856 pronounced a *fatwa* to defend Herat against the Iranian Shi'a.

The cheshtiyya

This brotherhood, which was founded by Maudud-i Cheshti (1142–1236), is most firmly established in India. In Afghanistan it is very much a minority group, and is mostly to be found in the Hari-rud valley, around Chest-i Sharif. At present, the *cheshtiyya* has two *pir*. The *'ulama* of the region are *cheshti*; the peasants see the brotherhood as being a *qawm* of *sayyad*, to which most of the people of the town belong. Until 1981, the brotherhood, a typical example of the *tariqat-e shariati*, ran some twenty *madrasa*, each of which had its own library. Here the identification of *pir* with *'alim* and of *murid* with *talib* is complete. Devoting all its financial resources to pay for the needs of teachers and students and the upkeep of the buildings, the brotherhood lives quite apart from the modern world.

In the north the brotherhoods are all orthodox and are therefore usually *naqshbandi*, but it is also possible to find *qadiri, cheshti, sohrawardi* and *ghausi*. These are very decentralised. In the south, the *qadiri* and *naqshbandi* brotherhoods, usually Maraboutic, follow the Gaylani and Mujaddidi families. The *naqshbandi* of Kabul, who are orthodox, also follow the Mujaddidis. There is no Sufism amongst the Shi'a. The differences between the different forms of Sufism are connected with the division between tribal and non-tribal zones. We shall find these networks appearing again when we talk about the resistance.

The *'Ulama*

As in other Sunni countries, in Afghanistan there is no such thing as an organised and hierarchical clergy. Nevertheless, there is a very clear distinction between the village mullahs and the more educated clergy. This "higher clergy" is defined as a body by its education and not by its place in the political institution. Having emerged from medieval Islam, this body has resisted change, in its study and in its general world view, to the present day, although its importance has been much diminished by the process of westernisation.

The madrasa

The *'alim* is called *mawlawi* in Afghanistan. After having left the village Qur'anic school (*maktab*), the religious student (*talib*) spends several years studying with a dozen other students under a local *mawlawi*, in an ordinary mosque transformed into an "upper" religious school (*madrasa*), whose prestige depends on the personality of the master. The study is carried out at a pace which suits each individual and consists in learning a certain number of didactic books in a fixed order.[21] When he has got the diploma, (*ijaza*) the graduate can open his own *madrasa*, or leave to continue his study in a school of higher learning. In Afghanistan, there has never been a *madrasa* capable of offering a first-rate education, in spite of the attempts of the Amirs to bring one into being. The most gifted Afghan *'ulama* used to go to India, in particular to the great *madrasa* of Deoband; and after partition in 1947 Peshawar became the centre where the traditionalist *'ulama* pursued advanced studies.[22] Until 1917, the *'ulama* from the north used to go to Bukhara, to the *madrasa* Diwan Begi.

Parallel with this network of private *madrasa*, the state has attempted to establish a government network so that it can shape the education that the *'ulama* receive, and play a key role in their selection. In 1951, a faculty of theology (*fakulte-ye shariati*) was set up with the help of Al-Azhar University in Cairo, and large *madrasa* were opened in the more important towns. This network has been integrated into the secular education system: the faculty of theology is part of the University of Kabul and the provincial *madrasa* function like ordinary secondary schools, with regard to the selection of pupils and the curriculum, with the exception, of course, of religious subjects. The difference between the *'ulama* who have been educated in the private and the government networks is very clear: the former, who are still clearly in the majority amongst the Afghan clergy, are more traditionalist, while the latter are more modernist in approach and closer to the intelligentsia. The difference between the two networks has nothing to do with the "secular-religious" divide. The state is concerned to monopolise religious instruction, not to destroy it, and has always attempted to restrict the sphere of activity of the *'ulama* who have been educated abroad. Conversely, the private network also provides a secular education, including such subjects as classical literature and traditional medicine. The private *madrasa* cover more or less the whole country, while the government network only exists in the towns.

The *'ulama* are scholars and not intellectuals.[23] They follow the age-old curriculum common to the whole Muslim world: classical Arabic, theology (*kalam*), interpretation of the Qur'an (*tafsir*), traditions of the Prophet (*hadith*), and Muslim law (*fiqh*). The *'ulama* feel that they belong to the Muslim community, the *umma*, rather than to a particular nation. It is true that what is being transmitted is a culture based on commentaries inculcated by repetition, but it is a culture which escapes the confines of parochialism; nevertheless it is ill-equipped to provide an ideology capable of making sense of the modern secular world. As in all Muslim countries, the *'ulama* seem incapable of adapting to the modern world and have allowed power to slip into the hands of new elites.[24]

The decline in the influence of the 'ulama *in the twentieth century*

Although at the end of the last century there were references to great *'ulama* belonging to the tribal aristocracy, this is no longer the case. The majority of the *'ulama* come from the non-tribal country areas (but there are as many Pashtu-speakers as there are Persian-speakers). On the economic level, the partial nationalisation of the *waqf* (religious possessions) by Abdurrahman at the end of the nineteenth century deprived the *'ulama* of their financial autonomy, for unlike their brethren in Iran, the Afghan clergy have never owned extensive lands or property. In the towns, the *'ulama* generally depend on stipends and government salaries; in the countryside, like the mullahs, they live from gifts and payments in kind made to them in the form of the *'ushr* and the *zakat*; but the families of the *mawlawi* are generally better off than those of simple mullahs.

The growing secularisation of the legal system, and the fact that a professional body capable of administering the law has come into being, whose members are graduates from the faculty of law, has deprived the independent *'ulama* of their legal responsibilities. In addition, the network of schools has already slipped from the control of the *mawlawi*; in instances where the small Qur'anic school was able to survive, it had to face the competition of the government primary school, where religion was also taught, but by students from the state secondary school. Many young people preferred to continue their study in the secondary schools or even the state *madrasa*, which guaranteed them work as state employees when they finished, whereas the diplomas awarded by the private *madrasa* were not recognised by the state.

The decline in the political influence of the *'ulama* has occurred more recently in Afghanistan than elsewhere. Until the end of the fifties, the monarchy could not do without their support. It was the *'ulama*, in alliance with the tribes, who caused the downfall of King Amanullah in 1929. The consensus of the tribes and the ceremony of enthronement carried out by the body of the *'ulama* were the two sources of legitimacy available to the sovereign. In 1932, King Nadir institutionalised the *'ulama* in the form of the *jama 'at ul 'ulama*, a council of the principal *'ulama*.[25] But the adoption of a policy of modernisation by Minister Daoud in 1953 rendered it powerless, and replaced it by the myth of the nation-state. The gulf between the government and the *'ulama* began to widen, while the tribal elites remained close to the regime: the coalition of the tribes and the *'ulama* which took place in 1928 was shortlived. In any case, the *'ulama* have never held the reins of political power.

The influence of the *'ulama* has also been reduced by their integration into the structure of the state as employees: where the state did not have enough people to take their place, the traditional *qazi* have become state officials. The clergy in the large towns now receive a salary. The creation of *jama'at ul 'ulama* is purely symbolic: this council may only give its opinion as to whether new laws are in conformity with the *shari'at*. More subtly, the monarchic state has attempted to draw the great religious families into the vast network of dependents, at whose centre is the royal family, by means of marriage, posts as ambassadors, and gifts of land. But when this policy of integration has been seen to fail, the state has not hesitated to have recourse to force: witness the arrests of the members of the Mujaddidi family in the late fifties and the great round-up of *mawlawi* in April 1970 at the Pul-i Khishti mosque (see below).

Finally, the *'ulama* network had no clearly defined centre: the Mujaddidi family which led the revolt of the clergy in 1928 lost a great deal of its influence. There was no specific place where the clercial opposition might come together, for the faculty of theology was in the hands of the Islamists (see chapter 4), who were regarded with some suspicion by the traditionalist clergy. Although in the elections of 1965 twenty-five *mawlawi* were returned as deputies, they did not constitute a party (theoretically forbidden) nor even a unified pressure group. Nevertheless, some kind of reawakening of political consciousness did occur amongst the *'ulama* of the towns, faced as they were with the rapid increase in support for Marxist political parties during the liberal period of 1963 to 1973. In December 1966, there was the famous occasion of the row which broke out within the parliamentary precincts between Muhammad Nabi Muhammadi and Babrak Karmal. In April 1970, following the publication by *Parcham* journal of a poem by Bareq Shafi'i, using, in order to celebrate Lenin's centenary, a religious benediction (*dorud bar Lenin*) which was reserved in Afghanistan for the Prophet, a demonstration by a number of *mawlawi* took place in the Pul-i Khishti mosque. This was the first occasion when the clergy and the militant Islamists worked together. The demonstration was violently repressed. At this time, at the instigation of the Mujaddidi family, two *'ulama* movements were created: the *harakat-i 'ulama-yi muhammadi* and the *khuddam ul-forghan,* the first by Sebghatullah, the second by his uncle, the *pir.* In spite of all this, when the communist coup took place, there were many networks of *'ulama,* but with no political organisation.

In the countryside the prestige of the 'ulama *remains high*

Thus, the decline in the influence of the *'ulama* has occurred only recently and is by no means complete. In the small towns and in the countryside, where state institutions have made only a partial impact, they are still active, especially in the non-tribal zones. They leave the business of local politics to the *khan,* a fact which has usually led to sociologists underestimating the importance of the *'ulama.*[26] The private *madrasa* have continued to exist in those places where the network of government schools is fragmentary. Thus, the *'ulama* have fallen back upon the countryside, where in earlier times they were less well established. Perhaps it would be true to say that a revival of Islam has occurred in the countryside as a result of the return to the villages of those *mawlawi* who were unable to find employment in the towns, where the government was busy replacing them with young people educated in the state system. In any case, the *mawlawi* are close to the rural world. There are several reasons why the prestige of the *'ulama* has remained high.

As we saw in the first chapter, the *'alim* embodies a principle of universality in a country which is highly fragmented, a principle which is both cultural and religious. In the non-tribal zones, the *'alim* is the only source of political legitimation: the nation-state has not taken root because it is, first and foremost, Pashtun. The *'ulama* also embody a principle of historical legitimacy: they have always been the ones to rally the people with a clarion call for a *jihad* and have always been in the forefront of the resistance to colonialism. They even, when necessary, opposed the more pragmatic Amir,[27] to such a degree that Abdurrahman forbad the *'ulama* to preach *jihad.*

Deprived of *waqf,* the *'ulama* have little in common with the new class of big property owners and modern capitalists, whose social origins lie in those influential groups open to secular ideas. Moreover, those more negative aspects of progress (destitution, the breakdown of social structures and the increase in bureaucracy) give a certain resonance to Islamic preaching on social justice, conceived not in revolutionary terms but as a result of moral reforms carried out in the name of laws accepted and understood by all. In opposition to the infiltration of social life by the state and the rhetoric of Marxism, which also emanated from the seat of power (the army and the teaching profession), the preaching of the *'alim* portrayed a familiar, stable, just universe and offered a guarantee of personal salvation.

The political vision of the 'ulama

Why were the *'ulama* not able to build upon this trust in order to create a political movement to be reckoned with? Nostalgia for a past which existed only in their imagination, withdrawal into a narrow legalism (even though, on the personal level, this was accompanied by an intensely spiritual life), and the inability to view the modern world as anything other than a source of alienation all contributed to the *'ulama* being unable to present a coherent political programme.

The *'alim* as such does not seek political power. Here we should examine more closely the idea that Islam knows no separation between spiritual and temporal. Islam has always recognised that there is such a thing as a de facto power (the Sultan) based on force, which may bring into being the whole machinery of the state (*hukumat*) with its own legal system (*qanun*) and its penal sanctions (*ta'zir*). While able to command its citizens' loyalty, to be legitimate this power must work for the defence of Islam (and thus receive the approbation of the *'ulama*), and it must promulgate the *shari'at*. The Sultan must act in accordance with the teachings of Islam, but this very willingness to conform to religious teaching presupposes that the ruler exists apart from and outside religion, an idea which the Islamist is unwilling to accept. The duty of the scholars is to ensure that the policies (*siyasat*) of the prince are in accordance with the *shari'at*; for this purpose they act as the prince's counsellors, and provide him with legal advice (*fatwa*). Public order, which is a prerequisite of all that is socially desirable in society (*maslahat*), has always seemed, to the *'ulama*, preferable to the demand that politics should be completely open to the promptings of religion. It is easy to imagine a number of compromises with the ruling power entailed by such an attitude on the part of a body which has no other means of enforcing its will than censure or the call to revolt.

This view of politics has nothing to do with the era of the first four Caliphs (the *rashidun*) who were, at one and the same time, both religious and military leaders. *'Ulama* politics are "medieval" and go back to the period when the body of the *'ulama* was first emerging as an institution, and when the secular – that is to say virtually non-religious – power was being established. When the sovereign becomes simply the cornerstone of an ordered society and no longer has any inherent legitimacy (through being linked to the Prophet or being placed on the throne by the *umma*), then it is necessary to provide a counterweight to possible misdirection by embodying a principle of legitimacy in some other institution to ensure that no abuse of power occurs. In the final analysis, the weaker the claim of the government to represent the duly constituted authority, the more closely do the *'ulama* become identified with that very same principle of legitimacy. Except amongst the Shi'a, the *'ulama* have no ambition to create a theocratic state.

In Afghanistan, the *'ulama* have never opposed the power of the Amir and have rarely become involved in his appointment, something which (except in 1919 and 1929) has been left to the tribes to decide. What concerns the *'alim* is civil society and not the state. The state must promulgate the *shari'at* within society, and outside it he must defend the Muslim *millat*. The *'alim* is thus a fundamentalist in the strict sense of the term: he seeks to get back to the original scriptures and the practice of the law. His is not a political role: he can allow the form of the government to vary. Opposition to the state after the fifties came not from any assertion on the part of the *'ulama* of their right to power, but from the fact that the government justified its authority not by appealing to Islam but on other grounds, which automatically removed from the body of the *'ulama* their function of underpinning the legal authority of the government. But even in this conflict, the *'ulama* can only be described as reacting to events, not directing them, and thus their position is essentially a negative one. One has to go to the Islamist intellectuals to find an alternative conception of the state.

The Shi'a

The Afghan Shi'a belong to the Jaffarite branch, that is to say they recognise, as do the majority of Shi'a in the Muslim world, the twelve *iman* starting with 'Ali, the son-in-law of the Prophet and the fourth Caliph. The Shi'a represent about 15 per cent of the Afghan population. They include almost all of the Hazara ethnic group, living in the central part of the country, but they also form substantial urban minorities in Kabul and Ghazni and at some time in the past still others migrated to Quetta and to the eastern part of Iran. The second Shi'a group comprises the *qizilbash*, descendants of the soldiers and officials who were brought to Afghanistan in the eighteenth century by the Shah of Persia, Nadir; although this group, which lives mainly at Kabul, is few in number, they are well educated and have always played an important role in the life of the urban intelligentsia. There is a third group, whose native tongue is Persian, in Nimruz province, living in the marshes of Seistan and in the plain of Khashrud; known as *fars* they are virtually indistinguishable from the Iranians across the border. There is also a Persian-speaking

Shi'ite minority at Herat, a relic of feudal times when Herat belonged to one of the vassals of the Shah of Iran. Finally, there are small Shi'ite groups, the *khallili*, whose native tongue is Pashtu, at Kandahar, in Logar and in the north. The Isma'ili, few in number, are considered by the Shi'a to be heretical: they represent a Hazara subgroup at Kayan (near Doshi), whose leader (the *sayyad* of Kayan) is the leader of all the Isma'ili, and also of all the other linguistic minorities of Pamir (the Tajik of the mountains: *munjani, shughni, rushani, ishkashemi, wakhi*). In general the Isma'ili are very poor, not particularly zealous and are regarded with suspicion by the others. The Shi'ite minority has always been far removed from the centres of power; they have been looked down upon and, until 1963, were practically outside the law. Their religious practices (praying with palms upraised, the procession of the *moharram*) were forbidden and the Jaffarite law was not recognised by the state. It was impossible for them to pursue a career in the army or in politics. The Shi'a living in the towns worked hard at building up their businesses and gained a great deal from the development of education from the fifties onwards. Shi'a students were very politically aware and formed the hard core of the Maoist movements. The educated Shi'a are very conscious of their position as a minority and are noted for political activism, but the Hazara peasantry are untouched by the modern world.

The clergy and the influence of Iran

Amongst the Afghan Shi'a there is a tendency to adopt Iran as a model, but this has nothing to do with the political regime in power there at the present time. In the inns of Hazarajat where, ten years ago, you would have found a portrait of the Shah of Iran, you will now find that of Khumayni. The educated Shi'a speak a form of Persian influenced by usages current in Iran (the use of "sir" (*agha*) and patronymics ending in *i* (Tawakolli, Beheshti)). A large proportion of the Afghans working in Iran are Shi'a.

Nevertheless, Iranian influence has not made itself felt amongst the traditional clergy, which has nothing resembling the hierarchy to be found in Iran. It is hard to tell the difference between a Shi'a and Sunni village mullah. On the other hand, the *'ulama* (called *shaykh*) are educated either at Qom, or at Najaf in Iraq (but by Iranian teachers); they return provided with a certificate awarded by an Iranian *mojtahid*. Personal relations between the Iranian clergy and the upper levels of the Afghan Shi'ite clergy are therefore very close, but no Afghan has ever been awarded the title of Ayatullah, even though the desire to model themselves upon Iran has caused certain *shaykh* to adopt the title for themselves. Nevertheless, the influence of the Iranian revolution has been very marked amongst the young Afghan Shi'a since 1978, and this applies both to those who have worked in Iran and to those who are members of the clergy. They have adopted Iranian religious practices (*taqlid*: the choice of a moral counsellor) and the politico-religious slogans of the revolution. Relations between the traditional clergy and young people who have returned from Iran are very tense.

For the Hazara, their ethnic (*qawm*), political (*millat*) and religious (*mazhab*) identity are often one and the same thing. The three terms are often employed interchangeably, though *qawm* in Hazarajat means ethnic group rather than extended family. This feeling of cultural identity has developed, especially amongst the young intellectual émigrés, into Hazara nationalism.

The Shi'ite religious revival

Until the fifties the Shi'a community was politically dormant. At that time there spread through the community a revivalist movement, the instigators of which were certain religious leaders who had returned from Najaf (Iraq). The movement, which began as a preaching campaign and which was marked by the opening of *madrasa* to produce a clergy better equipped for their tasks, soon became an assertion of cultural, social, and even political rights. The mosques were transformed into cultural centres, dispensing community welfare at Kabul and Kandahar, and the Shi'a demanded their political freedom. Around 1953 there was even a Hazara uprising at Kezel. The whole Shi'ite movement was repressed by Prime Minister Daoud, who continued to meet Shi'a demands with further repression when he became president.

In the sixties, several Shi'ite *madrasa* were opened in the provinces and those already existing in the towns experienced a revival. In Hazarajat, Sayyad Beheshti opened the *madrasa* of Takht-i Waras, which secondary school pupils also attended during school holidays. In Kabul, Wa'ez, who was later to be assassinated when Taraki was in power, was the head of the *muhammadiyya madrasa*, and he founded a cultural association which was very influential with the young Shi'a; he was arrested under Daoud's ministry, and wrote *Khaterat-i zendan* (Memories of prison). Kandahar produced the greatest living Shi'ite religious leader, Shaykh Asaf Muhseni, a former disciple of Ayatullah Khuy at Najaf; he was in charge of the *husseyniyya madrasa* and founded the *subh-i danish* (dawn of knowledge) movement, which at first had purely cultural goals. But under the influence of a disciple from Kabul, networks were set up which bore a close resemblance to those of the Muslim Youth organisation. A large number of small Shi'ite groups were established, ranging from the Iranian *mujahidin-i khalq* tendency to Maoism and representing all the subtle gradations of politico-religious ideology. Shi'a youths were introduced to radical thinking by their membership of cultural associations. We should not forget that young educated Shi'a are noticeably more politicised and more assertive in their demands than their Sunni contemporaries. We shall meet these movements again in the resistance. Nevertheless, the Shi'ite clergy of Herat and the Shi'ite population of Nimruz in general, very much influenced by secularism, have stayed outside the Shi'ite revivalist movement.

Chapter 3

The origins of Afghan fundamentalism and popular movements up to 1947

Afghanistan has always been at the crossroads between the Indian subcontinent, Iran and Central Asia. Although a tradition of popular uprising stems from the Iranian Khorassan,[1] the religious currents which swept Afghanistan from the sixteenth to the twentieth century all came from India and it was in the east of the country, on the frontier, that rebellion took place. Afghanistan, on the threshold of the subcontinent, has invaded India many times. Many dynasties in northern India, including that of the Moguls (1526–1852), were founded by princes who had come from Afghanistan. The cultural similarities between the countries are very marked, and Persian was for a long time the language of the court at Delhi. Above all, until 1947 India was the main educational centre for Afghan *'ulama*; it also provided them with the opportunity of coming face-to-face with other religions (Hinduism, Sikhism, Christianity) or with heresies (the syncretism of Akbar), which acted as a stimulus to Muslim reform. There was little dispute concerning the frontier with Iran, apart from the conflict about Herat. The north of Afghanistan was disputed between the Uzbek *khan* and the Amirs of Kabul, but no popular religious movement (this area was Sunni) made itself felt until the arrival of the Bolsheviks. The general decay which set in during the Bukhara regime also had its effect on intellectual life.

Religious reform movements in India at that time had some aspects in common with Islam in Afghanistan. First of all, there was fundamentalism, the desire to return to the *shari'at* and to the original scriptures. Secondly, there was Sufism, the predominant figures of which were *naqshbandi*. Finally, political issues played a more and more important part, a prelude to the Islamist movement of the present century (chapter 4). These were characterised by a nostalgia for the caliphate, a denunciation of social injustice (especially Waliullah), an increased emphasis on *ijtihad* in order the better to come to terms with the modern world, and, after Sayyad Barelvi (see below), an effort to find the most appropriate form of organisation. Despite the lack of agreement amongst contemporary writers,[2] from Mujaddid Alf-e Thani to Maududi a common strand of thought had great influence on the ideas of the *'ulama* and the Afghan religious intellectuals.[3]

Reformism in the Indian subcontinent in the seventeenth and eighteenth centuries: Mujaddid Alf-e Thani and Shah Waliullah

What has been termed the *"naqshbandi* reaction"[4] began with Shaykh Ahmad Sirhindi Faruqi, who was born in India at Sirhind in 1564. He was both a *naqshbandi khalifa* and an *'alim*, and opposed to the new syncretist religion (*din-i ilahi*) which Emperor Akbar promulgated in 1582. He wanted to get back to an Islam purified of all Hindu influence, while at the same time ensuring that its spiritual dimension remained untouched by the legalistic formalism which passed as orthodoxy amongst the *'ulama* of his time. He therefore advocated that Sufism should free itself from its tendency towards monism. This merging of a fierce orthodoxy with a Sufic spirituality runs right through Indo-Afghan revivalism, and in this respect is quite clearly at variance with the Wahhabi movement in Arabia, which is fundamentally hostile to Sufism.[5] The work of Shaykh Ahmad bore fruit during the reign of Akbar's son Jahangir: his writings (the "epistles": *maktubat*) have endured as a fundamental inspiration for religious revivalism in the Indian subcontinent. He was given the title of Mujaddid Alf-e Thani, "the reformer of the second millennium", which in itself is indicative of a latent millennialism within the movement. One branch of the family, the Mujaddidi, established itself at Kabul in the nineteenth century.[6]

Shah Waliullah (1703–62) was also an *'alim* and a Sufi. He saw himself as continuing the work of Shaykh Ahmad Sirhindi, but with a stronger streak of mysticism. In particular he stressed that the tradition of *ijtihad* should be reintroduced and he began to preach Islam in political and social terms, advocating greater social justice. He did not recognise the religious authority of the Mogul emperors and revived the idea of the caliphate, which was to be very influential in the subcontinent.[7] Faced with the threat presented by the Marathes, he called for a *jihad* and urged Ahmad Shah Durrani, the Afghan sovereign, to come to India to fight against them: this led to the great victory of Panipat in 1761. The call for a *jihad* was to become a commonplace of Muslim revivalism in the region.

While Shah Waliullah scarcely mentioned the British, his son and successor, 'Abdul 'Aziz, promulgated a *fatwa* declaring India *dar-ul harb*, a land where war between believers and unbelievers was being waged; and in 1803 obedience to the British was deemed to be a sin. Resisting the infidel now became a central issue, but it was still linked with Muslim reform: the main thesis was that it was only the rejection of Islam that had permitted the infidel to triumph, and that the way to liberation was through a return by the whole society to its former faith. Once again, we have here a constant theme which reappears with Barelvi, the Deoband school, the caliphate movement, Maududi and the members of the Afghan resistance. It is only in the Hindu areas that one finds a secular form of nationalism. For the majority of Muslim thinkers, nationalism is a secular idea, and those who fiercely opposed the British later opposed no less fiercely the establishment of Pakistan, which they saw as being both a negation of pan-Islamism and also of the dream that one day there would be a general conversion of all the Hindus.

The Mujahidin movement under Sayyad Ahmad Barelvi (1826–31)

From then onwards, religious reformism, still led by *naqshbandi*, was increasingly to take on militaristic overtones. Sayyad Ahmad Barelvi (1786–1831), a native of north-east India and disciple of 'Abdul 'Aziz, was the first person to realise the necessity of a movement which was at the same time religious, military and political. Working with great thoroughness, he established a network of people through the length and breadth of India to collect funds and encourage volunteers, and he himself travelled widely through the subcontinent, attracting a following from amongst the faithful. He chose first to oppose the Sikh kingdom of Ranjit Singh, which was expanding towards Afghanistan (the river Indus was crossed in 1823). Probably his idea was to establish a Muslim bastion on the north-west frontier before attacking the British.[8] Barelvi preached *jihad* amongst the Pashtun tribes, and demanded that they renounce their tribal customs and adopt the *shari'at*. The *khan* were ousted and the *'ulama* took their place, and a system of Islamic taxes was established, the money thus collected going towards the war effort. For the first time, the call to engage in *jihad* was addressed directly to the people, over the heads of the traditional leaders. The beginnings of a political party (*jama'at*), the chief aim of which was to carry out propaganda amongst the people, came into existence; it was not simply a question of carrying out religious preaching, for group activity depended on networks of preachers, collectors and judges, all seeking to carry out a common programme of evangelism (*nizam-i da'wat*) based on the village and not the court. The call for an armed uprising was only made after the final link in the network had been put in place. In spite of this, the campaign against the Sikhs was a failure, due to the treachery of the local *khan*, and Barelvi was killed by the Sikhs in 1831. Numbers of the Mujahidin (Barelvi's followers) took part in tribal uprisings in the north-west province until 1897, the date of the battle of Ambala against the British.

The movement belongs to the tradition of tribal uprisings led by charismatic leaders (we shall return to this subject) and was also a forerunner of the notions of Afghan resistance held at the present time by the Islamists and the *'ulama*: the concept of *jihad* presupposes that a revival of Islam has already occurred within traditional society.

The Deoband school

The great rebellion of 1857 against British rule in India was actively supported by the survivors of the Barelvi movement and by the majority of the *'ulama*, but the Amir of Kabul, Dost Muhammad, refused to take part. The rebellion was the last attempt by the Indian Muslims to regain political power. There followed a period in which activity of this kind died down, making way for two strategies, both claiming the authority of Shah Waliullah. The modernists, with Sir Sayyad Ahmad Khan, chosing the path of loyalty to Britain and the westernisation of the Muslim community, founded the school at Aligarh. The orthodox wing, led by the *'ulama*, founded the *madrasa* of Deoband, near Delhi, in 1867.[9] Most of the great Afghan *'ulama* were to be educated there. The curriculum, which could take ten years to complete, comprised 106 books having to do with theology (according to the Ashari doctrine), the commentary on the Qur'an, the Hanafite *fiqh*, and the *hadith*, and also included Arabic and Persian grammar, literature, Greek and Arab philosophy, astronomy and medieval geometry, the branch of medicine known as 'Greek' (*yunani*) and logic. In Panjshir, in 1981, the author met an *'alim*, Mirajuddin, from Astana, who had graduated in India and who still taught children geometry based on an Arab manuscript of the *Elements* of Euclid. Deoband was the second university to be created in the Muslim world after Al-Azhar. The Deoband school rejected innovation (*bid'at*), kept to a strict orthodoxy and would not permit the cult of the saints; nevertheless, it accepted Sufism and many of the teachers were *naqshbandi* or *qadiri*, which, in itself, clearly shows how the fundamentalism of the school is distinct from that of the Saudi Wahhabi. Once again, the link between fundamentalism and Sufism was to be the hallmark of the orthodoxy of the *'ulama* of the subcontinent, Afghanistan included.

To this dimension of religious fundamentalism there was added a militant strain of anti-British and pan-Islamic sentiment. Nevertheless, following in the footsteps of Barelvi, those responsible for the direction of affairs in the school considered that liberation presupposed the return of

57

society to the Islamic faith. But instead of directing their campaign towards the people, they sought primarily to influence the clergy. In spite of the attitude referred to above, just before the First World War, the 'ulama of Deoband took up positions which were more nakedly political under their new leader Mahmud Al Hassan (1850–1921). They campaigned in favour of the Ottoman caliphate and against the British Empire and found much to be hopeful about in Afghanistan, one of the few independent Sunni Muslim countries. As long ago as 1908, the head of the royal *madrasa* at Kabul, Abdurrazzaq, a former pupil of Deoband, tried to mount anti-British operations on the frontier, but was prevented from doing this by Amir Habibullah. Up to 1919 he led a campaign, the aim of which was to arouse the Pashtun tribes along the frontier.[10] Afghanistan and the north-west province were of great importance to the 'ulama of Deoband and they established a chain of *madrasa* right along the frontier. These still operate today and have provided the majority of the Afghan 'ulama since partition in 1947. The historical influence of Deoband has certainly been crucial to the development of Islam in Afghanistan; the only opposition to this tradition has been provided by the secular parties and by the Islamists and the Wąhhabites, who, in their turn, set about establishing *madrasa* in the north-west province from the fifties onwards.

Loyal to the pan-Islamic ideal, which was also a central plank of the fundamentalist – later to become Islamist – movement of the subcontinent, the 'ulama did not favour the idea of an independent Pakistan and preferred to support the Indian Congress. The contradiction, as was the case with Maududi later on, was only on the surface; an independent Pakistan would no longer be able to pursue policies designed to promote the spread of Islam beyond its frontiers and would be forced to withdraw into a narrow nationalism which retained no vestige of religion, while a united India seemed to them to present greater opportunities of restoring Muslim hegemony. Nothing illustrates more clearly their vision of what Islam might become – an evangelising and triumphant force – once it had been reformed and freed from British tutelage. From Afghanistan to Bengal, the Deoband school embodied a spirit of universality which transcended the limitations of ethnic groups and languages. It is understandable that the Afghan 'ulama, whose own country of origin was equally divided, should feel more at ease in this environment than in the ethnocentric Arab world. But, paradoxically, pan-Islamism developed in the Indian subcontinent at the very moment when the Ottoman Empire, which for so long had provided it with a historical point of reference, broke up under the pressure of warring nationalism.

Charismatic leaders and tribal movements

Of the three confederations of Pashtun tribes (Durrani, Ghilzay and the eastern Pashtun), only the first two evolved political institutions, shortlived in the case of the Ghilzay (1707–38) and more durable in the case of the Durrani (from 1747 onwards). The eastern tribes, who have always been very much attached to their customs and jealous of their independence, have never produced a political confederation. On the other hand, from the sixteenth century onwards, they were regularly thrown into turmoil by great millennarian movements led by charismatic religious leaders. None of these achieved anything, but present-day struggles are rooted in the memory of *jihad* of former times. In fact, one should make a distinction between tribal warfare and *jihad*. The former involved relatively few people and usually did not go beyond the level of the tribe; battles were fought intermittently and the cause of hostilities was a desire for vengeance or a struggle for material possessions. Few casualties were involved – the conflict was symbolic more than anything else, and the combat was really no more than the prelude to the bargaining that always followed. It was warfare waged between equals and, although it might have produced a number of heroes, there was never any question of a charismatic leader emerging. The *jihad*, on the other hand, always involved a coalition of tribes formed around the person of a leader fired with religious zeal. Even though there may have been similarities in the two cases on the question of tactics and general behaviour (such as pillaging), in the latter case they were fighting against an enemy who was irredeemably alien (the infidel, whether heretic, Sikh, British or communist). The charismatic leader nearly always stood outside the tribal framework; his point of reference was not tribalism, nor even the Pashtun community, but the Muslim *umma*. The figure who welded the tribe into a unit could only come from outside the tribal world. The factionalism of tribal life is thus effectively ruled out both, as it were, from below, because the leader has no significant ethnic origins, and also from above, because he points to something which transcends all the differences between Muslims. As a *hadith* puts it: "There is no genealogy in Islam" – and thus no tribalism.

Religious uprisings have not altered in any fundamental way over a period of four hundred years: they have had the same leaders and the content of their preaching has not changed. Bayazid Ansari, the founder of the *rushaniyya* sect (1525–85?), was an Ormuri from Kaniguram (Waziristan), a small ethnical minority which still survives today; he and his descendants led the tribes of Afridi, Orakzay, Mohmand, Bashgash and Khalil in uprisings for nearly a century.[11] Mullah Darwaza, his adversary, who led the Yusufzay in an uprising in the name of orthodoxy, was a *tajik*,[12] a disciple of Sayyad 'Ali Shah from Termez (he was also a non-Pashtun), whom the tribes revered under the name of Pir Baba. The aforementioned Sayyad Ahmad Shah Barelvi, who led the tribes in an uprising in 1826, was a Hindu. The Akhund of Swat[13] was probably a Gujar rather than a Yusufzay, the tribe he belonged to from choice. Shami Pir, who whipped up the feelings of the Sulaymankheyl and the Waziri in 1939, was, as his name indicates, a native of Syria. The Mujaddidi family came from India and the Gaylani from Iraq. Finally, we should remember that all the *sayyad* are by definition seen as standing outside the tribal structure, and are regarded as being Arabs even if they speak Pashtu and they have married wives from Pashtun circles for a number of generations. Even if a charismatic leader is not a *sayyad* and does not come from a different ethnic group, he cannot possibly be a *khan*; by definition the role of *khan* is limited to extending favours and increasing the number of people who are dependent upon him. He cannot be regarded as having a social status which places him outside and above the system of clans. The rule cannot be broken in this respect. It is also the nature of the present war (*jihad* and not a tribal war) which explains the absence of *khan* at the head of the Mujahidin.

The charismatic leader unites the tribes for the purpose of the *jihad* by his religious preaching and his call for reforms. In particular, his aim is to do away with injustice by a return to the *shari'at*. The *rushani* provides the only example where this preaching is based upon heretical ideas. In the other instances, the religious doctrines were the fundamentalist ones that we have already seen at work among the Afghan and Indian *'ulama*; the leader is a Sufi who directs his followers to return to the *shari'at*. The tribes are gathered together to re-establish "the true faith of Islam", and to meet a threat coming either from infidels, or from a sovereign deemed to have become a *kafir* (as was the case with Amanullah in 1928). Leaders of this kind included Hadda Mullah from Nangrahar, who was hostile both to the English and to Amir Abdurrahman, and influential amongst the Shinwari and the Mohmand (1880–1900). Others were Mushk-i Alam (a self-proclaimed *sayyad* from India but married to a Ghilzay Andar), who brought about a shortlived tribal coalition and attempted, without success, to wrest Kabul from the English (1879), Mulla-i Lang, who led the Mangal in an uprising against Amanullah (1924), and finally the Hazrat of Shor Bazar (a Mujaddid) calling for a holy war against King Amanullah in 1928.

What, then, is the relationship between tribal structure and religious movement, since such charismatic leaders only appear in the context of the tribe? For the majority of Western authors the *jihad* is no more than the ideological dressing of tribal warfare.[14] But, as we have seen, the course pursued by these two kinds of warfare is quite different, even if the attitude of the warrior in the heat of the battle (and more particularly with regard to the booty gained or desired) is the same. In particular, the *jihad* always implies a shift in power relations in favour of religious leaders and to the detriment of the *khan*. The ideal type of insurrection led by a charismatic leader is the one which had Sayyad Ahmad Barelvi at its head,[15] but one can also find typical examples in the siege of Kabul by Mulla-i Lang and in the many armed exploits of the Afghan resistance.[16] Because the new leader's authority has its source in religion, he attempts to oppose tribal customs in order to impose upon his followers the *shari'at*, the professional *qazi* and a new system of taxation.[17] While the movement is in the ascendant the *khan* takes a back seat. The warriors, on scenting victory, turn their attention to the distribution of the spoils and the new hierarchical relations which their armed exploits and the circulation of newly acquired goods will create; rather than admit that one of their erstwhile equals has gained a position of superiority, they prefer to play their own game, which usually leads to the army being disbanded. Thus, the *khan* appeal to tribal solidarity against the encroachment of the religious leaders and attempt to undermine the *jihad* in order to restore the traditional mode of politics within the tribe. This should not be seen as an act of treachery: for a *khan* what counts is his prestige in the eyes of his equals and not victory won against an external enemy. Political intrigue within the tribe takes place behind closed doors and the loser may always hope to overturn the result some time in the future. Tribal warfare occurs in a space which is inside the tribal world, whereas the *jihad* takes place outside it. It is better to come to some agreement with an enemy who recognises your local standing than to gain the *jihad* and risk losing your identity within the tribe. This was well understood by the British, who maintained their power by strengthening tribalism,[18] and it is also the policy being followed by the Russians in Afghanistan.

Of course, it is not always easy to distinguish between a tribal war and *jihad* for, even if a charismatic religious leader is involved, the combatant may regard the conflict as a tribal one if it is limited to a small area,[19] and the inner motivation of the ordinary soldier may be quite different from that of the leader. The elites experience conflict stemming from the contradictions between the tribal structure on the one hand, based on the *pashtunwali* and the interlocking circles of dependents (*mlatar*), whose focal point may range from the *malik* to the *khan*, and on the other hand the *jihad*, which presupposes the replacement of the tribal code by the *shari'at* and the emergence of non-tribal religious chiefs. It is not surprising that life is not simple for a common soldier having to act in conformity with the two systems at the same time. His personal faith is very important to him and Islam is the only means he has of escaping from the narrowness of his own experience; but at the same time tribalism is the code by which he lives. It is the external threat which gives Islam its energising power, with all the reorientation of values and ideas that that implies, but tribalism reappears in his relationships with other Pashtun, and the tension between these two poles is a recurring theme within the Afghan resistance movement.

Political pan-Islamism

The concept of the *umma*, the Muslim community, is of great importance in Afghanistan. It is a theme which constantly recurs in times of popular unrest and features prominently in the preaching both of the *'ulama* and of the charismatic mullahs. But until the beginning of the twentieth century, pan-Islamism was not a political doctrine; it was an ideology which arose as a result of infidel incursions against the Muslim community, now separated from the Hindu world and the British by a moveable frontier. For the *'ulama*, pan-Islamism is a basic fact of Islam, a truth both eternal and supreme, not linked to the uncertainties of the political world. The first to think of pan-Islamism in political terms were the Afghan sovereigns. For them, up to and including Amanullah, pan-Islamism consolidated the naissant state, and was a factor in its foreign policy which gave Afghanistan an enhanced role in the region, while carefully avoiding any temptation to be caught up in a policy of destabilising British India or Soviet Turkestan. With the arrival of Nadir Khan in 1929, pan-Islamism disappeared from the vocabulary of those who favoured the development of a modern state and once again became the monopoly of the *'ulama*.

In Afghanistan the rulers have always been able to evoke a favourable response from the people by referring to Muslim solidarity. They have presented themselves as the protectors of Islam and have made it seem as if their wars of conquest were carried out for religious motives – for example the struggle against the Shi'ite heresy or the Zoroastrians, during the invasion of Persia in 1709, or the struggle against the Marathes in 1761. The last Afghan sovereign to respond to an appeal from the Muslims of India for help against the infidels, the Sikhs as it happened, was Shah Zaman in 1795.[20] But harping on the pan-Islamic theme has never been anything more than a means of strengthening the power of the state, and this has always been a major aim of those in power.

Thus, every time that the people's fervour for pan-Islamism rises to such a point that it endangers the Afghan state, the sovereigns have always chosen to play safe and resist the pressure of the *'ulama* in favour of intervention. Dost Muhammad refused to support the great Indian Mutiny of 1857 in which the Muslims played a major part. Abdurrahman opposed the charismatic mullahs who wanted to hurl the frontier tribes into battle against the British. Habibullah refused to take the side of Turkey during the First World War and yielded to British pressure to prevent agitators bringing about an uprising amongst the frontier tribespeople. Finally, Amanullah, the ruler who was the most sympathetic to the pan-Islamic idea, refrained from helping the Basmachi after 1923 and did his best to block the Khilafat movement in India (see below); he also forbade *'ulama* educated abroad, and thus at Deoband, to teach in Afghanistan.

The history of modern Afghanistan represents a number of short periods when the *'ulama* and the ruling circles came together under the banner of pan-Islamism, followed by longer periods when Islamic opposition condemned those in power for making pacts with the infidel. This thread can be traced from the *fatwa* of excommunication pronounced in 1881 by the *'ulama* of Kandahar against Abdurrahman[21] to the demonstrations of the young Islamists in 1972 because of the way that Kabul was supporting India against Pakistan.

The great period of political pan-Islamism stretches from the war in the Balkans in 1911 to the abolition of the caliphate by Ataturk in 1924. This was the only time when pan-Islamism offered the chance of a political strategy which would have allowed Afghanistan to play a regional role. The call to defend the Muslim world came from the Indian Muslims. It was taken up by the Afghan *'ulama* and also by the modernist movement of young Afghans, whose mentor was Mahmud Tarzi, a disciple of Jamaluddin Afghani and founder of the newspaper *Seraj-ul Akhbar* (1911–19), which led to the progressive and liberal movement.[22] The assassination of King Habibullah in 1919, after he refused to support Turkey against Britain, represented the high point of this coalition.[23] The new king, Amanullah, made a unilateral proclamation of his country's independence. He then declared war against the British, which led to a military defeat but a political victory in 1919. Amanullah was acclaimed by the clergy, the people and the modernists. He signed a treaty of friendship with the USSR in February 1921, one clause of which maintained the independence of Bukhara and Khiva, which, incidentally, was enough in itself to make any future allusion to this treaty worthless. He also signed a treaty with Turkey on 1 March 1921, which country was recognised by Afghanistan as the custodian of the caliphate.[24] The prestige of Amanullah was at its peak at a time when, both in Afghanistan and in India, a rather odd pan-Islamic movement was about to develop: the Khilafat.

The Khilafat movement was founded in India in 1919 by two brothers, Muhammad 'Ali and Shawkat 'Ali, with 'Abdul Kalam Azad, also a *naqshbandi*, at its head.[25] The members of the movement had links both with Deoband and with Aligarh. Its aim was to achieve the recognition of the Ottoman Caliph as the Caliph of all Muslims and it also preached the *hijrat* (exodus) of Muslims under foreign domination to independent Muslim countries. Amanullah supported the movement quite openly, until thousands of Indian Muslims decided that they would go and live in Afghanistan. This exodus of people, who had sold all their belongings, ended in August 1920, when Amanullah was finally obliged to call a halt to a human tragedy. The abolition of the sultanate by the Turkish National Assembly in November 1922, which withdrew recognition of the Caliphs' temporal power, followed by the outright abolition of the caliphate in March 1924, meant that the Khilafat movement no longer had anything to campaign about, and it soon fizzled out.

At the same time, King Amanullah embarked upon a policy of modernising Afghan society,[26] which meant that he lost the support of the clergy. This was the end of the alliance between the tribes, the clergy and the modernist establishment under the banner of pan-Islamism. The basic disagreement had to do with the relation between the defence of Islam and westernisation. For the fundamentalist *'ulama*, the defence of Islam was to be achieved by the return of society to Islam, which, for them, involved a return to the *shari'at*. For Amanullah, the defence of Islam was one strand in a policy of resistance to imperialism and was to be achieved by westernisation; in fact, the term "Islam" meant different things to each of the two parties. The *'ulama* identified Islam with religion, and thus with the *shari'at*. The modernists, on the other hand, defined Islam, from a more specifically Third World viewpoint, as a cultural form; it enabled them, when the Japanese defeated Russia in 1905, to see it as a victory of downtrodden Asia over the West, achieved by westernisation.[27] For the *'ulama* all forms of westernisation were a defeat and could not possibly be a means of opposing the West.

This is an ambiguity that is to be found throughout the history of the Muslim world: is Islam a culture or a religion? Some Muslims who have also been out-and-out atheists, such as Sultan Galiev in the USSR and even Hafizullah Amin in Afghanistan, have defended the thesis that "Asiatic" revolutions have something unique about them which sets them apart from the Soviet model, while at the same time they have been engaged in a bloody struggle against Muslim clergy.[28] Lenin saw the pan-

Islamic movement as anti-imperialist, as is shown by the appeal of the Council of Commissars of the People to the Muslims of Russia and of the Orient (24 November 1917), but a few years later the Russians came to see pan-Islamism as a reactionary ideology. All Soviet historical writings on the subject of popular movements are marked by this ambiguity. As all popular movements in Afghanistan have always claimed to represent Islam, the problem for Soviet authors has been to know whom they were directed against: if their target was the British they are regarded as progressive, but if they arose as a backlash against social reform they are regarded as reactionary. But the problem is that they have usually been directed against both these enemies at the same time, which accounts for contradictions in the views of Soviet authors on Afghan rulers who carried out reforms.[29]

Popular movements in the name of Islam and the policies which seek, by strengthening the state, to secure the independence of the Afghan nation-state are not necessarily opposed to one another, but neither are they necessarily working in the same direction. Rather, the political forces just mentioned are rooted in totally different assumptions. We cannot even say that the popular uprisings are systematically "re-actionary" or "traditionalist". This is a quite different conception of politics, as is shown by the revolt of Bacha-yi Saqqao, whose popular movement (see below) has been caricatured more than any other in Afghan history, both by the royalists and by the Marxists.

The fundamentalist revolt of Bacha-yi Ṣaqqao

With the exception of the resistance of the Hazara and the Nuristani to the troops of Abdurrahman, the only non-tribal popular movement rose in Shamali, the plain which stretches round the north of Kabul as far as Salang, and then becomes part of Kohestan and Panjshir. The native language of the majority of the people here is Persian, but south of Istalif as far as Kabul and Koh-i Safi are Pashtun; the two peoples are very much interlinked and it is not unusual for mixed marriages to occur. The Shamali region has always been opposed to the Durrani dynasty, not because it is Pashtun, but because it is tribal. There is no tribal organisation in the Shamali region. It is a fertile, agricultural area, mostly farmed by smallholders. The standing of the religious leaders is very high there. Almost all the *'ulama* are *naqshbandi* and the local *pir* have thousands of *murid*; the most famous is the *pir* of Tagao – the last holder of this title died in 1981, after having fled from the regime of Taraki.

The people of Shamali played an important role in the second Anglo-Afghan war of 1879–80. Mir Majedi and his brother Mir Darwesh, two *naqshbandi 'ulama,* gathered together troops which, led by Mir Bacha Khan, harassed the English cantonments, while an armed band of tribesmen led by Mushk-i Alam attacked to the south of Kabul. After this the Shamali region remained calm until 1928, despite a number of anti-tax revolts led by romantic outlaws, sometimes linked to the Sufis, like the bandit Imamuddin in 1906–7, supported by a *fakir.*[30]

Shamali is a bastion of fundamentalism: their movement involved a return to the *shari'at* led by *'ulama,* generally *naqshbandi.* Nevertheless, there is one aspect which clearly distinguishes this movement from those occurring in the tribal zones. The leaders of the non-tribal zones are not charismatic figures; they come from the locality and are related to some of the more important families, but their influence is less than that of similar families in the tribal zones. The opposition between secular power and the clergy is less significant than it is amongst the tribes, which explains why there is less need for a charismatic leader. Even though there are, of course, local customs and it is not unusual for the *khan* to constitute an economic force which has little qualms about acting in conformity with the *shari'at,* the tension between the secular and religious modes of social behaviour is less acute than in the tribal zones, and so religious movements here are less extreme and have greater staying power.

There can be no doubt that the uprising of the Basmachi against the Soviet regime had repercussions in Shamali and Panjshir, where Mawlawi 'Abdul Hayy, an *'alim* and a former student at Deoband, joined Enver Pashah in 1920. And Amanullah sent a Safi from Tagao as his representative to the Basmachi in 1919.[31] Finally, Ibrahim Beg, the Basmachi leader, who had come to live in Afghanistan, supported Bacha-yi Saqqao at the beginning of 1929.[32]

Bacha-yi Saqqao, "the son of the water carrier", was the son of a soldier who had taken part in the second Anglo-Afghan war. A native of the village of Kalakan, he was an outlaw, whose exploits of robbing the rich to give to the poor took place in Shamali. When the Shinwari of Nangrahar revolted against Amanullah in November 1928, Bacha-yi Saqqao launched an attack on Kabul and took the city on 16 January 1929. He was crowned king with the title of Habibullah by the *pir* of Tagao.[33] For the majority of Afghan and Western historians,[34] the Bacha-yi Saqqao affair represents a rather bizarre episode, an interruption in the course of traditional politics. But in fact it should be interpreted as a visible manifestation of a deep structure: the fundamentalist network. Kabul does not fall, even in a period of anarchy, by mere chance. Moreover, it is quite clear that Bacha-yi Saqqao benefited not only from the moral support of the *'ulama* in the north, but from their actively backing his cause in their preaching,[35] particularly in the *naqshbandi* areas. He was the candidate of the fundamentalist coalition which was able to sap the power of Amanullah, while the revolt of the Shinwari was not directly inspired by activities within religious circles. At that time there was no charismatic leader to spur the tribes into open revolt and the tribal movement was controlled by the Durrani aristocracy, in the person of Nadir Khan. The recapture of Kabul in October 1929 and the defeat of Bacha-yi Saqqao were not the results of a *jihad*, but represented the regaining of political power by a tribal confederation, no longer restricted to the Durrani but now embracing all the Pashtun. Proof of this was the fact that Nadir Khan chose to legitimate his authority, after the fall of the capital, by invoking the great *jirga* in preference to the council of *'ulama*.

Hamidullah Khan Akhundzade, the *pir* of Tagao who crowned Bacha-yi Saqqao, was the son of Mir Sayyad Jan Padshah, who crowned Nasrullah in 1919. It is said that Bacha-yi Saqqao was himself the *murid* of Shams-ul Haq Mujaddidi Kohestani, *pir* of Gulbahar.[36] His entrance into Kabul was approved by the Mujaddidi family of Shor Bazar, which had, at first, wanted to crown Inayatullah, the clergy's candidate against Amanullah in 1920. As always the fundamentalist *'ulama* wished to see on the throne a sovereign who would re-establish the *shari'at* and who would undo the modernist reforms of Amanullah. Popular support for Bacha had the same foundation: it was first and foremost a cultural revolt, rather than a political or economic one.

What, then, brought about the downfall of Bacha? Two facts were crucial: the reaction of the tribes and the fact that the Mujaddidi family rallied to the aristocracy. While the issue of religion and culture played a part in the uprising of the tribes, once Amanullah had left the scene the traditional struggle for power was unleashed and this was far removed from a *jihad*. The tribes were unwilling to countenance the presence on the throne of a Tajik, whom they regarded as a usurper, and they therefore lent their support to the first tribal chief who emerged as a potential leader. There was no question of imposing the strict discipline of the *shari'at*: the *pashtunwali* was, on the other hand, solemnly confirmed. The Mujaddidi family, who had at first supported Bacha-yi Saqqao, became worried by the advent of anarchy and, having far closer links to the establishment than the *'ulama* and the *pir* of the provinces did, they switched their support to Nadir Khan, a development which explains the ambiguous role that the family were to play later on in the resistance.

The people of Shamali kept alive the memory of Bacha, whom they called Habibullah, and his shade hovered over the resistance to communist rule. These were the same groups which formed the backbone of the resistance of 1979 and 1980, but now they were joined by the Islamist intellectuals. Continuity was even closer than it may have appeared on the surface. The few influential families (like the Khallili family) who had supported Bacha were now to be found, either the same individuals or their descendants, supporting the *jam'iyyat-i islami* (see p. 219) and not the establishment parties. The strongholds of the revolt led by Bacha were now the strongholds of the *Hizb-i islami* (see p. 219) or of the *Jam'iyyat-i islami*, with one exception: Bacha's own village of Kalakan was now a Maoist bastion. The surviving *'ulama* and *pir* played a role in establishing the first Islamist groups in 1960, which explains why Shamali was one of only two places where the *'ulama* rejoined the *Hizb-i islami* of Hekmatyar. Let us take as an example Mawlawi 'Abdul Ghani of Qala-yi Boland. Educated at Deoband and *khalifa* of the *pir* of Tagao, he was at the heart of Bacha-yi Saqqao's revolt and symbolises the transition from fundamentalism to Islamism, since he formed part of the small group who founded the Islamist movement in the 1950s; the village of Qala-yi Boland was a bastion of the *Hizb-i islami* of Hekmatyar (see p. 190). 'Abdul Ghani and the *mawlawi* of Qala-yi gholam Shah educated several generations of local *'ulama*, the former being a specialist in philosophy, Sufism and general culture, the latter in the *fiqh*. The son of 'Abdul Ghani, Mawlana Iblagh, had studied at Al-Azhar, another symbol of transition between two generations of *'ulama*. Finally, while the last *pir* of Tagao, Mian Gul Jan, was apparently, not a member of the Islamist movement, one of his sons supported the *Hizb*, and Tagao was still a stronghold of this movement. The tradition established by Bacha-yi Saqqao flourished again in 1979, although we must qualify this by saying that behind the idealistic outlaw we should see the fundamentalist tradition, the essence of which was handed down to the young Islamist intellectuals and then interpreted by them in a more progressive light.[37]

From fundamentalism to Islamism

In a short work devoted to the revivalist movement, the Islamist Maududi examines the reasons for their failure.[38] He finds that there are three. First, an excessive devotion to Sufism; and we know that the young Afghan Islamists, even if they are not opposed to Sufism, are less fervent in this respect than their elders. Secondly, the absence of any real political organisation; we shall see that the theory of the party is one of the principal contributions that Islamism has made to revivalism. Finally, the necessity of coming to terms, not only with modern technology, but also with modernity itself. The Islamist movement was born in the modern sectors of society, and developed from a political critique of the popular movements which preceded it.

Chapter Four

The Islamist movement up to 1978

The phenomenon of Islamism in Afghanistan is of recent origin and owes more to the Egyptian Muslim Brothers than to Indian fundamentalism (in spite of the importance of Maududi). While it stands within the fundamentalist tradition, it nevertheless represents a complete break from Afghan cultural tradition. The Islamists are intellectuals, the product of modernist enclaves within traditional society; their social origins are what we have termed the state bourgeoisie – products of the government education system which leads only to employment in the state machine. Except for the group of "professors" in the faculty of theology, they do not consider themselves to be scholars ('ulama) but as intellectuals (roshanfikr).

The Islamists are almost all products of the government education system, either of the scientific schools, or of the state madrasa. Very few of them have had an education in the Arts. On the campus, they mostly mix with the communists, to whom they are violently opposed, rather than with the 'ulama, towards whom they have an ambivalent attitude. They share many basic beliefs in common with the 'ulama (Qur'an, sunnat, etc.), but Islamist thought has developed from contact with the great Western ideologies, which they see as holding the key to the West's technical development. For them, the problem is to develop a modern political ideology based on Islam, which they see as the only way to come to terms with the modern world and the best means of confronting foreign imperialism. The Islamists have played a decisive role in the Afghan resistance movement.

The political history of the Islamist movement

Origins

Originated in 1958 in religious intellectual circles, the movement was supported and protected by Dr Gholam Mohammad Niyazi, the future dean of the faculty of religious sciences (or faculty of theology), when he

69

returned from Egypt. The founders are known as the "professors" (*ustaz*). They had received their education within the government system and not in the private *madrasa*, and they completed their studies not in Pakistan but in the great Al-Azhar University in Cairo, where they encountered the Egyptian Muslim Brothers; later, they taught in the faculty of theology at Kabul. At first it was a group without clear definition rather than a party: in addition to professors such as Niyazi, Rabbani and Tawana, there were other intellectuals like Sebghatullah Mujaddidi and Minhajuddin Gahiz, who in 1968 founded the newspaper *Gahiz*. In 1958 there was a sharp conflict between religious circles and the government (led by Muhammad Daoud, a cousin of the king). Sebghatullah Mujaddidi was among many arrested, and in part the movement was forced to operate secretly. It was called *Jam'iyyat-i islami* (Islamic society); also known as *tahrik-i islami* or *nihzat-i islami*, and it concentrated mainly on cultural activity within the student body. The group introduced translations of the works of foreign Islamists, such as Sayyad Qotb, and Maududi, brought up to date religious terms and teaching methods, and in general presented Islam as a modern ideology. They also found it necessary to confront the new ideologies which were spreading in intellectual circles.

The first translations of the work of Sayyad Qotb were published around 1960 by Mawlawi Khalis, under the title *Islam wa edalat-e edjtemay* (Islam and social justice), the translation being by M. Reshad and A. Sittar. Then Rabbani, who was in Egypt from 1966 to 1968, undertook the translation of *In the Shadow of the Koran* (which was never completed) and of *Pointers to the Way*.

There were no links with similar movements in other countries, beyond a network of people who knew one another. (However, a cousin of Mujaddidi, Harun, was later imprisoned in Cairo by Nasir, as a Muslim Brother.) Two Egyptian professors, Jamal Amar and 'Abdul Al Ahmad Atwar taught in the faculty of theology, followed by Al Nadawi, an Indian Muslim and a supporter of Maududi. Nevertheless, it is clear that the Afghan Islamists found their inspiration in Egypt rather than in Pakistan, although Gahiz (murdered in 1972) tried to establish institutional links with the Pakistani *jama'at*, the party founded by Maududi (whose future "Amir", Qazi Husseyn Ahmad, a Pashtun, came frequently to Kabul). Because the more radical Islamists were hostile towards him, Sebghatullah Mujaddidi was not a member of the movement, but he participated in the delegation to the Islamic conference held in Tripoli in 1973. Unlike the Pakistani *jama'at*, an elitist party which resembled Opus Dei in the way it operated, the Afghan Islamists had as their goal the establishment of a mass movement.

Muslim youth

The "professors" greatly influenced their pupils and in 1965, the year of the foundation of the communist party, the Islamist students demonstrated openly by distributing a leaflet entitled *Shabname-yi jihad*, the 'tract of the holy war'. The period 1965 to 1972 was one of political turmoil on the campus at Kabul, which had never had so many students before. The liberalism of the regime and the violent debates occurring in parliament provided a climate favourable to political activism of this nature. The student branch, called *sazman-i jawanan-i musulman* ("organisation of Muslim youth"), was to become the most militant section of the movement. Western observers considered the movement to be conservative,[1] but it had a revolutionary and reformist side to it; and, in any case, European progressives have consistently favoured a conservative but secular establishment to the possibility of religious conflict.[2] The students demonstrated against Zionism during the Six-day war, against American policies in Vietnam and the privileges of the establishment. They were violently opposed to important figures on the traditionalist side, to the King and especially to his cousin Daoud, and in this last instance the struggle was particularly vicious. They were totally against Pashtun nationalism and they opposed those who wanted to establish an independent Pashtunistan, just as they opposed the partition of Pakistan in 1972.[3] They protested against foreign influence in Afghanistan, both from the Soviet Union and from the West, and against speculators during the famine of 1972, by demanding that there should be curbs on personal wealth.[4] But they were also very much opposed to communism, and a great number of violent fights broke out on Kabul campus between them and the Maoists. Although at the beginning they were outnumbered by the communists, the Islamists' influence steadily increased and they gained a majority in the student elections of 1970.

The Islamists recruited members from the government education system, principally from the scientific faculties, the *madrasa*, and the secondary schools. In this way they acquired the services of Massoud and the engineer Habiburrahman from the Polytechnic; Gulbuddin Hekmatyar, Ishaq and Nurullah Emmat from the engineering faculty; the "professors", and Sayyaf, Mawlawi Habiburrahman, Abdurrahman Niyazi and Tareq from the *madrasa*; and Zabiullah of Mazar, Sayfuddin Nasratyar, and Sayfurrahman of Ghorband from the secondary schools. Geographically their strongholds in the west were around Herat (with support coming mainly from the government *madrasa*, and therefore more moderate); and in the east at Baghlan, Takhar, Mazar, Panjshir, Ghorband, Laghman, Kunar and Nangrahar, with most members coming from the better educated products of the government and not the religious education system. In tribal zones they had absolutely no support. We shall study the interconnections of these groups in greater detail in chapter 7.

Mistrust of the 'ulama

Immediately, there arose the problem of relations between the Islamists and the traditionalist *'ulama*. The student youth movement was mostly hostile towards the mullah and to the *'ulama*, who considered them to be conservative. The "professors", on the other hand, were very anxious to keep contact with the clergy. In effect, there was no collaboration before the *coup d'état* of 1978. Nevertheless, in the provinces of Nangrahar, Kunar and Laghman, a certain number of local *'ulama*, such as Mawlawi Khalis from Nangrahar, joined the movement as well as the majority of the *mawlawi* from Nuristan. The Najmulmadares *madrasa* of Hadda, near Jellabad, was also an Islamist stronghold. Even at Kabul, the *mawlawi* of Jamal Mina (the "parish" of the students) was Islamist, as well as Mawlawi Fayzani, who opened a library at Pul-i Khishti and who was popularly supposed to have begun to establish a network in the army. (He was executed by Daoud in 1975.) These links can be explained in two ways. First, the *'ulama* of *Mashriqi* (the three provinces to the east of Kabul) had a well-established tradition of fundamentalism and anti-imperialism; a mullah of Hadda had been an important figure in the struggle against the British and in opposition to the monarchy in the nineteenth century. Many *mawlawi* of the region had led tribal uprisings against the "infidels". The mullahs of Nuristan had kept up the militant tradition of a "land with a mission" (Nuristan was only converted to Islam at the end of the last century). The fundamentalism of the Mashriqi *'ulama* had always been more radical and anti-traditionalist than in other regions. From 1950 onwards the region had been shaken by movements inspired by Wahhabism, such as the *panjpir* movement (from the name of a village in Pakistan): a certain "Sayyed Mullah" influenced the Shinwari of Kunar towards both Wahhabism and *Hizb-i islami*. These local *mawlawi*, who were the most sectarian part of the movement, often became supporters of *Hizb-i islami*. But most of the Afghan *'ulama*, since they were hostile to the government *madrasa* and were worried about the radicalism of Muslim Youth, remained aloof, even though they were distressed by the government's repression of the demonstration of traditionalist mullahs against Parcham at Pul-i Khishti in April 1970.

The influence of the Deoband school remained strong amongst the *naqshbandi pir* in the Kabul region and a certain number, such as the *pir* of Tagao, the *pir* of Qala-yi Boland and Hafezji Saheb of Kapisa were close to the Islamist movement and in many instances their sons actually belonged to it. Tagao and Qala-yi Boland were strongholds of the Islamist movement.

Structure and political activity

The movement functioned on an open level, the Muslim Youth, and a more secret level, centred upon the "professors". A council (*shura*) was in overall control and elected an "Amir": until 1972 this was Gholam Niyazi, and later Rabbani. In 1972, the year in which the movement's constitution was drawn up, the *shura* was composed of a president (Rabbani), his deputy (Sayyaf), a secretary (engineer Habiburrahman, replaced by Hekmatyar in 1975), who was also responsible for supervising the military wing, someone responsible for cultural affairs (Tawana), *'ulama* (including Mawlawi Habiburrahman), and peasants. Small cells, each having five members, were established as part of a pyramidal structure (five cells made a district, *hawze*, and five districts a province, *wilayat*). Meetings were held in private houses, Until 1972, the members placed emphasis on spiritual growth and not on the pursuit of power. The faculty of theology published the review, *Majalle-ye shari'at*, (review of Muslim law), edited by Rabbani, which provided much support for the Islamists in intellectual circles. But the threat of a communist coup caused the leaders (in particular Rabbani) to set about attempting to infiltrate the army.

In theory, the student movement was answerable to the *shura* but in fact it operated quite openly. The four leaders of the youth movement, Abdurraman Niyazi, Engineer Habiburrahman, Mawlawi Habiburrahman and Gulbuddin Hekmatyar (the only survivor after 1975) were better known than the members of the secret organisation. Until 1970, the movement did not go beyond the campus: it restricted its activities to an endeavour to build mosques there, to preaching political sermons and to engaging in fights with the communists. Towards 1970, the movement attempted to come out from the campus ghetto. The young Islamists inaugurated a campaign of politico-religious preaching throughout the country, with a branch called *da'wat o tanzim* (preaching and organisation) as its spearhead. In the town, the students preached in the local mosques, effectively depriving the urban clergy of some of their influence. For their part the clergy were few in number, ill-educated and pro-government – the mullahs of Kabul were paid by the government. In the countryside, the students used their holiday period to preach in their home villages. Unlike their communist colleagues, the young Islamist

73

teachers were not averse to working in the backward areas. They tried to introduce reforms into everyday life, by employing the kind of terms used by the reformers of the last century ot rationalise actions sanctioned by religion (for example, ablution was presented as a hygienic act rather than a form of piety, which thus assisted them in the spread of health education). For instance, in the village of Ri-Jang, Balkh province, Mawlawi Alam, a young student in the faculty of theology, and thus a pupil of Rabbani, set up near the mosque a cooperative providing seed for peasants.[5] This is a typical example of the social progressivism of the Islamists, both more reformist and more practical than that of the communists. Apart from the mullahs, most of the peasants welcomed the young intellectuals, but had no real idea of the political dimension of their action. The significance of the uprising of 1975 was lost on them, although the Islamists who survived became natural leaders of the resistance movement after 1980.

At Kabul, the Muslim Youth, known by their enemies as *ikhwan* (brothers), had a more combative approach. The student leaders did not shun the limelight during demonstrations, but the teachers tended to remain in the background. Although it is true that there were two tendencies within this movement, radical and moderate, which in 1976 became opposed to each other, up to this point there was a sharing of tasks rather than a divergence.

The young Shi'a, especially the *qizilbash*, also became politicised because of the influence of spiritual leaders such as Wa'ez at Kabul and Muhseni at Kandahar; they set up clandestine Islamist organisations, quite distinct from those of the Sunni.

The coup d'état led by Daoud and the failed uprising of 1975

From 1970, the Islamists noted with anxiety the degree to which the communists, whose methods they were better acquainted with than were foreign observers, were infiltrating the state machine. In 1972, they decided to plant Islamist cells in the army. Engineer Habiburrahman, who was entrusted with this task, recruited the future commander, Massoud, as his assistant. (After the death of Habiburrahman, Hekmatyar was briefly in charge.) But it was too late.

The coup led by Prince Muhammad Daoud, on 17 July 1973, was carried out with the assistance of the Parcham faction of the *PDPA*. Daoud, a Pashtun nationalist, and a man of secular outlook whose support came from the communists, was in every respect totally and implacably opposed to the Islamists. The Minister of the Interior (Faiz Muhammad) was a member of the Parcham group and thus it was that the coup was soon followed by the arrest of the more militant Islamists. Niyazi and Rabbani made a final attempt to come to terms with Daoud, promising him their support if he would break with the communists. This attempt ended in failure and the principal leaders of the movement, with the exception of Niyazi, fled abroad.

The movement was then divided into two factions which fore-shadowed the split between *Jam'iyyat-i islami* and *Hizb-i islami* (hence-forth 'Jamiat' and 'Hizb'). The younger members wanted a general popular uprising, but Rabbani was of the opinion that people were not ready for this and opted for a longer-term policy – infiltrating the army in order to lay the ground for a counter-revolution. The radicals, led by Hekmatyar, carried the day. It appears that Bhutto, the President of Pakistan, was then stirred to immediate action to counter Daoud's pro-Pashtunistan policies; to achieve this end he lent his support to Hekmatyar.[6] The Islamists regrouped at Peshawar, received training from the Pakistan army and carried out clandestine missions in Af-ghanistan. The uprising was planned on a regional basis: Massoud was responsible for Panjshir, Mawlawi Habiburrahman for Laghman, Dr Omar for Badakhshan, Nasratyar for Herat and Hekmatyar for Paktya.

From July 1975, groups of armed men attempted to incite the people. The fiercest conflicts took place in Panjshir (with Massoud and Ishaq), Laghman (Mawlawi Habiburrahman), Kabul ('Abdul Haqq), Bad-akhshan (Omar and Ismael Pasokh, a Muslim from Shughnan), Ghor-band (Issa and Sayfuddin) and Nejrao (Engineer Habiburrahman). In fact, only in the north-east was there anything approaching an uprising; in the rest of the country, including Paktya, where Hekmatyar was, nothing happened. At Herat, Nasratyar was arrested as soon as he arrived. People were not with the movement, and the young activists were either arrested or barely escaped imprisonment. The attempted uprisings in the various regions were badly coordinated and there was no support from the army. On occasions militants made suicidal attacks on police stations. The repression which followed was terrible: hundreds of young people and dozens of *'ulama* disappeared and were summarily executed. Professor Niyazi was murdered in prison, as was Mawlawi Fayzani. Two hundred militants, including Nasratyar, were to remain in prison without trial and were finally executed in June 1979. Political observers in the West knew only of the uprising at Panjshir, which they thought was the work of the *Sitam-i milli*.[7]

The lesson to be learned from the failure of the rebellion is clear. The only regions to be at all affected by the uprising were those in the north-east, where the most radical militants were well established, and which were later to become the bastions of resistance against the Soviet forces.

The towns and the tribal areas took no action, and neither did the west of the country. There was no revolt by the armed forces. The people did not see the Islamic political movement as being a bulwark of Islam, any more than they considered the Daoud regime to be pro-communist. Above all, the movement had completely failed to come to grips with the requirements for a successful guerilla campaign and the level of secrecy it required. The authorities had no difficulty in arresting the militants, who were still hooked on the myth of left-wing guerilla warfare so central to the thinking of the sixties generation: Guevara's idea of revolutionary cells that infiltrated the peasantry with groups of intellectuals whom the peasants were supposed to follow.

The setback and the subsequent repression represented a grievous blow which has continued to weaken Afghan resistance to the present day. The hundreds of intellectuals who disappeared are cruelly missed by a resistance movement deprived of leaders, all the more so because of all the intellectuals only the Islamists joined the campaigns after 1979. Nevertheless, some lessons have been learned by those who survived: there could be no uprising without close links with the *'ulama*, the people of influence within traditional society; neither could it succeed without close contact with the peasants; and it was clearly necessary to coordinate a peasant uprising with a rebellion in the towns and on the part of the army. This was the conclusion Rabbani came to, which took visible form in the uprising of Herat in March 1979. The radicals like Hekmatyar, on the other hand, who had hoped for more from the revolt of 1975, generally acted more cautiously when they opposed the communists in 1978 and 1979, since they had no wish to suffer another equally crushing defeat; it was the Soviet intervention which really involved them in the war.

Exile at Peshawar and the split

After the failure of the uprising, the surviving militants took refuge at Peshawar, where Bhutto allowed them to open offices. At that period the Islamists enjoyed the support of the left in Pakistan (Bhutto's People's Party), the army and of the Pakistani *Jama 'at-i islami*, as well as receiving a certain amount of money from the Saudis during the first year. Pakistan's support was not ideological but strategical: the Afghan Islamists were opposed to a nationalist ideology and the claim made at Kabul concerning Pashtunistan, and they rejected the traditional Kabul–New Delhi coalition in the name of Muslim solidarity. They were, therefore, the best defenders of Pakistan's integrity.

Nevertheless, things soon became very difficult for the exiled Islamists.

They ran out of money, because Saudi Arabia and Iran, who were pursuing a policy of support for Daoud, did not help them, and Pakistan did not wish for an open confrontation with Kabul. Finally, dissension broke out openly.

The movement polarised around the leadership of Borhanuddin Rabbani and Gulbuddin Hekmatyar. The former attracted the moderate element, especially amongst Persian-speakers, the second the radicals, especially the Pashtun. Rabbani, who was born in or about 1940 in a family of small landowners at Yaftal (Badakhshan) with a Sufi background, had followed the typical course of study pursued by a modernist *'alim*: government *madrasa*, then studies at Ankara and Cairo. He was a graduate of Al-Azhar. His studies and published works developed in three different directions. In literature, he wrote a thesis on the mystic poet Jami of Herat; in theology, he published a refutation of the rationalist philosophers known as Motazilites, and he began a translation of the political thinker Sayyad Qotb's *In the shadow of the Koran* and *Pointers to the Way*. He represents the meeting point of three currents of thought which characterise the Jamiat: classical culture, spiritual (almost mystical) orthodoxy and political Islamism. Such a mixture is rare in the Muslim world. The personal prestige of Rabbani was very great in the government *madrasa*, the Sufi brotherhoods in the west, in literary circles and amongst the Persian-speaking Islamist intellectuals.

Gulbuddin Hekmatyar is a Pashtun from the Kharrut tribe, a native of Baghlan; thus, he belongs to the Pashtun communities who have moved to north Afghanistan. He was a student of engineering, but he did not have the time to take his diploma; the whole of his academic career was spent on the campus at Kabul. A man of great talents, radical and with undoubted charisma, he had great influence over the students, and led most of the demonstrations from 1965 to 1972. But because he had not had a classical education and was hostile towards the traditional clergy, the *'ulama* had no confidence in him. As a radical he was quite at home with the vocabulary of the Iranian revolution. His influence was strongest amongst former students, especially those who spoke Pashtun, amongst the Pashtun communities in the north and the few *mawlawi* from the east who had joined the Islamist movement.

There were two main reasons for the split. On the one hand, it may be represented as following the line of cleavage within the social structure which underlies everything else: the social environment of the government *madrasa*, the brotherhoods of the west and the Persian-speaking Islamists were pro-Rabbani, while the radical students, especially the Pashtun, were pro-Hekmatyar. On the other hand, we may see it as corresponding to another line of cleavage which runs through the whole cluster of Islamist ideas in the Muslim world and which, in my view, revolves around the question of the *takfir* (literally: "the action of declaring a Muslim a heretic"). Historically this concept originated with Ibn Taymiyya (1263–1328); for him it was a question of whether it was right to pronounce *jihad* against the Mongols, even though the latter had been converted to Islam.[8] Thus, the good Muslim was no longer defined by his religious attitude, but by his political actions, and it was possible to define someone as a heretic for purely political reasons, as happened in the case of the assassins of Sadat. Rabbani rejected this interpretation, following in this respect the traditionalist *'ulama*. The Hizb of Hekmatyar anathematised its opponents, and thus gave the Islamic revolution pride of place in the struggle against the communists and the Soviets (an attitude which was close to that of revolutionary Iran), while Rabbani sought the broadest possible coalition of all Muslims, whatever their political attitudes.

In fact, these views represent two quite different and contradictory conceptions of political action. Hekmatyar adopted a theory of the avant-garde party, homogeneous and disciplined, which was not far removed from that of Lenin. Rabbani, after the creation of the Jamiat, spoke in terms of united fronts and new groupings; in particular, he realised that it would be impossible for them to establish themselves in tribal zones by means of a simple party structure and that it was necessary to adapt to tribal institutions. He underlined the necessity of accommodating liberal intellectual circles. He was equally opposed to the elitist views of the *Jama'at* in Pakistan, which had absolutely no interest in developing into a mass movement; what Rabbani had learned from the Egyptian Muslim Brothers was precisely this notion of a mass movement, so foreign to the revivalism of the Indian subcontinent.

The split took place during 1976–7 in obscure circumstances. Hekmatyar then set up the *Hizb-i islami*, "the Islamic party", and the choice of the term "party", borrowed from the communists, was not a neutral one: it echoed the whole theory of the militant and enlightened avant-garde. The other movements would be forced to submit or disappear. But the continued use of the term *jam'iyyat* ("society") by Rabbani is an indication of his desire to achieve unity.

The Hizb suffered a second split in 1979. Mawlawi Yunus Khalis broke away from Hekmatyar, but kept the title for his section of the Hizb. The cause of the split was once again the acceptance or rejection of radicalism, but this time the rift reflected regional geography: it affected the Pashtun of Nangrahar and the followers of Jallaluddin Haqani in Paktya. Rabbani and Khalis, who got on very well together, shared the same view of political Islam.

It was at this time (1978), when the Islamists, weakened by these quarrels, were on the retreat that the communist coup occurred. The repression of the Islamist movement by Daoud opened the way for the communists, and that year there was nobody to oppose them except for the discredited government led by Daoud. Daoud had dug his own grave.

Islamist ideology

The term "Islamic ideology" (*ideolozhi*) appears frequently in the writings of Afghan Islamist intellectuals, though these writers were not the first, nor indeed the only ones to demand a return to Islam. The fundamentalist *'ulama* share the same intellectual points of reference in, for instance, the Qur'an, *sunnat* and *shari'at*. Since implicit in Islam is the notion of a global view of society, it may not be apparent, at first sight, what additional meaning the term Islamic ideology could possibly convey. The Islamists' reply to this is that, up to the present, no truly Islamic society has ever existed, with the exception of the period of the Prophet and first four Caliphs. But since there have, indeed, been societies where the *shari'at* played an important role, we must conclude that what the Islamists mean by Islamic society is something different from anything which has existed up to the present.

The sphere of politics

The Islamists have absorbed Western thought, if only to reject it, while the *'ulama* simply have not come into contact with it. First and foremost, Islamism represents the conviction that it is necessary to introduce modern conceptual categories.[9] The employment of Western concepts such as sovereignty, the state, democracy and revolution has wrought a transformation in the intellectual paradigm through which the problems of society were viewed. The Islamists reject Western political concepts because they do not wish to be involved in the slavish imitation which characterised Muslim reformism in the last century. Nevertheless, the fact that these concepts do appear in their vocabulary itself opens up a new political dimension in which the terms used are, in fact, the traditional ones. The contribution of Western thought has not been in the form of new concepts but in the provision of the very notion of an autonomous political sphere. Islamist thought owes its originality to a double shift of focus: from the West they have borrowed a novel idea emptied of all its concepts, from the *'ulama* a terminology which has undergone a semantic shift. This is certainly not a mere cultural imitation of the West. It remains to be seen whether their programme will be fulfilled.

The point of departure for the Islamists is not the everyday experience of Islam, that is to say Islam interpreted as a cultural form, but a political insight. For many of them, the return to religion has been brought about through their experience in politics and not as a result of their religious belief. The *'ulama* define politics on the basis of relations within society as established by law: the state is the means by which justice is able to operate within Muslim society; it is the Muslims, or rather the community of Muslims, who provide the basis for political thought; politics is an extension of law. For the Islamists the nature of society is predetermined by the nature of the state. Whence comes the distinction, and this is one that an *'alim* would certainly dispute, between the Muslim state and the Islamic state: "the objective [of Muslims] must be the setting up, not of a national Muslim state, but an Islamic state" (Maududi).[10]

There is a great need for someone to formulate a theory of the Islamic state, since, as Maududi emphasises, the traditional thought of the *'ulama* does not recognise politics as an autonomous realm, because it conflates ethical, legal and political problems.[11] The word "ideology" has been chosen to signify this different approach to the problem of the state, indicating that it should no longer be thought of in juridical terms, as for the *'ulama*, but in political terms. The *'ulama* deal with political problems by looking for an analogous instance in the Qur'an or the *sunnat*. The Islamist, for his part, begins with abstract concepts: what is society, what is power, what is nature? Questions which, in Europe, would be thought of as belonging to an eighteenth-century political theory. Once the definitions have been arrived at, the Islamist then corroborates them with verses from the Qur'an. Many Islamist manuals begin with a course on political philosophy and only get on to the strictly religious aspect later.[12]

The theological questions implicit in Islamism

A constant theme, on the theological level, of the reformers of the nineteenth century as of modern Islamists is the rejection of *taqlid* (imitation) and the importance of *ijtihad* (personal interpretation).[13] Tradition did not completely rule out the need to adapt to new situations. The Hanafite school recognised four sources of law: the Qur'an, the *sunnat*, the *qyas* (reasoning by analogy with a known example) and the *ijma'* (the consensus of the Doctors of the Law). However, only the *'ulama* are entitled to be involved in *qyas* and *ijma'*. When the nomination of the Amir occurs – theoretically he should be chosen by a consensus of all believers – the *'ulama* generally claim to be the interpreters of the consensus. From the orthodox point of view, the Islamist intellectuals, not usually being *'ulama*, are excluded from *ahl ar-ray* (the people of decision), on both ideological and political issues.

Thus, there are two possible ways open to the Islamists if they wish to participate in decision-making: to extend the concept of *ijma'* to include the whole community of believers, which would mean the authorising of universal sufferage, or to claim that they are also part of those termed Doctors of the Law, in so far as they are intellectuals,[14] leaving the *'ulama* the monopoly of the *fiqh*. In both cases, the Islamists prefer to see the Qur'an as having pre-eminence over other sources of law, because its edicts are more general in nature; this makes it possible to bypass the complex construction of tradition, casuistry and scholasticism which the *'ulama* use to justify their existence as a body of technical experts. What the Islamists look for in the Qur'an is the general sense rather than a system. Their broader theological approach is their way of coming to terms with modernity and rejecting a tradition which seems to them to be more medieval than Muhammadan.

The theme of the party and of the Islamic revolution

The appropriation of Western political concepts, now filtered through a re-reading of the fundamental documents of their religion, has made it possible for the Islamists to adopt the political (Leninist) formula which has served liberation movements elsewhere so well, whatever their relations with Marxism have been: the theory of the party and the myth of the revolution. The Islamists, also, have a theory of the avant-garde, centralised, relatively disciplined party whose members are linked by a common ideology, reinforced by a certain political training. It is in this sense that the three Islamist parties in the resistance (the two Hizb and the Jamiat) are true political parties, and thus also relatively efficient war machines; while the three nationalist parties are nothing more than clubs for people of influence and traditionalist *'ulama*. The party is a modern concept which has no place in the world-view of the *'ulama*, who recognise only the community of believers and the body of scholars.

A final theme is that of revolution (*enqelab*). This has its place in the millennial tradition of popular religion, where the establishment of an Islamic state brings justice and happiness.[15] The Islamists are certainly revolutionaries who take social justice seriously; more so than the *'ulama* who have a more gradualist approch, and for whom the important thing is to act in conformity with the law. The *'alim* hopes for justice to be attained when the individual respects the law, the Islamist seeks the same goal by redefining social relations through political action and therefore by means of the state. Nevertheless, revolution is no more than a way of attaining a timeless justice and is not to be considered as merely one stage in the historical process.

The programme

The political programme of the Islamists has always been open to change and in the period which separates their origins as an underground political force and the present resistance movement it has quite clearly developed, becoming more moderate and closer to the doctrines of the *'ulama*. Let us consider the essentials of their present programme.[16] Sovereignty belongs to God alone. The Amir is only a representative and the only source of true authority is religious. The Amir is selected by a consensus of the whole community, expressed concretely by election. The electoral principle is, in fact, widespread in the resistance, both at the local level and within the parties. The powers of the Amir are considerable, but he is assisted by a *shura* or council. The body of the *'ulama* retains its autonomy with regard to the political power and may censure or depose an Amir. Civil society is under the control of the *'ulama* acting within the limits of the *shari'at*. The fact that all Muslims have equal rights is clearly stated. The principle of private property and economic profit are acknowledged, but corrective mechanisms are provided to prevent social inequalities from becoming too marked. It is forbidden to lend money in order to exact interest, there are taxes on income and on capital, and the poor and the sick must be provided for by obligatory donations. It is recognised that women have a right to education, but coeducation is ruled out.

The Islamists have no wish to see an all-powerful leader at their head (unlike the Shi'a, influenced by the mystique of the hidden Imam), although theirs is a system which favours the emergence of a single leader. The rule of law within the state is maintained, thanks to the autonomy of the *'ulama*, the fact that the Amir may be dismissed and the electoral system. This very broad programme would, because of its reliance on the doctrines of Islam, stand a good chance of gaining the support of a majority of Afghans, but it leaves open the precise form that the constitution of a liberated Afghanistan might take.

One must not overlook the fact that this political position has a certain ritualistic aspect. Rather than being a well-defined programme, Islamist ideology has carved out a space for itself which enables it to confront both tradition and modernism, and to remain separate from the *'ulama* while standing on a common platform with them. Finally, Islamist ideas make it possible for them to continue the dialogue with the West because the framework within which they work has originated there. The West (both liberal and Marxist) is attempting to reject a world of archaism, feudalism, the Middle Ages and obscurantism, ideas that are, in fact, products of modernism. The traditionalist 'alim is a far more reassuring figure than the young Islamist intellectual educated in our schools. And yet he is our mirror image.

We have seen how Islamist political thought aimed principally to give some coherence to the workings of politics in Afghanistan. In this context, the reader will recall that in the first chapter we described the void which exists between the reality of the day-to-day operation of the qawm and the aspiration for a Muslim universalism bereft of any precise political form. We shall see how the political institutions set up by the Islamists, that is to say the parties, are as carved out by the qawms as the central state was, but to a lesser degree, for the Islamist intellectuals are subject to the rivalries of the qawm to a much lesser extent than the state machine, or, indeed, than the Communist Party. For, in so far as the Islamist parties have become mass parties, the rivalry of the qawm, at least on the local level, has reappeared. At the summit, the political views of the 'ulama have played a negative role. For example, Rabbani's willingness to compromise led him to strike unfavourable deals with Sayyaf and Hekmatyar which were violently attacked by his subordinates. This may be seen as a result of a legalistic attitude which owed more to his training as an 'alim than to political calculation: if the person with whom one has dealings is accepted as a Muslim, one must, however shady his character may be, do one's utmost to come to an agreement with him. Certain improbable alliances, like the former fundamentalist alliance, are shored up by the arguments of the 'ulama, not only those from Afghanistan, but also from Saudi Arabia and Pakistan, who are concerned only with professions of faith and not with political action. The soothing words of the 'ulama, concerned with unity at any price, have resulted in a failure to consider the problems of the resistance in a political context and this has allowed political intrigue and the exercise of naked force to flourish beneath the surface.

Chapter Five

The communist reforms and the repression, 1978–9

The Communist *coup d'état* is outside the limits of the present study.[1] But after having studied the historical background of the Afghan resistance movement, we should analyse in greater detail the popular uprisings and the coming into being of the resistance. The prime cause of the uprisings was the authoritarian way in which the new regime imposed its reforms a few months after the coup of 27 April 1978.

The ideological framework of the reforms

The three major aspects of Khalq policy were agrarian reform, the elimination of illiteracy and the strengthening of the state machine. The communist leaders have always been conscious of the fact that they have been creating a revolution by proxy, faced with a nebulous working class and an apathetic peasantry. Obsessed by Amanullah's precedent, they thought that it was necessary to strike swiftly and ruthlessly before the "counter-revolution" was able to organise itself. To achieve this they adopted three means: repression, made possible by the existence of a loyal and well-equipped army; agrarian reform which, they thought, would win the support of the mass of the people; and the elimination of illiteracy, in order to rescue the people from the influence of the clergy and to spread the new ideology.

The Khalq are, at one and the same time, theoreticians and activists. The mistakes made by the government can be traced to "Khalq thought". They include a superficial acquaintance with Marxism, a total failure to analyse the existing situation, and a profound conviction that they were inventing a new brand of socialism, suitable for Third World countries and without any intermediate stages. This theme crops up again and again in every history of oriental revolutionary movements, from Sultan Galiev to Pol-Pot.[2] Amin stated: "we are struggling to uproot feudalism in order to pass directly from a feudal society to a society where the exploitation of man by his fellow man will be unknown",[3] "Our Khalq state is the best and the *first* example of a proletarian state of this type"[4] (such an ambition cannot have been very much to the liking of the Russians). Quoting Taraki, he continued: "our great revolutionary leader . . . did not think it necessary to wait for the growth of an autonomous popular movement led by the party. On the contrary, he thought that the party should attract the active and practical support of the people." A final quotation, printed in the *Kabul Times* of 19 April 1979, encapsulates the schoolmasterly voluntarism of the Khalq: "Our great leader hit upon the truth that due to the fact that in developing nations the working class has not yet developed as a political force, there is another force which can overturn the feudal and oppressive government, and in Afghanistan that force was the army. He also gave a firm order that working-class ideology should be spread through the army . . ." We should not forget that Amin had a degree in education and that the college of education where teachers were trained was a Khalq stronghold. However, according to this way of looking at things, the machine-gun soon replaces the rap over the knuckles, and any peasant who does not understand the master's lesson is considered to be a dangerous counter-revolutionary.

For the Khalq, Afghan society is feudal. The peasants (*dehqan*) are exploited by a handful of feudalists (the *khan*) with the support of the clergy. The peasants are alienated by religion and do not see where their true interests lie. It follows that all that was necessary was to make a sudden break with the past and give them their own land (agrarian reform) and provide them with "enlightenment" (the elimination of illiteracy), and their support for the revolution would be total. According to the fantasies of the Khalq, the peasant has no independent existence: he doesn't think, he does not have his own forms of organisation or of culture. He is like clay in the hands of the potter, living only to satisfy his immediate needs and mirroring the thought of whichever person happens to be dominating him at the time, the mullah or the teacher.[5] Although there is no space here to consider Afghan agrarian society in depth, we can be sure that it bears no similarity to the simplistic view of the Khalq. The latter, unlike Soviet authors, never take into account the possibility that there might be such a thing as a "tribal" mode of production: in economics as in politics, tribalism is not comprehended by Khalq ideology (and yet it is a constant as far as their political action is concerned). Finally, the concept of mode of production is defined in strictly economic terms, while, in reality, economic considerations are contained within broader societal relations.

The agrarian reform

Details of the agrarian reform were contained in two decrees. Decree 6, passed in August 1978, did away with the mortgage system (*giraw*) and usury (*sud*): debts and mortgages which had been in existence for more than five years were cancelled, and the land was returned to its former owner without quid pro quo; lands which had been mortgaged for less than five years were returned to their owners but a modified payment was made for the loan. These measures only applied to poor peasants – those who came below the threshold of 10 *jerib* (2 hectares) of fertile land. Only organisations and individuals selected by the local commission for agrarian reform were permitted to use the Development Bank, which was presided over by the district headman.[6]

Redistribution of land was dealt with by Decree 8 (30 November 1978). Article 1 announced the intention of getting rid of feudal and semi-feudal conditions. No family should own more than the equivalent of 30 *jerib* of good agricultural land. The land was divided into seven categories each with its own coefficient (ranging from irrigated orchards to arid land which had been left uncultivated for more than two years, and the coefficient went from 1.00 to 0.10). The beneficiaries of the reform were placed in six categories in order of priority: (1) peasants without land who were already working on the land being redistributed, (2) peasants without land and day workers from the village where the land being redistributed was situated, (3) small landowners of the same village, (4) peasants without land within the district and nomads who frequently resided there, (5) peasants without land and day workers from the region, (6) peasants without land and nomads from other regions. Land in excess of the limit (*ezafe*) was confiscated without compensation and re-distributed to the beneficiaries in order of priority, and provided that they did not exceed a certain limit, which was below the legal limit of property ownership. The law also established the juridical framework for agricultural cooperatives reserved for those who had less than the equivalent of 20 *jerib* of good agricultural land.

The failure of the agrarian reform

It would have seemed that the reform was sufficiently well worked out to have been accepted by 80 per cent of the peasants who possessed less than 20 *jerib*.[7] It was first put into practice in January 1979 in zones around the towns where the large estates were (Herat and Kandahar especially). Yet, as the sequence of events shows, it was often the arrival of the commission involved in the agrarian reform which sparked off active resistance. Why?

Rejection on ideological grounds. The idea of land redistribution was in sharp conflict with the notion of the intangibility of property to be found in the *shari'at*. For the Afghan peasant what was unjust was not owning property in itself, but the abuse of a position of power, either in the form of money (usury), or through the exercise of power itself (authoritarianism and corruption). What the peasant wanted was a reform, not of the system of landownership, but of financial practice and the way in which power was exercised. Moreover, the imposition of the reforms was achieved precisely by means of those very channels of power that the peasant rejected, and the reforms were presented in an ideological framework (class struggle) which was alien to his everyday experience.

The unrealistic nature of the reforms. The criteria on which the reforms were based did not correspond to socio-economic reality. There has never been a distinct stratum of exploiters opposed to a mass of the exploited: many share-croppers own a small amount of land and live just like landowners, whereas many landowners are in debt, and moneylenders are not necessarily people who own land. Unlike moneylending, mortgage is not at all unpopular. It is the only way in which the peasant can have ready money and at the same time avoid the burden of high rates of interest. The decline of living standards in the countryside (more specifically in the fertile plains near the urban centres) was the result not of a feudal economy, but, on the contrary, of the introduction of capitalist norms. The exchange of goods was expressed only in money terms, and relationships which were both social and economic became purely economic; but the government would not accept that Afghanistan had ever entered a capitalist stage.

The question of communal goods and services was not even touched on by the reforms, and yet these benefits (pastures, and often water supplies) are very real and are much sought after by the peasants. Nomadic groups were persistently defined as being poor and represented as wishing nothing so much as to be able to settle down. On the contrary, in many regions, such as Logar, nomads are important property owners. In any case they are better off than most of those who live in one place (as in Hazarajat) and their own view of themselves has little in common with the reformers' definition.

According to the reformers the criteria to be employed in defining exploitation in agriculture were: (1) the nuclear family: by law a family comprises one adult aged over eighteen with his wife and his children, or an unmarried person living alone;[9] and (2) the area of land. But Afghans live, in general, in extended families (brothers living on land which has not been partitioned after the death of the father) and exploitation is defined not, strictly speaking, in terms of the area of the land (except for irrigated land) but in terms of seed, plough (*qolba*) or the right of access to irrigation. Redistribution which is based only on calculations of the area of the land has little meaning. This is all the more true in that there are no reliable land registers. During the royalist period, local communities, faced with a government official who, not recognising the existence of communal property, demanded that land should be registered under a single person's name, and registered these communal lands under the name of the chief of the clan or the tribe. As a result, on paper great landed estates were created, although in reality they did not exist at all. The reformers did not recognise rights created by custom, neither did they accept principles derived from the *shari'at*. Rather, they assumed the existence of a state of law which was purely imaginary: peasants were supposed to provide juridical acts,[10] the committee carried out its work on the basis of a tax register which never existed, and the concept of a nuclear family was not in harmony with the real familial structure of Afghanistan.

The question of irrigation rights was referred to a commission which was to sit in future under the chairmanship of officials of the Ministry of Agriculture which, of course, had not been set up by the time that the peasants needed to irrigate their fields.

In a word, the agrarian reform was carried out to fit in with a preconceived theoretical model of Afghan society which bore little relation to the real thing, a model which had been developed, not as the result of a painstaking inquiry carried out on the ground, but to be consistent with party dogma. It is not surprising, therefore, that, instead of setting 98 per cent of the people against 2 per cent of the exploiting classes, these "reforms" led to a general revolt in 75 per cent of the rural areas.

The ill effects of the reform. The complex system of share-cropping which was most common in Afghanistan was far from egalitarian, but it worked and there was an element of give and take about it. The reforms put an end to this traditional way of working based on mutual self-interest (sharing of work, of property, of seed, of beasts of burden and of irrigation rights between the landowner and the share-cropper) without introducing any alternative. The landowners who had been dispossessed of their land were very careful not to distribute any seed to their share-croppers; people who traditionally had been willing to provide loans now refused to do so. It is true that there were plans for the creation of a bank for agricultural development and for setting up an office to oversee the distribution of seed and fodder, but none of this had been done when the reforms actually took place. There is one specific instance of poor peasants, never doubting for a moment the promises of the reformers, who were transported 1,000 km from their homes to occupy confiscated land. No preparations had been made for them – no seeds, no finance, no houses – so they were forced to return home, poorer than ever.[11]

So it was that the very act of announcing the reforms cut the peasant off from his seed supplies. He was no longer able to buy seeds in the bazaar, for the traditional moneylenders refused to grant loans because moneylending and the provision of mortgages had been banned. Many landowners, fearing that their land would be confiscated, did not sow the fields, and this occurred to such an extent that agricultural production fell by one third in the spring of 1979.[12] One final disaster: the reform broke up the few extensive properties where mechanisation had raised the level of profitability. This example comes from the region of Herat: a big landowner with 300 *jerib* used to give 170 of these to be worked by a single share-cropper, who employed fifteen agricultural workers who were provided with a tractor; after the reallocation of land, the share-cropper had no more than 5 *jerib* (like all the agricultural workers in the village). None of the farms could make a profit, so immediately the peasants demanded, not the return of the absent landowner but the re-establishment of the farm under the direction of the share-cropper (personal observation, October 1982).

But what the reform destroyed was not just the economic structure, it was the whole *social* framework of production and, indeed, of the very life of the peasant. Community work (repair of irrigation channels, for example) was now explicitly the sole preserve of a state which was totally incapable of matching up to the task.[13] Both the *malik* and the *khan* had, as we have already seen, a social function as intermediaries in relations with the state, and as "bosses" who provided the share-croppers with protection and social stability. But it was the intention of the regime to get rid of them. It is thus clear that the aim of the reform was to destroy the whole socio-economic framework of the Afghan countryside. So much so that one may ask whether it is justifiable to continue to speak of the "mistakes" which were made when the reforms were thought out.

Was the agrarian reform ever a viable proposition? The official aim of the reform was to create a great number of smallholdings of between 20 and 30 *jerib* in good agricultural land. In theory, such farms should be capable of making a profit, but it would be necessary for the peasants to have loans available, since the law forbade them to mortgage the land which had been redistributed to them. A rapid calculation shows that wiping out the debts and getting the farms off to a good start would cost the state 10 billion *Afghanis* (£100m), whereas the total amount of all agricultural loans for 1977 was only one billion *afghanis*.[14] In addition, 20 to 30 *jerib* was the maximum amount of land that could be owned; this meant that the farms actually set up as a result of the reform were far below this ceiling, and unprofitable simply because the total quantity of land available was insufficient.[15]

The government must certainly have been aware that the agrarian reform would not work. If we bear in mind how committed they were to bypassing the capitalist stage of social development, the following hypothesis might carry weight. The agrarian reform was intended to break down traditional social structures and not to create a viable system of smallholdings; later on the government planned to set up cooperatives which would group together the small farmers who had benefited from the land reforms, and who would now have come to realise that it was impossible to make a living from their farms by themselves. In support of this view we might add that the official document which published the article dealing with the establishment of agricultural cooperatives appeared in September 1978, that is to say *before* Decree 8. The agrarian reform may not have been a collectivist reform, but it seems that it was worked out with the clear intention that it should be the first stage on the route to a collectivist society of the future. That is why the leaders did not really try to provide an efficient network of banks to provide credit, which might have had the unfortunate result of placing smallholdings on a firm financial footing. However, it goes without saying that when the new system was seen not to be working, the peasants who had initially welcomed reform felt they would be better off going back to the old system rather than venturing into the unknown.

The attempt to put the agrarian reform into practice

It is possible to distinguish three zones: (1) those where the reform did not even get off the ground: this, of course, was the area in which the rebellion broke out in 1978, but it also includes the very distant or very mountainous regions, such as Hazarajat; (2) those where the rebellion actually broke out because of the arrival of the commission working on the agrarian reform (we shall deal with these later); (3) those where the agrarian reform was successfully implemented. These are interesting, because, although some of them remained loyal to the government, others joined the opposition in their struggle a few weeks after the agrarian reform.

As a general rule, the zones where the agrarian reform took place were those where vast estates were a significant factor, where the landowners were often absent and where the previous state of affairs which had worked to the mutual benefit of the *khan* and the *dihqan* had been replaced by naked economic exploitation. In cases like this, often neither the *khan* nor the *dihqan* belonged to the same *qawm* or even to the same ethnic group (Pashtun *khan* for Tajik *dihqan*, for example). The lands in question had generally been acquired only a short time before, using capital derived from commercial activity, which explains the absence of any socio-political links between the *khan* and the *dihqan*. (But there have also been cases where the links of traditional solidarity between groups within the same *qawm* were dissolved.)[16] These zones included Herat (the length of the Hari-rud valley from Obe to Ghoryan), Farah, Nimruz, Logar and Kunar and the suburbs of Kandahar, as well as the outskirts of certain towns. In all these cases, the landowners were often rich traders from the town who had invested their capital in land. However we must not exaggerate the extent of these lands, which ranged from a few hundred to a few thousand *jerib* in area, or rarely more than 1,000 hectares of land, which were not all irrigated. It seems that in those cases where the landowner was a member of the local tribal aristocracy (Durrani, Baluchi) and where the share-croppers were members of the same tribal group, the latter refused to take part in the reform.

On the other hand, in the regions where different *qawm* were very closely involved with one another, the reform served as an excuse to redistribute power between groups which were political rivals, without any "class struggle" being involved. This was the case in the region of Fayzabad (Badakhshan), where land which had belonged to families involved in the resistance was granted to the relatives and allies of the ex-Maoist Taher Badakhshi, a member of an important and influential local family.[17] In the same way, in the Kunar valley and in the Khost region, and thus in a tribal zone, the reform made it possible for "junior" clans to gain the upper hand over other "senior" clans of the same tribe, who up till then had traditionally held political power because they were able to call upon more warriors and were able to exert more influence. Thus, behind the fine phrases, the key to understanding the way in which the reform was operated is to be found in the traditional in-fighting of different political factions in Afghanistan.

How did the beneficiaries of the reform act when the rebellion broke out in their region? It is difficult to generalise on this, seeing the many obstacles in the way of the inquiry, but there is one interesting fact worth noting. In those regions where there were many absentee landowners, the peasants joined the resistance in great numbers (at Herat, for example, the uprising only broke out some weeks after the beginning of the redistribution of land). When landowners did not return, and this was usually the case as far as those who owned extensive land were concerned, the peasants kept the land which had been granted them. In areas where most landowners owned medium-sized holdings of about 100 *jerib*, the landowners remained, and the clergy urged that the land should be returned to them on condition that the harvest should be more equally divided. On the other hand, in those regions where the segmentation of society into rival *qawm* and clans was still the major problem of local political life, the groups which seized the land now became militant supporters of the government.

When the peasants acted it was virtually never as members of an economic group, but as members of a *qawm*. This was equally true for the landowners. In the zones where there were many absentee landowners, neither group (peasant or landowner) had any strong feeling of belonging to a *qawm* and the landowners were in no position to lead an uprising in a place where they had not laid down any roots. In those zones where the *qawm* phenomenon was still a powerful influence it was the latter which mediated relations between people and land, a source of power rather than of wealth. Very often the members of the commission for agrarian reform used these reforms to advance their own group in local rivalries.

Finally, there were the mullahs, opposed to the reform for religious reasons, but not on economic grounds for the Afghan clergy did not own very much land. The clergy used their influence in every region to try and block redistribution of land with two exceptions, which confirm the accuracy of the analysis which we have just given. They did not support the absentee landowners, who were accused of having deserted the resistance movement and especially of having acquired the land with illicit profits (loans which produced interest). And they could not support tribal groups deeply involved in competition for land who preferred to follow the tribal code (where the appropriation of the land belonging to a rival group is a praiseworthy act) rather than the *shari'at*.

In any case the reform only affected a very limited area, and it was stopped after the Soviet invasion. The statement published in the *Kabul New Times* of 17 November 1983, that 650,000 peasants without land had received land in a five-year period, seems barely credible, all the more so since only five days later the same newspaper gave the figure of 300,000 peasants. The reform did not succeed in providing the government with a social basis of support, but, on the contrary, it created a hostile consensus of opinion amongst the peasants. In short, it only worked to the advantage of a few isolated groups who later became members of local militia. As far as the movement which was later to become the resistance was concerned, opposition to the reforms not only strengthened the feeling that the ownership of land was sacrosanct, but it also caused the landowners to offer more favourable contracts to those who farmed their land (except in Hazarajat) and it ensured that the resistance movement could not avoid coming to terms with the social question.

The fight against illiteracy

In the make-believe world of the government, the campaign to eliminate illiteracy played a role which was as important as the agrarian reform. The essential idea was that all that was necessary was to enlighten people and they would become firm supporters of the new regime. The campaign had to take place immediately and it embraced the whole country: children and adults, young and old alike, had to learn to read and write in a single year. The programme envisaged 18,500 teachers being sent into the countryside (of whom 16,000 would be volunteers), beginning in early 1979; it actually began in May 1978, using whatever resources were available. It was estimated that it would take 150 hours to teach someone to read and write. The teachers were provided with a new manual. Every Thursday morning, they gathered in the main town of the area to receive political instruction. In fact, it was quite clear from the very beginning that there was a close link between the campaign against illiteracy and the process of political indoctrination. The textbook showed European and urban lifestyles in a good light, a tendency which was already at work under the preceding government. One particularly grotesque page represented people marching towards the future – three intellectuals wearing suits and ties and equipped with a shoulder-belt against an undifferentiated background of a crowd in traditional costume. A way of life centred upon the land and the lifestyle of the peasantry were here associated with the grandparents' generation; the father, on the other hand, was a worker in a modern factory. *The* book was no longer the Qur'an but the school textbook. A whole page was devoted to the tank as a symbol of the people's liberation, and a third of the pages were taken up with slogans and catch-phrases invented by the government. We should recall that this campaign was supported by UNESCO advisors at Kabul, who, with natural delicacy, described the section of the course devoted to propaganda as "lessons with a socio-economic content".[18]

As in the case of the agrarian reform, the people's attitude towards the campaign against illiteracy was somewhat complicated. They certainly did not want to miss the opportunity to learn. The teachers enjoyed a certain esteem in the countryside, providing they did not go against tradition. Contrary to what has often been said, the government which was in power before the King was deposed had spared no effort to bring education to the countryside, and the increase in membership of the PDPA was a direct consequence of this policy. It has been estimated that 30 per cent of boys were receiving education under the previous regime, against 5 per cent of girls, and these two figures were increasing.[19] The method that was used to bring schools to new neighbourhoods – a very progressive one – was to stimulate interest in the idea of having a school among the villagers, and then to encourage the whole village to participate in putting the school buildings up, after which the government would be responsible for paying the teacher's salary. The Khalq regime rejected this progressive policy. The teams whose task it was to wipe out illiteracy had to go everywhere straight away. Their members were not teachers (there were not enough of these) but students and secondary school pupils who supported the regime.

Opposition to the literacy campaign did not focus on the idea of such a campaign in itself (which was quite well received in urban quarters) but on the way in which it was carried out. First of all, the fact that the teachers often behaved in an authoritarian and arrogant way, especially when they found themselves in a different region from the one they had been brought up in, was extremely annoying to a society which had great respect for hierarchy and politeness. Next, the fact that old men were forced to attend the courses was a source of profound humiliation to them. The element of propaganda was an affront to the devout. Above all, what sparked off the revolt was the requirement that girls should attend the courses. Contrary to popular belief, the issue was not whether women should receive instruction or not; only the very traditional circles, which were not necessarily also very devout, were opposed to this. But there was general agreement that any mixing of the sexes should be violently opposed. Also, because there were not enough women teachers, all the courses had to be conducted by men, who had come – and this was worst of all – from the town which was seen as a hot-bed of vice. It was this, and not the idea of a literacy campaign in itself, which led to the rejection.

There was a close correlation between the areas involved in the literacy campaign and those where uprisings took place. The literacy campaign was at its peak at the beginning of 1979, but after the spring it was in retreat. By winter 1979–80, the literacy campaign had come to a halt in the countryside and now only affected the town areas which were firmly in the grip of the regime.

The reform of the dowry system

The outlawing of the custom of providing dowry by Decree 7 (October 1978) did not produce the reaction which one might have expected, for Afghan society was, in any case, very much divided on this subject. Of course fathers of girls of marriageable age saw in the new measure a lost opportunity to do business, but young unmarried men welcomed the new law. The clergy were split between modernists and traditionalists. The modernists carefully distinguished between the *mahr*, the provision of a guarantee provided for by the *shari'at*, which was paid to the woman and the amount of which was strictly limited; and the dowry proper (*shirbaha*) which was customarily paid to the father. The traditionalists saw the dowry as a cornerstone of morality and the stability of the family (in fact it is very rare for a wife to be repudiated in Afghanistan compared to the remainder of the Muslim world). Since the *mahr* was continued, Decree 7 did not present an affront to Islamic law.

Reforms versus traditions?

The communists, like many Western observers, interpreted the uprisings as a rejection of the reforms, a continuation of the traditional interpretation of the events which led to the downfall of King Amanullah in 1928. But a more detailed study has shown that things were more complex than that. While it is true to say that there was a traditionalist party in Afghan society (especially in the tribal sectors) which was opposed to any kind of reform, there was also a growing proportion of the population, including, as we have seen, members of the clergy, which held that far-reaching reforms were necessary. By studying the way in which the uprisings occurred, we can see that it was not the principle of reform which caused the population to revolt but the way in which these reforms were being carried out (with the ensuing repression), or the contradictions in which the peasant population found itself as a result of them. Next, the cultural factor played an important part: instead of being introduced pragmatically, the reforms were presented ideologically, using an explicitly Marxist terminology which was a real affront to the religious beliefs of the population. Finally, the implementation of the reforms involved the incursion of the state machine into the village communities in a particularly brutal and unprecedented way. The revolt was as much anti-state as anti-communist.

The repression

During the period of government of Taraki–Amin, the Afghan people suffered cruel repression. In February 1980, the government of Babrak Karmal admitted that 12,000 people were "officially" dead, but this number only involved those who had disappeared in the prison of Pul-i Charkhi. (The number of executed and missing persons in the countryside was also very great although these victims received less publicity than those at Kabul.) In all, between 50,000 and 100,000 people disappeared. Here also the attitude of the government was consistent

95

with its view of Afghan society: if the exploiters were only a small minority and the people were insufficiently mature to unmask them themselves, it was necessary for the forces of repression to directly eliminate the handful of counter-revolutionaries. Mass arrests began in the autumn of 1978 and reached a peak the following year. In the towns, the victims were in the upper echelons of the clergy, intellectuals opposed to the government and a mass of ordinary people rounded up on the least pretext; there was scarcely any family at Kabul which was not affected. In particular, the government showed great zeal in attacking those close to it, such as the liberals, the Maoists and, from August 1978 onwards, members of the Parcham faction. The Maoists had strong support amongst the students but had no means of taking cover in the countryside, and had no links with the great families of the capital (although they often had links with the local squirarchy). Moreover (and this particularly damned them in the eyes of the Pashtun Khalq), they belonged to non-Pashtun ethnic groups. For all these reasons they were the object of a particularly savage wave of repression which left them politically broken by the end of 1980. In the towns, where the reforms applied, and where people were more receptive to the idea of change, it was the policy of blind repression which alienated them from the regime.

In the countryside, the victims were to be found amongst the clergy, the Sufi orders and people of influence in the local community. But tribal solidarity proved more important than political differences: for example, Sayyaf, who was later to become President of the Islamic alliance (see p. 122) and who belonged to the Kharruti tribe (to which Hafizullah Amin and Hekmatyar also belonged), was spared during his stay at Pul-i Charkhi.

In the villages, the potential opposition was led away by "security groups" who had come from the provincial capital; nothing more was heard of them. It is surprising to see the large number of *'ulama* or *pir* who allowed themselves to be captured in this way – an indication that they did not expect to be arrested and that they had not engaged in anti-government activities. It would be impossible to deal with all these arrests and killings in detail. They included the murder of the *pir naqshbandi* of Purchaman (Farah), who was extremely influential amongst the Aymaq: Hajji Baha'uddin Jan, killed with his two sons. The main *modarres* of Maymana, Mawlawi Ala'uddin was killed in the summer of 1979 with a number of his students and several dozen secondary school children, and a dozen influential people disappeared in the small town of Lawlash (Faryab), taken hostage by the army at the same time. At Ghalmin (Ghor) the former deputy and two religious leaders disappeared, as did two *mawlawi* at Kandahar. These are only by way of example. In addition to these selective arrests, massacres of whole civilian populations occurred at Samangan, in Kunar (Kerala), at Farah and at Darrah-yi Souf. Partial inquiries have been made but the story of this wave of repression has yet to be written.[20] For this period, the aim was the total elimination of certain social categories (the clergy and people of influence) rather than genocide. Specific examples of the working of this "principle of selection" can be given. In January 1979, the whole of the Mujaddidi family who still lived at Kabul was arrested and taken to Pul-i Charkhi, where all the male members of the family were executed. In the same way, in June, several hundreds of Islamist militants, who had been arrested during the Daoud period and who had remained in prison without trial since 1975 were executed in a single night. The Shi'ite clergy were a particular target: Sayyad Wa'ez, who was in charge of the Muhammadia *madrasa* and who was one of the instigators of the Shi'ite revival, disappeared in February 1979 with the majority of his teachers. Dozens of devout Shi'a were arrested at Charkent, Darrah-yi Souf, Yakaolang and Jaghori. Some of the religious leaders and local *pir* had a narrow escape (the *pir* of Tagao, and all those in the Herat region), as well as Shaykh Asaf Muhseni, Shi'ite leader from Kandahar.

The areas affected were those where the government exercised a certain degree of military control but where it was conscious of the fact that it had no hold over the population: the west, the north and Kabul. Very often in these regions the harshness of the repression concealed old ethnic antagonisms, and the Hazara living on the boarders of Hazarajat paid a particularly heavy price. The tribal areas in the east (and the establishment) were protected by tribal solidarity.

The goal was clear: to cause the "old" Afghanistan to disappear, by dissolving the social structures and uprooting them from the memory of a whole people, by striking down middle-class people of influence (rather than the aristocracy, considered to be less dangerous because cut off from the people), the *'ulama*, guardians of the age-old Islamic culture, and finally young non-Marxist intellectuals, who might have shown a different way towards modernity.

Chapter Six

The uprisings, 1978–9

When the coup of 27 April 1978 occurred, the new regime was not regarded as being communist either by political observers or by the ordinary citizens of the country. On 20 May, a specialist in Afghan affairs, Louis Dupree, published a letter in the *New York Times* under the heading: "A communist label is unjustified". Nevertheless, the rhetoric of the regime left little room for doubt: it called for unity between workers, poor peasants and enlightened intellectuals to bring about the downfall of feudalism, talked of solidarity with socialist countries in their fight against imperialism, and published telegrams of support sent by international para-communist organisations. But long experience of Third World "revolutions" has led Western observers to expect a gap between revolutionary rhetoric and a more moderate approach to the exercise of power. Both the Afghan communist movement and the degree of Soviet penetration were largely underestimated. Babrak, Taraki and Amin, who were all well known as individuals, were regarded as political amateurs. It was thought that the USSR already had sufficient influence in Afghanistan and would therefore not wish to run the risk of a major political crisis by openly taking over a country already under its control.

Daoud was not popular in the country. The coup was generally seen as yet another example of *padshahgardi*, "political in-fighting within ruling circles", which meant that power changed hands at the top without bringing about any fundamental change in society. Nevertheless, there were certain elements which were totally new. Apart from the brief rule of Tajik Bacha-yi Saqqao in 1928, it was the first time that power had passed out of the hands of the Durrani Pashtun and into the hands of the Ghilzay Pashtun. Those who now held power came from the lower middle classes (officers and officials) and openly professed allegiance to socialism. The rhetoric employed – like the ethnic and social origins of the new ruling groups – was something quite new. To understand the way the Afghan people reacted to the takeover, it will be helpful to divide them into five somewhat unequal groups. First, members of the PDPA and those who were generally in sympathy with the movement immediately took over all positions of authority in their work places in advance of official confirmation of their new posts: their reaction was, of course, one of enthusiasm. Secondly, the small group of Islamist students and *'ulama* who had become politicised knew very well that those who had seized power were communists, for they had moved in the same circles and fought against them for ten whole years in the schools and the faculties. This group immediately went underground, soon to be followed by the majority of the Maoists, whose cause would not be advanced by the pro-Soviets. A third group was made up in part of that minority of the urban population which was modernist without being communist and in part of impoverished peasants living around the towns. They reacted favourably towards a government which, in their eyes, was not communist and which was expected to carry out the reforms that had become necessary due to the worsening economic situation (the expansion of the market economy and population growth). Fourthly, the great majority of the rural population deferred judgement, although in certain regions, such as Laghman, meetings held to explain the agrarian reforms attracted much interest. Finally, a certain number of communities reacted towards the new government on the basis of their ethnic and tribal loyalties: the Ghilzay were in favour of the change because it meant that it was now their turn to be in power, while the Nuristani were violently opposed because they had had close links with the preceding government. The uprising began in July 1978 on a tribal basis, but soon turned into an ideological struggle. We shall study the chronology of the uprisings and look more closely at the places where they occurred, and then analyse the reasons for the peasants' revolt. As a definition of what constitutes an uprising we shall take any attack on a government district (*uluswal*) post carried out by the local people.

In July 1978, the people of the Nuristani valley of Waygal sent a delegation to the government post at Manugi, which was in the Pashtun territory of the Safi, to find out what had happened to members of their valley community who had disappeared just after the coup. Although no one knew it at the time, these officials had been summarily executed because they were suspected of remaining loyal to the Minister of the Interior. Such loyalty could be taken for granted since they were members of the same *qawm*; from the beginning the new communist regime made great use of the social structure of the tribes ("Never trust anyone who is not a member of your own *qawm*") in order to maintain itself in power. Although in the early days this policy gained them the support of the Pashtun, it also meant that the non-Pashtun were automatically forced into opposition, whereas they might have been won over by a more flexible policy, such as the one which the Russians tried to follow after 1980. However this may be, the events at Manugi degenerated into a riot,[1] the government post was captured on 20 July and the revolt spread to the Nuristani valleys of Waygal, Bashgal (Kamdesh) and Ramgal (Upper Laghman). In October 1978, the two government posts in the Bashgal valley (Kamdesh and Bargimatal) were captured. It is interesting to observe that, when it came, the counter-attack was made on tribal not political lines. The government offered weapons and money to tribal groups who were hostile to the Nuristani: the Gujar, nomadic cattle-breeders who lived on the upper slopes of the valleys and who had a longstanding dispute with the Nuristani about pasturage, and the Pashtun tribes of the Kunar (the Meshwani, the traditional enemies of the Nuristani) and of Nangrahar (the Shinwari). A mechanised battalion accompanied this coalition of tribes, who were driven by their desire for gain. Kamdesh was recaptured by government forces in November. But, in February, the Nuristani formed a coalition of people from the three valleys which was able to crush the government battalion at Mirdesh and recapture Kamdesh. Peace was made with the other tribal groups and the government forces did not set foot again in Nuristan. A new element now appeared: a number of Islamist intellectuals who had come from outside, including Massoud, the future commander of Panjshir, took part in the fighting on the side of the Nuristani. At the same time there developed amongst members of different tribes (such as the Safi) a spirit of solidarity which transcended tribal loyalties, and which led to a refusal to take part in pillaging. Already there were signs of the tension which was to develop between traditional tribal chiefs, such as Amin Anwar Khan of the Kam, and fundamentalist mullahs, like Mullah Rustam (Kam) and Mullah Afzal (Kati). However, the fighting in Nuristan had little effect on the country at large, since Nuristan is very remote and something of a special case.[2]

So it was that the uprisings began in the north-east of Afghanistan in 1978. The whole of the west of the country rebelled from March 1979 onwards, beginning in Herat and spreading through the province of Farah. Then it was the turn of the centre, with Darrah-yi Souf (Hazarajat), beginning in December 1978, followed by the northern part of Uruzgan in April. The anniversary of the revolution of 27 April saw uprisings in Hazarajat (with Yakaolang, Nahur, Malestan, Lal and Shahrestan), in the Aymaq country (Daulatyar) and the north-west (Faryab and Badghis provinces, with the capture of Jawand in April). Maymana revolted in June. By autumn the whole of the centre, from Ghazni to Maymana, from Farah to Darrah-yi Souf, was free.

Apart from Wardak, Uruzgan and Logar, which took part in an

uprising in April, the Pashtun regions were less troubled by conflict than the Persian-speaking regions. This relative state of calm was due to two factors: the new Khalq power was Pashtun and thus retained a certain "national" legitimacy which in the eyes of the other ethnic groups it did not possess. Since the influence of the Islamists was not so strong in tribal zones, ideological factors took longer to come into play; the tribal framework made it easier for the regime to consolidate power locally, and the tribal policies the regime pursued strengthened them in their attitude.

The uprisings in the Pashtun zones started after those in the Persian-speaking zones. A good indicator is the state of insecurity of the teams involved in the literacy campaign which had come from the towns. In May 1978 there occurred the first murders of these teachers in Shamali, to the north of Kabul, then in the autumn there were more killings at Herat. In the spring of 1979 the literacy campaign came to a halt in the provinces: the government was no longer in control of the countryside.[3] The Ghilzay also became restive at this period, although they were well represented in the government. The people of Wardak, who had been asked by the government to lead a punitive expedition against the Hazara (another example of their tribal policies), demanded weapons – and then went on to capture a government post (April 1979). Also in April, at Barak-i Barak in Logar the census commission was slaughtered, and in the area around Jellalabad a mutiny took place. By now it had become dangerous to leave the tarmac road between Kabul and Herat.

Summer 1979 saw the outbreak of resistance in Panjshir (6 July) and in Takhar (August). More serious still for the government, the first disturbances occurred at Kabul with riots in the Shi'ite quarter of Chendawol in July. Worse still, on 5 August, a mutiny occurred at Bala-Hissar, the major barracks in the town, which was said to have been led by a group of Maoist officers (whose importance has been overestimated in the West, since the members of the Jamiat also played their part with other dissidents). At this time, the former Maoist militants, now scattered in a great number of different organisations whose ideological stance was not very clear (of which the most important was the Liberation Organisation of the Afghan People – SAMA), played an important role in the urban opposition at Kabul by handing out pamphlets and organising strikes. The town suburbs, which had supported the regime in 1978, now became unsafe, and it was impossible to leave the centre of Kandahar at night. The bazaars to the south of Mazar-i Sharif, such as Sangcharak, were captured by the resistance.

Curiously, up to that time there is little reference to the Paktya tribes. The government never had very firm control in that region and, with the exception of Khost, was careful not to send literacy campaigners or agrarian reformers there. Many Khalq officers were natives of Paktya and were careful to do nothing that might be harmful to the interests of their tribal group. Nevertheless, in Afghan tradition the tribes have always been the spearhead of movements opposed to the government of the day and any call for an uprising of the tribes was an alarm signal for the Kabul regime. This is why the government reacted so firmly when the Jadran tribe became disaffected after the harvest of summer 1979. This was the only major military operation carried out by the government in the eighteen months that it had been in power. But the revolt of a single Paktya tribe (the others remained passive) was much less of a threat than the revolts which had taken place in Herat or Hazarajat. In this instance, also, one is led to the conclusion that the government was a prisoner of its tribal view of Afghan politics and of its understanding of the recent past. According to this view the key to political power had always been in the hands of the tribes; for example – so the argument ran – when paid sufficiently well by the British they had been able to bring about the downfall of the reformist King Amanullah.[4] The myth of tribal power was so deeply rooted that Amin decided to launch a full-scale military operation in Paktya which lasted from September to October. It was a crushing defeat, and the road from Gardez to Khost is still strewn with hundreds of burnt-out vehicles and armoured cars. This defeat, together with the ousting in September 1979 of the pro-Soviet Taraki by Amin, who was more of a nationalist, was one of the major factors in the Soviet decision to intervene.

The number of uprisings in tribal zones multiplied: Zabul, Kunar and Ghazni in September. In November the Asmar affair took place when the commandant of the garrison led a mutiny in the course of which he executed Soviet advisors and other members of the party. The weapons of the mutineers were recovered by the Shinwari of Kunar who were members of the *Hizb-i islami*.

Thus, on the eve of the Soviet invasion, three-quarters of the country was in a state of rebellion, a situation which had begun in spring 1979 in the centre and the north, and in the autumn in the tribal zones. Many details remain obscure, all the more so because observers tend to overemphasise events in Kabul, Kunar and Paktya because they were more easily accessible. Nevertheless, it is possible to be reasonably confident about the accuracy of the general outline: apart from the incident of the Nuristani, the revolt began in the Persian-speaking zones (Tajik and Hazara). Where Pashtun took part in the first revolts, it was always in the non-tribal Pashtun zones (Logar and Laghman, Wardak and Uruzgan as exceptions) in which the influence of the Islamist militants was often very strong. The tribes were no longer the force they had been in Afghan political life.

(1)   The Ghilzay and the Pashtun of the east became disaffected in the autumn, after the harvest, which was the traditional pattern of tribal warfare. Their spirit of aggression was as strong as those in the Persian-speaking parts, but the tribal structure had its effect on the form of organisation and the actual warfare.

(2)   Shi'ite Hazarajat became independent from the very beginning and remained so.

(3)   Except at Herat, there was no coordination between the military revolts and the popular revolts, neither was there between the urban and the peasant movements.

These general points apply to all the stages of the combat: there were three main types of resistance movement (non-tribal, tribal and Shi'ite) and a lack of coordination between the town, the army and the countryside.

The zones which were not affected until the Soviet invasion took place may be classified on the basis of what kind of community they were or by using sociological categories. Let us take first the community groupings:

(1) The Uzbek remained unaffected by the revolts going on around them, except in the lands of the Hazara and the Tajik (Takhar, Samangan and Sangcharak), where they became involved in the movement. In addition, from Shibergan to Kunduz there was no involvement in the fighting. In the Uzbek ethnic group traditional structures had broken down, and being more socially differentiated than the others, they were more receptive to the attractions of modernism (even though the number of people who joined the PDPA was very limited).[5] During the war, the Tajik, more than any other group, formed the backbone of the officers who led the resistance in the north. The information we have concerning the attitude of the Turkmen during this period is, unfortunately, somewhat sketchy, but they seem to have been very much opposed to the new regime.

(2) The Durrani tribes (from Kandahar to Farah) waited to see how things would turn out. This attitude, no doubt, reflected the degree of prudence which characterised the high aristocracy until the Soviet invasion occurred. The town of Kandahar remained calm.

(3) The Baluchi tribes did not get involved, and neither did the province of Nimruz, divided between the influence of the Baluchi aristocracy and the Maoists.

(4) The Pashtun communities of the north, although influenced by the Hizb, were slower to revolt than the Tajik. Perhaps this was a reaction

born from the community solidarity between the Pashtun minority and the government officers who came from the same background, and who had traditionally acted as their protectors.

(5) A certain number of tribes in the east collaborated (Shinwari in Nangrahar, not to be confused with those of Kunar), or were "passive" (Mohmand, Jaji, Mangal, Tani, Waziri) and remained so. In fact, many Khalq had been brought up in a tribal environment, and, by tradition, the tribes have always played a double game (receiving arms and sums of money from both sides, taking advantage of their key position to make deals, like the Mohmand). Finally, the old rivalries with the tribes involved in the resistance as well as the smaller impact of Islam, ensured that they remained largely untouched by the current enthusiasm for *jihad*. Strangely enough, these were the tribes which caused most trouble to the British in the last century.

(6) The nomads, out of necessity, are great opportunists, except the Taraki, who, for straightforward reasons of tribal solidarity, were supporters of the government until September 1979, the date of the murder of Taraki, their fellow-tribesman.

(7) The Isma'ilis, traditionally victimised and despised by the other ethnic groups, for the most part very poor, not very zealous in their practice of religion and uncritically following the lead of their chieftains (the *moqi*), remained neutral and even provided members for the militia in Badakhshan as well as the governor of Doshi (from the *sayyad* family of Kayan).[6]

On the sociological level, three different social strata remained neutral at the beginning:

(a) The urban lower middle class of officials and employees: dependent on the state, modern in their outlook and deprived of any possibility of withdrawing to the countryside because they lacked the personal resources, the officials (*mamur*) stayed at their posts at least until the Soviet invasion occurred, and preferred exile to resistance. Their passive attitude is understandable in so far as they, more than anyone else, formed the social basis of support for the regime and in that they had been little affected by the revival of Islam (at least at Kabul, for many provincial officials reacted favourably towards Islamist ideologies or, in the case of the older ones amongst them, to Sufi preaching). By contrast small shopkeepers were very quick to join the opposition.

(b) Downwardly mobile peasants, especially in the suburbs: here, where large estates had grown up and where the social relations between *khan* and share-croppers had been replaced by a simple relationship of economic exploitation, the landless peasants who had nothing to lose accepted the agrarian reforms and were quick to enrol in the government militia (for which they were well paid). This is how the situation was around Herat, Kandahar, Jellalabad and Pul-i Khumri, but not at Kabul, where small landowners were in the majority. In certain places (Khost, Kunar) these groups represented "younger" segments of the tribe (*qesher*) which had lost political and economic power to family networks having more members and being wealthier (like the Mandozay and the Ismaelkheyl of Khost, who were confronted by the powerful Jadran tribe). In other areas they represented a population which had become detribalised and isolated within a tribal environment: thus in Kunar, the Dihgan, detribalised Pashtun-speaking peasants, who lived on the banks of the river, were in favour of the regime, while the tribes in the adjacent valleys (the northern Shinwari, the Safi from Pech) were, from the very beginning, in the resistance. The ranks of these collaborators were swollen by members of the lower working class and a section of the urban youth who saw no future for themselves. From the beginning, it was these groups which formed the basis for the government militia.

(c) The establishment: paradoxically, apart from religious dignitaries, the establishment was less affected by the repression than the lower middle class or people of standing in the provinces. Many high officials of the previous social order retained their positions even though real power was now exercised by incompetent young Khalq. It was not until the USSR invaded that this group left the country, and sometimes even later than that. It is more difficult to understand the reasons for their actions, but the protection provided them by tribal solidarity (it is known that the Khalq often came from tribal environments in the east), the certainty that it was not the right time to defect, and finally the fact that the resistance movement had had its birth in non-tribal and non-Pashtun areas (reminders of Bacha-yi Saqqao, who still ranked highly in the demonology of the Westernised middle classes), all these factors militated against the establishment joining the resistance.

Geographically, the bastions of the regime were, at the beginning, the centre of Kabul and Jellalabad, a whole series of small villages, such as Sarobi, Pul-i Khumri, Khost, Urgun and Lashkargah, certain clans and certain tribes (such as the Jaji, and the Shinwari of Jellalabad). Some isolated villages were won over by people of influence in their midst, which thus gained possession of land belonging to rival communities. As a general rule, zones which had a strong mixture of uprooted tribal elements, migrants of all kinds and a hotch-potch of ethnic groups were more subject to government influence (which was able to play upon the rivalries and the frustration plaguing subordinate groups) than zones which were homogeneous from an ethnic or a tribal point of view. These zones, as one would expect, lay primarily on the main tarmac roads through the country or in isolated basins (like Khost) in the middle of the mountains or in the deserts. Certain regions which later were to become strongholds of the resistance were untroubled by violence until the Soviet invasion occurred; they included Shamali, Kandahar and the towns in the north.

Finally, the resistance movement was, of course, quicker to get off the ground in the zones such as Hazarajat, Badakhshan and the west, where, for reasons having more to do with cultural and ethnic factors than socio-economic ones, the Communist Party had failed to take root; in these zones, those inclined towards Marxism had become Maoists in opposition to the Pashtun communism of the PDPA.

It is necessary to make a distinction between the uprisings which occurred spontaneously and those organised by Islamist militants. The former always followed a regular pattern: they started as a popular and local reaction to a direct and coercive intervention on the part of government militants who had come from the provincial capital to the major town of the district, either with the aim of imposing land or literacy reforms or to make arrests. Those who led the first revolts were religious leaders, people of influence such as village headmen, or other individuals who were usually elderly. The revolt usually took the form of a mass uprising preceded by preaching and followed by an attack on the government post of the principal town of the district, using smallarms (including flintlock guns). The post was usually captured with heavy casualties on both sides. The communist militants were executed, non-communist soldiers and officials allowed to go. Then the revolt would spread to the whole area in which there was tribal solidarity. The people who had taken part in this attack then spread out throughout any neighbouring villages of their own ethnic affiliations. When the frontier of the territory of the ethnic or tribal group was reached, the dynamic phase was over. Members of the resistance did not attempt to go beyond their own territory. They were then confronted by two problems: weapons and organisation. A second phase began when people rallied to the different parties at Peshawar. If government forces still remained within the tribal or ethnic territory (usually this would be in the plains, but also in Bamyan and Chakhcharan), they served as a focal point for the Mujahidin who could then organise themselves to deal with their military problems. If the territory was totally liberated, as in Hazarajat and Nuristan, civil society gained the upper hand and internal quarrelling poisoned the atmosphere. Most frequently a liberated territory would be bordered by a "front" (*jabha*) which was relatively static. In these cases, a frontier guard would be set up, the members of whom would, of course, be the most highly motivated resistance fighters.

On the other hand, in the areas where militants of Muslim Youth had long been established (Panjshir, Herat, Mazar, Badakhshan, Laghman, Nangrahar and Baghlan), the sequence of events was different. When spontaneous uprisings occurred there before the summer of 1979, they had been led by young intellectuals. If the region remained calm, the militants tended to go underground earlier and to create guerilla "cells" without any popular uprising (the most telling example was Panjshir). Finally, Herat represented a case apart, since this was the only example of a major uprising which resulted from a pre-arranged plan, between the militants, the clergy and the officers of the opposition.

One spontaneous uprising

The spontaneous uprising in Aymaq territory, Daulatyar and Chakhcharan can be taken as an example. While the Chakhcharan region had a few Islamist teachers, the neighbouring valley of Daulatyar was the stronghold of traditional *arbab*. On 20 April 1979, a delegation bent on agrarian reform, comprising a dozen armed Khalq militants, came from Chakhcharan, the provincial capital, and established themselves in the school. Their arrival unleashed a wave of agitation: the local *mawlawi* declared the reform to be contrary to the *shari'at* and, on 27 April, the anniversary of the communist coup, the post was besieged. The delegation was well armed and held out for two days, but finally ran short of ammunition. An old man succeeded in setting fire to the buildings, and the delegation surrendered and was massacred. No reinforcements arrived from the provincial capital, which was three hours jeep-ride away. In the days immediately following, the rebels came under bombardment as a reprisal, but the revolt still spread. To the north of Chakhcharan, the Ghalmin valley rose in revolt at the beginning of June, against the agrarian reform and because of the way in which people were being coerced into taking part in the literacy campaign. The incident which sparked everything else off seems to have been the abuse hurled at old men who refused to attend the classes. The communist teachers were killed, and the school and weather centre were burnt down. There was no garrison there. It appears that at this time the bazaar at Chakhcharan fell into the hands of the insurgents; it was only recaptured in January 1980 by the Russians who had come from Shindand.

One organised uprising

The uprising which occurred at Herat differed from others in many aspects. First, the agrarian reform had been set in motion without opposition (although it was brought to a halt later). Secondly, this was the only uprising where evidence shows that different groups were acting in unison. Finally, contrary to what Vercellin states,[7] ethnic factors did not play an important part in the affair and there was no question of it being an anti-Pashtun revolt. On the contrary, this uprising bears the marks of the strategy advocated by Rabbani immediately after the communist coup, that the army should attempt a counter-coup supported by a general uprising of the urban population. Hekmatyar's opposition to this strategy caused the whole operation at Kabul and elsewhere to end in failure.

A month before the uprising, several dozen militants of the Jamiat returned secretly from Iran. They had formed a rough plan for a revolt, though the date was not fixed, and were in contact with captains of the division stationed at Herat, (including Ismael Khan and Ala'uddin Khan), who were secret members of the Jamiat. The uprising began in the morning of 16 March 1979, in the oasis villages of Herat, when communist officers, especially teachers, were massacred. The uprising gained great momentum: peasants interviewed three years later described it as unplanned, but the link between the Jamiat militants and the *mawlawi* who preached in the mosques the evening before has been established.

The villagers then converged on the town where another revolt broke out: communist officers, and dozens of Soviet advisors and their families, were killed, though other foreigners were spared. The next day the army mutinied, led by the captains. By the following evening the whole town was in the hands of the insurgents, who retained control for a week. Then a government force of armoured cars appeared on the road from Kandahar brandishing the Qur'an and the green flag. The general staff of the resistance, convinced that the rebellion and the mutiny of the troops was going to spread throughout the country, gave the order to allow the column to pass. Whereupon the government troops, supported by the air force, a part of which came directly from the USSR, retook the town. The population suffered enormous losses, estimated variously at from 5,000 to 25,000 dead. The defeated rebels abandoned their heavy arms and regained the safety of the surrounding mountains of Kuh-e Doshakh, where they lived out in the wilds until the Soviet invasion occurred. A general insurrection now broke out simultaneously throughout the whole province of Herat.

The areas where uprisings were organised were areas where the Jamiat was strong. Strangely, Hizb strongholds (Laghman, Ghorband and Baghlan), which also had a network of young activists who had gone underground, remained calm and did not rise in rebellion until after the

Soviet invasion. Since the determination and discipline of Gulbuddin's men is well known, this lack of action can only have been part of a detailed plan. What were the Hizb waiting for? As always, it is not easy to provide an explanation for the policies of Gulbuddin.

Chapter Seven

The establishment of political parties

After the insurrection, the local members of the resistance sent deleg-
ations to Peshawar or to Iran to get arms for the various parties. It was
necessary to belong to a party, mainly for logistical support in negotiating
aid from outside and organising supply networks. A party made it
possible to hope that the traditional segmentation of society might be
overcome. It could also be represented politically in the outside world,
which would be quite impossible if the resistance was no more than an
aggregation of warring fronts. In a word, a party provided access to the
political arena. At the same time, the ideology of the *jihad*, which is
always dominant in Afghanistan in time of war whatever the sociological
structures, brought to the forefront feelings of identity of purpose and
unity amongst members of the resistance. For the peasant population and
the traditionalist *'ulama*, neither of whom are influenced by Islamist
ideology, the party is a way of giving visible reality to the *umma*: to belong
is to refuse to accept the divisions within society and to affirm unity.
Nevertheless, while one may accept the fact that it is necessary to belong
to a party, the choice of party remains unexplained. Knowing that the
Afghans have not much interest in ideology, one might think that the
choice of party is a pragmatic decision: you belong to the group which
provides you with weapons. But a map showing support for the different
parties reveals a distribution of support which seems to take into account
the following three criteria: the physical distribution of ethnic groups, the
political antagonism which exists between Islamists and traditionalists,
and the fact that certain social networks were already in existence. This
model provides a rough guide only, but it does serve to clarify the
situation.

The ethnic map and the political map

Three large areas stand out. In the tribal Pashtun south the so-called
traditionalist parties of Nabi, Gaylani and Mujaddidi are well represented, the choice being made according to the existing social network.

This area, which forms an arc, includes Farah in the west and runs as far as the Kunar valley to the north-east. The Shi'ite Hazara centre belongs, of course, to the Shi'a, whose representatives have established themselves at Quetta and not at Peshawar. The north, where Persian and Turkish are spoken, is mainly Islamist – more precisely Jamiat. Nevertheless, the influence of Nabi's *Harakat-i inqilab* was strong there in the first three years of the war, although it declined later.

This tripartite division runs through the whole resistance movement. Indeed, pockets of support for the Hizb correspond almost exactly to the areas where the Pashtun migration, starting in the nineteenth century, occurred. In Badghis the Pashtun are Harakat, the Tajik Jamiat. The nomads and the Baluchis support the traditionalists. The people of Nuristan are divided between the two groups on socio-political criteria: influential families are traditionalists and mullahs fundamentalist. Finally, in the west of the country, it is not so much the ethnic difference which is important (Pashtun against Tajik) but the fact that different languages are spoken: the Nurzay, who speak Persian (west of the line Shindand–Farah), are supporters of Jamiat, the Pashtun-speaking Nurzay (to the east) are members of Harakat – supporting the contention that an individual's conception of himself owes more to cultural than ethnic factors.

The *Hizb-i islami* of Khalis (see p. 78) was at the beginning no more than a regional schism in the Hekmatyar party, comprising the largely detribalised Khugiani of Nangrahar, the Pashtun to the south of Kabul and those of Paktya. The transition from tribal zones in the strict sense of the word, such as Paktya, to the zones where Pashtu is still spoken but which are not tribal (Shamali), is a gradual one and it is in this area of transition that political fragmentation is most apparent.

The influence of Islamism is very noticeable in the north and in the centre. It also exists among the Sunni groups (Tajik supporting the Jamiat, Pashtun supporting the Hizb) and in Shi'ite areas (with the Nasr, the Sepah and the *Harakat-i islami*). As we saw in chapter 1, this may be explained by the closer connection which exists between the clergy and the general population and by the weak sense of nationalist ideology.

There are of course exceptions to the correspondence between parties and the three criteria mentioned above. In the south there are some flourishing Islamist groups (especially the Hizb), particularly around Ghazni, Zabul and Helmand. The establishment of Hekmatyar groups is a phenomenon which transcends tribal alliegance, but it occurs most frequently in Pashtun areas and amongst young intellectual groups. It is to be found most frequently in pockets where tribal structures have broken down or which have a mixture of groups originating from

different tribes. Inversely, *Harakat-i inqilab* groups are to be found in the
north; these are the networks of traditional *'ulama*. In all, use of the
concept of social networks provides a more detailed analysis of the
support enjoyed by the various parties.

The social networks

Each of the four types of network, Islamist, clergy educated in the
traditional *madrasa*, tribal, and Sufi, is quite different from the others.
With the Islamist network we have something which resembles a modern
party. The clergy from the *madrasa* have created a network of personal
links between teachers and pupils, comparable to the Sufi's relationships
between *pir* and *murid*. The tribal network is one which links "dependents" and "benefactors" in a series of power relations. Alliances
forged through marriage play an important part in the last three networks
(and also, incidentally, amongst the Parcham), but not amongst the
Islamists. The idea of a social network is fundamental to the way in which
politics operate in Afghanistan, as has already been shown in the first
chapter: it creates group loyalties which operate independently of any
political programme (except, once again, in the case of the Islamists).
Naturally, the networks described above are not completely independent
from one another: we shall see, later on, how the tribal, clerical and Sufi
networks merge in the persons of the Mujaddidi family; we shall also see
how in the north, the Sufi and fundamentalist networks interpenetrate.
Moreover, it is absolutely essential that the *qawm* of a political leader
should follow him, even though its members might not necessarily share
his political views.

The Islamist network

In chapter 4 we dealt with the institutional background from which the
Islamist recruits came (university students and pupils of the government
madrasa). This results in the following pattern: the militants who
graduate from the secular faculties join the Jamiat and Hizb in about
equal numbers (the Pashtun usually join the Hizb and the Persian-
speakers the Jamiat), while those from the government *madrasa* join the
Jamiat. The Sufi orders in the north-west, fundamentalist by tradition,
usually join the Jamiat, but apart from a few teachers who were members
of the party before the war, it seems that this surge of support for the
Jamiat occurred at the time of the uprisings. Although there was no
Jamiat political network in the brotherhoods (in spite of the fact that
certain Sufis belonged to the Jamiat), the personal prestige of Professor

Rabbani amongst the religious scholars and the *modarres* was very great.

The strongholds of the Islamists are to be found around the cultural centres in the north, that is to say in the towns and in the parts of the countryside traditionally linked to the towns.

In the north-west, a Jamiat stronghold, the hard core of the militants came from the government *madrasa*, but also included army officers, teachers and officials. The Sufi and clerical networks interpenetrated. The Jamiat network was established in more moderate and orthodox circles here than in Kabul. In contrast, Hizb militants were mostly teachers in the government secular schools, and Hizb influence almost disappeared in the west after 1983.

In the centre (Ghor province) the Hizb and Jamiat networks have more in common, both leaders being educated in a government *madrasa*; but once again one finds the same underlying pattern: teachers in the Hizb, students of government *madrasa* in the Jamiat.

In the north-east, both Jamiat and Hizb militants came from secular universities. The Islamist networks in the north-east were, therefore, more radical and militant, and the rivalry between Hizb and Jamiat (which predominates) was all the fiercer in that *a priori* there was very little difference between the militants. The survivors of the failed uprising of 1975 have today become the local leaders of the resistance movement in this area.

The mawlawi *networks*

The *mawlawi* networks are very informal and therefore more difficult to pinpoint than those of the Islamists. We have already seen how the typical curriculum vitae of a traditional *mawlawi* consists in moving up from a private and not very well known *madrasa* to a more prestigious one as his knowledge increases. Thus, the future *mawlawi* places himself under the authority of a succession of teachers, to whom he remains attached, in the same way that he forms links with his co-disciples. When a respected *mawlawi* establishes himself in the countryside, he quite naturally begins to exert an influence on the village mullahs, who come to him with their problems.

After partition in 1947 and the political decline of the Mujaddidi family, Afghanistan no longer had a focal point, either geographical or political, for the networks of *'ulama*. But the networks continued to exist. Most of the Pashtu-speaking *'ulama* carried out their studies at Peshawar and then returned to the tribal zones. The Ghazni *madrasa* provided many young officers for the *Harakat-i inqilab*, for its leader, Muhammad Nabi, had taught there as well as in Logar. Since he owned some land in

Helmand, he had acquired great influence there. The informal *mawlawi* networks seem to be particularly strong around Kabul and at Nangrahar (Khalis), Ghazni and Gardez (Nabi, Mansur), and the whole region of Ghilzay and Kandahar. To the south-west, the networks are not so tightly knit, to the north and at Zabul they are still very localised and, in the countryside, they merge with the orthodox Sufi networks.

The members of the *'ulama* networks joined the Harakat of Muhammad Nabi, thus giving this party the absolute majority in the Afghan resistance movement in the first year after the Soviet invasion. The *'ulama* saw the Harakat as an apolitical party, a sort of clerical association. Decentralised, without any rigid structure, without political militants and without ideology, the Harakat is very much the centrist party. Supporting a return to the strict application of Muslim law, but without wanting an Islamist republic, it was opposed both to the Islamists (for whom the question of the state was not one that could be avoided) and to the secular royalists. Nevertheless, it was in agreement with the Islamists on the question of the primacy of the *shari'at* and with the royalists on the compatibility between the monarchy and Islam. Fundamentalist without being Islamist, traditionalist without being secular, the Harakat is the catch-all party of the resistance. Its organisation consists in a series of local fronts, centred round a non-government *madrasa*, under the direction of *mawlawi* who incorporate their pupils into the movement as officers. There is a *jabha-yi tulaba* (front of religious students), something which often crops up in areas where the lack of formal education makes the *tulaba* the only literate members. Such fronts are also to be found in the provinces of Badghis, Nimruz, Farah and Zabul.

Nevertheless, not all the local *'ulama* networks joined the Harakat. There were some Islamist networks in Herat in the west and in Paktya in the east. But it was important for the *'ulama*, whatever their political affiliations, to keep up their networks and to give them official standing in the *jam'iyyat-i 'ulama* or *shura-yi 'ulama* (associations or councils), to preserve their independence from the political resistance movement and to confirm the uniqueness of Islam by maintaining horizontal and "professional" links with their fellow members.

The Sufi networks

The local influence of a *pir* and his immediate descendants plays a more important role than alliegance to one of the three great orders, the *naqshbandiyya*, the *qadiriyya* and the *cheshtiyya*). The prestige of a brotherhood depends more on the standing of recent *pir* than on that of their forerunners. If the disciples are asked which group they belong to, they will mention not the name of the order, but the *silsila* of so-and-so. The *pir* have a purely local influence, which varies according to their personal prestige. But there is also a hierarchy amongst them, and a given local *pir* will proclaim himself to be the disciple of another of higher standing, and this produces Sufi networks. (See chapter 2 for the various orders of Sufism.)

Maraboutic Sufism in the Pashtun tribal zones

In Maraboutic Sufism the *murid* have joined the two parties formed by their respective *pir*: the Islamic Front (*Mahaz-i islami*) for the disciples of Sayyed Ahmad Gaylani, and the National Liberation Front (*Jabha-yi nejat-i milli*) for the followers of Mujaddidi. The Islamic Front is also the party of the establishment of the old society. Since "Maraboutism" is opposed to the strict religious orthodoxy of the *'ulama*, it is understandable that this party should be the one most strongly opposed to the Islamists. Sufism, in this context, makes it possible to give outward expression to religious sentiment while still remaining secular in approach to politics.

The Mujaddidi front is very much in the minority, but the alliegance felt for the last *pir*, Muhammad Ibrahim, has carried over to the leader of the party, Sibghatullah, who is not a *pir*.

Orthodox Sufism

The brotherhoods of the north are, as we have seen, very orthodox – indeed even fundamentalist. They have provided many *'ulama* and local mullahs, especially in the countryside. Here, the network of brotherhoods and that of the *madrasa* overlap. They are difficult to make out at first sight, for the *pir* of the north always refused to take a political stand in the parties.

The brotherhoods of the north-east, from Maymana as far as Pakistan, are still very traditionalist. When they have many local *'ulama*, they generally belong to the Harakat, or at least they did during the first years of the war. Throughout the north, the brotherhoods are anathema to the Hizb, who hold that their particular brand of religion is contrary to true Islam. The local *pir* have either disappeared or emigrated and their personal influence is not what it was. But the brotherhoods have joined the resistance with their networks.

The brotherhoods in the west and in Aymaq territory joined the Jamiat and, in some cases, the Hizb. The structure of Sufism does not seem to be any different at Herat or anywhere in the north; the orders find new members in the suburbs, for which they provide the clergy, and the town *madrasa* are still in the hands of a legalistic and formalist clergy. Alliegance to the Islamist parties arises, without doubt, from the fact that its members are better educated, and are therefore likely to make contact with politicised intellectuals. Finally, branches which openly proclaim their allegiance to the Mujaddidi family (such as the *pir* Shaykh Agha Jan at Barnabad and the *pir* of Kabarzan) are members of the Jamiat.

There are two other interesting networks in the west. Around the town of Chesht-i Sharif, a real little Sufi republic has come into existence with the *cheshtiyya* brotherhood. It controls all the *madrasa*, which are hidden away in the mountains. The brotherhood recaptured Chesht from the government during the winter of 1983–4.

The second network is that of Aymaq Sufism, centred upon Purchaman, whose *pir* controlled a whole number of "itinerant *pir*", who, having been invested with religious authority by him, wander throughout the Aymaq territory as far as Maymana. Although these brotherhoods are less spiritual and more inclined to belief in magic than those of Herat, they have joined the Islamist parties, especially the Jamiat.

Finally, in the south there are also orthodox brotherhoods. For example, in Zabul, two *pir* head networks of *tulaba* which have developed from their respective *madrasa*. The first to rise in rebellion, their *murid* set up formidable *jabha-yi tulaba* (fronts of theology students). The Harakat organisation at Zabul is based on this Sufi and clerical network. The non-clerical Sufi belong to Gaylani if they are *qadiri* and to Mujaddidi if they are *naqshbandi*. Thus, the general rule throughout Afghanistan is that a local *pir* identifies himself with the political position of the leader of his order (Mujaddidi or Gaylani) only if he is himself not an *'alim*; if he is an *'alim* he joins the Jamiat or the Harakat, and in a few cases Khalis or Hekmatyar.

In war the *pir* are rarely military leaders (except for the *cheshti*). In contrast the Sufis, led by the *murid*, control the local committees in the suburban areas of the north, particularly at Herat and Maymana. On the local level, the brotherhoods make for unity and coordination. The fighters from groups belonging to the local *khanaqah* are reliable and well-disciplined, because they are accustomed to obey the *pir* and they are well known to each other. In general, they are older and more mature than the usual Mujahidin. While the brotherhoods are quite capable of absorbing moderate Islamism, they are very much opposed to Wahhabism or radical Islamism, and thus opposed to the growth of parties like the Hizb or Sayyaf's alliance (see p. 135).

While it cannot be said that the brotherhoods have been the political spearhead of the resistance, they constitute in the north the best established network of the resistance at the local level. In fact the role of the brotherhoods in Islam must be similar to that which they play in Soviet Turkestan.[1]

The tribal networks

The tribal networks have two aspects: the old Durrani establishment, which is above all, urban, and influential people in the local tribes. As the establishment essentially developed from the great Durrani tribal federation which took power in 1747, these two networks, having the same origins, were linked through matrimonial and political alliances. Other great urban families came to join the establishment – families which had not sprung directly from the tribes (such as the Mujaddidi and the Gaylani) and influential families from the provinces who were not Durrani but were generally of tribal origin. The task of reconstructing this network in detail would be too laborious,[2] and it no longer has any importance at Kabul. Where it is strongly represented now is amongst those who have emigrated and amongst the tribes, especially the Durrani, where it is in competition with the *'ulama* of the *Harakat-i inqilab*, with whom the first-mentioned network of families generally has no marriage alliances. In any case, the tribal networks are royalist and constitute the core of the Islamic Front or, to a lesser extent, Mujaddidi's Liberation Front. So it is not surprising that their strength lies in the tribes which were the cradle of the monarchy, such as the Popolzay around Kandahar, where the present head of the Karzay family, 'Abdul Ahad Karzay, is also for the leader of the tribe.

Nevertheless, the fact that none of the great families has been represented in the resistance inside the country is striking. The tribal aristocracy has lost political power at Kabul as it has in the resistance, although in the tribal networks there were a few Parcham, such as Shahpur Ahmedzay (chief of staff), killed by the Khalq; Sulayman Laeq, Minister of Communications under Taraki and Zia Muhammadzay Zya, in command of Daoud's bodyguard in 1973. Generally speaking, the tribal leaders have generally been replaced by the traditionalist *mawlawi* of the Harakat or of Khalis' Hizb.

As we have seen, the *khan* only exist in the context of rivalry with their equals. This is why it is difficult for them to establish a party. Even if the local *khan* belong to the same party, they bring their rivalries with them. At Wardak, rivalries between cousins ended in the establishment of a dozen fronts and local committees all claiming alliegance to Gaylani, while only one of them, that of Amin Wardak, had any real power. The parties which have developed from the tribal networks resemble clubs, where relations of dependence and personal relations are dominant. They have little political or military potential. Abroad, they essentially comprise the members of the royal family.

When the USSR invaded on 27 December 1979, two-thirds, of the country was already in a state of rebellion and Amin's government was on the point of collapse. The invasion produced a twofold effect in the resistance movement: first, regions and groups which had not as yet revolted went over to the rebel camp. This was especially true of the intellectual middle classes, the officers, the northern Pashtun and the ex-Maoists, except for the *Sitam-i milli*. Next, the Peshawar parties, which, bar the Jamiat and Hizb, up to that point were still in an early stage of development, gained in influence.

The spread of the resistance movement

The Soviet invasion met with no armed resistance in the first month because its target was not the countryside, which was in a state of rebellion, but the government's army and the government itself.[3] For two months, winter and the shock caused by the invasion, combined with the establishment of the new regime and the fact that repression was much less evident, dulled people's reactions. Nevertheless, the Babrak government was definitely seen as being no more than a Soviet puppet and a powerful wave of nationalist feeling surged through sectors of society which, to that point, had remained passive. In Kabul, there were bloody demonstrations on 21 and 22 February, and again in May. The driving force behind these demonstrations was the students, both male and female, of all political tendencies. Amongst them, and particularly active, were former Maoists, experienced militants of the Liberation Organisation of the Afghan People (SAMA). In a more general fashion, the lower middle classes who had been educated in the capital, and who had remained passive, passed into the rebel camp. But this urban opposition declined after 1980, through a lack of any efficient underground organisation. Many officials then left the country.

In the provinces, the whole country joined the resistance except for a few pockets of supporters of the regime (see p.105). In the north-east, the Pashtun-speaking areas around Ghorband and Baghlan generally joined the Hizb. In Shamali, the plain just to the north of Kabul, French journalists were taken by SAMA to Farza and Istalif.[4] At the other end of the country the Nimruz front started to attack government frontier posts. The few areas where the left was influential joined the uprising after the Soviet invasion. The *Sitam-i milli*, however, took the opposite point of view: very anti-Khalq, they were later to join in the struggle against the government in 1979, but rejoined Parcham in 1980. Finally, Kandahar, the second most important town in the country, joined in the rebellion.

At the same time, the army – more particularly the officer class – was hit by a wave of desertions. The officers had been comparatively loyal so long as there was an Afghan government at the helm, for they were more nationalist than Islamist; they were totally against the invasion and could not stomach the idea that in the future they would have to be advised by arrogant Soviet officers. In May the Ghazni garrison mutinied. Throughout the country it was no longer possible to travel, except on tarmac roads in a convoy escorted by armoured vehicles.

The Soviet invasion had the effect, not only of spicing the anti-communist revolt with a current of nationalist feeling, but also of driving underground thousands of government opponents – some of whom were long-established in their opposition and others who had only recently arrived at that point. The long-term opponents were political prisoners who had managed to survive, and whom the government had freed in February 1980. Those who had only recently joined the ranks of the opposition were mainly soldiers, who joined the resistance with their weapons and all their equipment. Usually, dissident officials and officers did not join the resistance but went into exile, as did the members of the establishment still remaining at Kabul. There were a few rare exceptions of army deserters who remained with the guerilla forces.

Starting in February, the Russians embarked on their first direct operations against the resistance: this was the offensive carried out at Kunar in February 1980, then in Badakhshan, Panjshir, Baghlan, Takhar and Ghazni. The main objective was to keep the supply routes open. The country was entering the classic spiral of repression followed by more resistance.

The constitution of the political parties in exile (1978–9)

The origins of the political parties before the Soviet invasion are shrouded in obscurity. We have seen that the Hizb (and the breakaway group led by Khalis) and the Jamiat had their own offices and organisation well before the communist coup. But these parties had their own very clear ideological line. They were not in a position to absorb the mass of fighters who suddenly came to seek either weapons or simply a framework to operate in without political conditions – all the more so since the Afghans find it extremely distasteful to be involved in a rigid organisation. Again, some political or religious leaders, who had up to that time been in exile, were not keen on joining parties where they were not in command. So three different patterns emerged, which have characterised the history of the resistance parties throughout:

(1)   A number of loosely structured parties, made up of local fronts, corresponding to the segmentation of Afghan society and indicative of the rivalries of potential leaders and their followers; these multiple groups joined in a loose coalition. They are the so-called "moderate" parties.

(2)   A dominant party which had renounced its quintessential character to absorb people who were not ideologically committed from the very beginning: this is the Jamiat.

(3)   A very homogeneous party, of the Leninist type: this is the Hizb of Hekmatyar.

The problem of "union" was to be the main question of political life at Peshawar. The parties fluctuated between attempting the useless task of uniting and accentuating their differences in a suicidal fashion. First, the illusion that believers must of necessity be capable of coming to an agreement led to the worst kind of compromise, especially when there was pressure emanating from religious circles. Secondly, there was no tradition of political activity apart from the wheeling and dealing indulged in by the *qawm*. The leaders, not to mention their followers, found it difficult to make a distinction between the party and the network of social obligations created by past favours received, all the more so because this involved the possession of weapons, traditionally the outward symbol of local power.

The parties were victims of the same evil which undermined the Afghan state and now undermines the government at Kabul: the corrupting influence of the *qawm*. This view of politics as nothing more than the operation of networks formed by interpersonal links explains the way in which the parties have evolved at Peshawar. Temporary alliances are followed by further splits. The president of a coalition transforms the coalition itself into a new party, which is then added to those which make up the coalition in question. Thus, in June 1978, the "Front for the Salvation of the Nation" (*jabha-yi nejat-i milli*) was set up. In the autumn, Sebghatullah Mujaddidi was elected president with Tawana, Rabbani's deputy, as his secretary. But very soon Mujaddidi turned this front into yet another party and Rabbani resigned. Another attempt, in which Hekmatyar was involved, was the creation of the Revolutionary Islamist Movement (*harakat-i inqilab-i islami*), one of the names used by the Islamists in the sixties. At first, this front was very broad. Muhammad Nabi Muhammadi, a traditionalist *mawlawi* and a former deputy, was elected leader. Some say that Nabi was chosen on the suggestion of Hekmatyar, who hoped that he would be a man of straw. But he took the

Harakat in hand, and even created an alliance with former Maoists to strengthen his position.[5] This process repeated itself with Sayyaf, elected president of a broad coalition in 1980, which was dissolved in 1985.

At Peshawar, as in the interior of the country, the Soviet invasion constituted a clear break with the past. Until the invasion the parties were more or less dormant, because they received virtually no assistance from outside. The Jamiat tried to organise a counter-coup supported by a popular uprising, but the only place where this had any success was at Herat. However, the Jamiat continued to be the most active party in the country during this period. The Hizb adopted a longer-term strategy: it strengthened its inner networks by keeping them carefully concealed, abstained from any call for an uprising and went on developing its international connections with Iran and the fundamentalist circles of the Persian Gulf. The split with Khalis took place in 1979 because the latter was much more anxious to engage in concrete action and became involved in the uprisings in Paktya and Nangrahar. Mujaddidi and Gaylani, who arrived at Peshawar in the winter of 1978–9, slowly gained influence there, especially through the networks of the frontier tribes. Once Nabi had gained control of the Harakat he concerned himself mainly with regrouping the traditionalist clergy. None of these parties was able to bring in arms (often bought in the famous Pakistan bazaar at Darrah) in any great quantity. Nevertheless, when the Soviet invasion occurred, the political map of the resistance movement was clearly formulated: the six parties of Peshawar[6] were established by that time and changed very little subsequently, as was also true of the three main Shi'a parties. The existence and the importance of the small groups (Maoist or Shi'a) is more difficult to evaluate.

The Soviet invasion and the Western view of the parties

The invasion completely changed the Western attitude to the Peshawar parties. Instead of being ignored, they became necessary links between the resistance inside the country and the outside world and were adjudged to be an important trump card to be played against the USSR on the international stage. Only two things counted: the war on the ground and diplomacy. The West, which had a purely pragmatic attitude towards the parties, was not interested in their structure, their social bases or their ideology, and because of this their hopes failed to be realised on numerous occasions. It was not long before the decision to provide practical help for the resistance movement was taken in Washington, Cairo and at Riyadh. Such outside assistance was cautious, and was provided through the intermediary of the Pakistan government, which was careful not to pour too many weapons into the country. On the diplomatic level, an Arafat was needed, or at least a PLO. The Western powers, therefore, sought to impose an alliance, even though an artificial one, using a recurring blackmail: if you want to receive aid, you must unite first.

In the beginning Pakistan placed much less emphasis than did the West on the issues of weapons and union. Pakistan, whose new military government was not fully in control, could not afford to appear as a mere American staging-post, all the more so because after the business of the Iranian hostages (and later the events in the Lebanon), American support seemed unreliable. Although the Pakistanis permitted weapons to flow through their country, they placed a quantitative and qualitative limit on these. They must not exceed a certain calibre (14.5 mm for machine-guns and 82 mm for mortars). And a ceiling was imposed on the degree of technological sophistication, which barred missiles, and really up-to-date weapons. On the political level, the Pakistanis were obsessed with the fear that the resistance might develop in the same way as the Palestinian groups had done, enjoying the support of millions of refugees. It seemed to them that the best protection against this risk was a divided resistance. The Pakistanis granted the same facilities to each of the six groups and closed their eyes to the activities of the minor groups, which they did not recognise. It was thus the Pakistanis who ensured the continuance of the major split in the movement, at least until 1984.

By contrast, the Americans and the Saudis made union the key of their diplomatic offensive against the USSR. Their emphasis on the use of diplomacy was evidence not so much of an optimism that these problems could be resolved but of pessimism with regard to the military situation, and it was this attitude which led them to attempt to frustrate the plans of the USSR on an entirely different level. Their strategy was to impose a general union on the parties.

Coalitions formed between 1980 and 1984

On 19 March 1980, all the parties except Hekmatyar's Hizb announced that they were forming an alliance: Sayyaf, a former member of the Muslim Youth, was elected president, with Mujaddidi as vice-president. Sayyaf was chosen first, because having only recently come out of prison and being an independent he seemed to offer all the advantages of a new man at the helm, one who would be unlikely to favour any particular party; secondly, he was a former student of the faculty of theology, had studied in Cairo and Saudi Arabia, and therefore spoke Arabic perfectly. He seemed an excellent choice as a go-between to enlist the support of the

Saudis and the Gulf States, which was the Afghans' major source of money and diplomatic support. But this choice soon proved to be a disaster: Sayyaf was ambitious and not troubled by too many scruples; he proceeded to play his own game to transform the alliance into his own personal party. Initially he joined with Hekmatyar to bring about a split with the moderates and to reduce the influence of Rabbani and Khalis in the alliance, then he turned against Hekmatyar and created a rift in the Hizb. Money counted for a good deal in determining the policies that he was to follow. Being in charge of the Treasury after the break with the alliance, he arranged for funds from Saudi Arabia to be paid into his own account, and literally bought groups of resistance fighters coming to Peshawar for arms by giving them what they wanted in return for their nominal support.

The alliance never remotely looked like working. From that time on, the Afghan resistance split into two camps: Islamism and Royalism. This polarisation corresponded, as we have seen above, to a split in Afghan society itself, but one which had sociological and ethnic rather than ideological causes. The Harakat, which consisted above all of fundamentalist *'ulama*, but which gained its recruits from tribal zones, gravitated to the Royalist pole.

Each of these two poles had its own extremists: Gulbuddin Hekmatyar for the Islamists, and the last remnants of the tribal aristocracy for the Royalists. The radical Islamists viewed with horror the secularism of Royalist government, which they identified with irreligion and believed to be responsible for Soviet penetration of the country. For their part, the aristocrats looked down on those who formed the Islamist ranks, because they did not come from distinguished families and in most instances were without tribal connections. "We don't know his father" was a formula frequently used to disqualify some of the Islamist leaders. But, if one excludes the extremes, the differences between the more central parties in the two camps (where Rabbani and Mujaddidi were the leading figures) were not all that great. In the alliances two contradictory impulses were at work: at Peshawar the tendency was towards polarisation around the extremists, but within Afghanistan itself there was a centrist coalition which was closer to the natural balance of forces in the resistance movement. Until 1984, the Shi'a parties were not seriously invited to participate in the alliances, which explains why we are dealing with them separately.

After the failure of the coalition based on the five parties, two alliances were established in April 1981. An assembly of *'ulama* called all the political leaders to Peshawar and announced that they would only be allowed to leave when a real coalition had been formed. Gaylani, suspecting a trap, refused to attend. After several days of confused debate, a "coalition of seven parties" was set up which included the three Islamist parties of Hekmatyar, Rabbani and Khalis, that of Sayyaf with splinter groups from other parties, two from the Harakat (the only important one being that of Mawlawi Nasrullah Mansur, which was quite firmly established in an area ranging from Paktya to Ghazni), and one from the National Liberation Front. Parallel to this a moderate coalition was established with Nabi, Mujaddidi and Gaylani: this was more stable, but had less support inside the country.

Thus, the political scene changed very little until 1984. The Islamist alliance had only superficial unity; on the one hand, Rabbani and Khalis continually dreamt of a more broadly based united front, while Gulbuddin Hekmatyar and Sayyaf, who had at first been at one in their aim of eliminating the others, engaged in 1983 in a struggle to the death.

In the spring of 1985, under Saudi pressure, a broad alliance was established with all the parties. It seems to work quite fairly.

The activities of the Royalists

While the "alliances" were being set up, certain Royalist circles, encouraged secretly by Gaylani, played the *jirga* card, the mode in which traditionally Afghan sovereigns were endowed with legitimacy. Officially, this operation was presented as an attempt to set up a democratic parliament. But choice of members (co-opted from the tribal elite) and the sociological and historical context in which the *jirga* had formerly existed, made these *jirga* seem like a final attempt by an aristocracy in decline to oppose the rise of Islamists in the north and clerics in the south, both of which questioned their right to rule in the name of Muslim egalitarianism. In the moderate alliance, only Gaylani and Mujaddidi supported these initiatives; the Harakat, more clerical than tribal, remained aloof.

There were three attempts to convene the *jirga*. In the spring of 1980, following the initiative of a Jadran leader of the Paktya, Omar Babrakzay, contact with other groups was made, but the *jirga* was sabotaged by the Gaylani family who felt that power was slipping from them. The most serious attempt was made in the autumn of 1981. The *jirga*, which had been prepared for several months by a committee of influential people, should have taken place at Quetta. It aroused a certain amount of enthusiasm in Pashtun tribal circles and thousands of people gathered in the town. But the Pakistan government refused to give permission for the meeting to take place. It was transferred to Pishin, where a group took advantage of the state of confusion to pass round a petition demanding the return of King Zahir. The *jirga* then broke up in confusion.

These events were typical: behind the intention, sometimes sincere, of bringing together a kind of National Assembly, the *jirga* were no more than stalking-horses of the tribal aristocracy and for that reason condemned to fail. The establishment of the old society had always been very much cut off from peasant uprisings, and as time passed their understanding of the Afghan resistance became even more tenuous. The sociological changes undergone by resistance fighters, both in non-tribal and tribal zones, reinforced the separation more and more. The establishment had learned nothing but it had forgotten nothing, and wanted to return in every detail to the status quo ante. It was dogged by a fear of Bacha-yi Saqqao rather than of communism, and much preferred an agreement with the USSR than the recognition that a new leadership had emerged within the country.

In 1983–4, the *jirga* was again placed on the agenda, after an appeal by the King.[7] But there was nothing to indicate that any fundamental change had taken place, even though the outward presentation was now more sophisticated. Nothing had been done to integrate the resistance movement within the country or the parties. The Royalists' solution would have had meaning only if the King had been able to present himself to his people armed with an acceptable agreement made with the Russians. This was not the case. After that, the King refused to be identified with the only nationalist alliance.

The setbacks which occurred whenever the parties attempted to find unity demonstrated that there was no place for a political space within traditional society, and that this tendency was still very strong in the parties. The concept of unity as far as the *'ulama* are concerned rests on an ecumenicalism which rules out the need for political structures; amongst the Islamists this same concept dealt a powerful blow against the practice of clientism. In both cases there was a sharp conflict between rhetoric which affirmed the need for unity, strengthened by reference to the *umma*, and everyday experience. Even the setting up of a flexible coalition presented problems, for, instead of building their relations upon an objective appreciation of the power and the real interests of each party, most of the leaders considered power or military problems from a symbolic point of view. Questions about who should take precedence over whom were to them more important than the sharing of real power. Weapons, like money, were more symbolic of power than a means to fighting the war, for power traditionally involved not a bank account, or a display of wealth, but the ability to distribute economic goods to others and in exchange receive their gratitude. This, at least, was the relationship to power which characterised the attitude of Sayyaf and the moderates. It cannot be said to be true of Rabbani and Khalis (or of Hekmatyar, who had other concerns), although they could not avoid giving the appearance of being involved in the pursuit of this kind of power.

Chapter Eight

The development of the parties between 1980 and 1984

The party spectrum in 1980

The distribution of support for the parties is not the result of chance but may be correlated with fairly precise social networks. The map showing the level of support for the parties in the different areas and their relative strength has yet to be drawn. Naturally, studies carried out at the time were almost non-existent, and the situation has to be reconstructed.[1] At the beginning, only the Hizb and Jamiat militants made mention of the idea of the party; they established themselves through their networks of militants, without exercising any overall control over the population. People in general followed their local leaders, who made up their minds according to their belief in one of the four networks described above. For this reason there was a great diversity of opinion, combined with frequent shifts in loyalties. Sharp divisions in people's political loyalties owing to a great number of parties being represented at the same time in the same place characterised much of the country at the outbreak of war. Nevertheless, it seems that in the south the sharp divisions were less marked at the beginning but remained a factor to be reckoned with, while in the north, which was more divided in 1980, the political situation became clearer and a certain amount of regrouping went on.

In 1980, the leading party was, without any doubt, the traditionalists' Harakat, for the network which underpinned its support, the *mawlawi* of the non-government *madrasa*, covered the whole of the country. It was the dominant force in an area which cut a broad crescent throughout the south. In the north, it came second to the Jamiat in Herat and Badghis, but led the field in the area from Maymana to Kunduz, that is to say in the Uzbek country and in the Pashtun pockets of the north-west, whereas the Tajik zones were more inclined to support the Jamiat. The Harakat was not well represented in the centre and in the north-east.

The second most popular party was the Jamiat. Its stronghold was in Badakhshan and Panjshir in the east, and in Herat in the west. It was essentially to be associated with the Tajik.

The Hizb had taken root in the small areas where Pashtu was spoken in the north-east (Baghlan, Kunduz, Laghman and Ghorband) and amongst the detribalised Pashtun of the south (Ghazni and Helmand), as well as amongst some of the Aymaq.

The support enjoyed by Gaylani's and Mujaddidi's parties was not widespread but remained stable throughout the war. It was based upon sections of tribes (clans) whose heads were in personal contact with one or the other of the two leaders. Which party they supported was largely determined by which one was able to provide them with weapons. Of the two only Mujaddidi had groups in the north (generally amongst the *murid*); but there is evidence of Gaylani groups amongst the Pashtun nomads of the north (Taraki), which is understandable, and amongst the Turkmen. Nangrahar strongly supported Khalis, as did the Jadran tribe.

Developments between 1981 and 1984

The growth of Khalis' Hizb-i islami *amongst the Pashtun*

Yunus Khalis left Hekmatyar in 1979, because he blamed him for avoiding combat. Khalis, who was linked both with the traditionalist *mawlawi* (he had been educated in private *madrasa* and studied at Deoband) and with the Islamists (he was one of the originators of the movement and had had a hand in producing propaganda when he worked for the state publishers), was at first followed by his tribe, the Khugiani of Nangrahar. Paradoxically, his social network was both political (Islamist) and tribal. As you travel away from the territory of the Khugiani, through the Ghilzay to the west, the Laghmani to the north or the Shinwari to the east of Nangrahar, you will find that the influence of Khalis declines abruptly. Moreover, when Jallaluddin Haqani, a Jadran from Paktya, joined Khalis because he had a similar political outlook, those who followed him did so on the basis of their tribal origins.

Khalis' party is unanimously considered to be well prepared for combat, well organised by Afghan standards and strategically well situated on the main Kabul–Jellalabad route. The prestige of its leader and the valour of its commanders, such as 'Abdul Haqq, cannot be gainsaid. For a long while this party had only a regional base in Nangrahar and Paktya, but from 1982, it made spectacular inroads into the region of Kandahar, where much-revered commanders (such as Mullah Malang and Obeydullah) joined it.

The front led by Jallaluddin Haqani was very tribal in character. Like Khalis he was a product of the private *madrasa* and had finished his studies at Peshawar. He does not seem to have engaged in any political activities before the war. He ousted the notables and the *khan*, by virtue of his energy and military skill. The Jadran tribe formed the backbone of the resistance at Paktya. However, Jallaluddin managed to extend his influence beyond his own tribal area. At the time of the coup the other tribes (Jaji, Mangal, Tani and Waziri) were either passive, or followed Gaylani. But in 1985 some tribally mixed fighting groups were established. It is through Khalis that the Islamists hoped to spread their influence among the tribes.

The decline of the Harakat

This event represented the most significant shift of power during the first four years of the war. In 1980 the Harakat was the major party. But from 1981 onwards, most of the local Harakat committees in the provinces of Herat and Faryab as well as those in the Persian-speaking area of the Farah joined the Jamiat. This shift of allegiance was connected with certain language divisions: in Farah the Persian-speaking Nurzay joined the Jamiat while the Pashtu-speaking members of the tribe stayed with the Harakat. The same thing happened in Badghis and in Faryab: the Tajik and the Uzbek changed their allegiance, while the pockets of Pashtu-speakers who had supported the Harakat, including many members of the *Jabha-yi tulaba* ("theology students' front") remained faithful to that party. The non-Pashtun groups blamed the leadership at Peshawar for giving Pashtun members an unfair share of weapons. But there were other and deeper reasons for this switch, especially in the west.

The fact that the Jamiat picked up support from the end of 1981 in the province of Herat and Farah was a direct consequence of the "affair of Shir Agha". As we have seen, the Harakat, based on the social network of traditionalist *mawlawi*, had always sought to encourage the development of the horizontal inter-party structures going by the name of the "society of *ulema*" (*jam'iyyat-i 'ulama*). This organisation was established at Herat by Gholam Maheddin, a *pir* of Obe. The true leader was Shir Agha of Herat. At the same time, the Maoists of the region, who were strong in numbers but were unable to act openly, decided to use the society of *'ulama* as a cover.[2] Immediately there was conflict between the Maoists who had infiltrated the party and the Jamiat, for they had already clashed in the schools during the King's reign, since the *mawlawi* considered the Maoists to be no more than expendable intellectuals. At the beginning of 1981, Shir Agha openly joined the government with all his *qawm*, which until that time had formed the most combative group of militia in the west. The core of the Harakat committees in the province joined the

Jamiat. In addition to the *qawm* of Shir Agha, a few Harakat groups near the Iranian frontier, who had been infiltrated by the Maoists, fought on the side of the government. The *pir* of Obe and the anti-government Maoists then fled to Iran.

The treachery of Shir Agha and the Maoist infiltration illustrate the fundamental weakness of the Harakat: it is a party lacking in any firm organisational structure, no more than an aggregation of local fronts established around *mawlawi* without political experience. It is not surprising, therefore, that the Harakat should be a prime target of infiltration, either on the part of the Maoists, or opportunists like Shir Agha, who sought to raise the stakes and then negotiate their defection to the other side on their own terms.

The weakness of the central leadership, incapable of controlling its followers, and the very traditional way in which arms were distributed (the commanders had to go themselves to obtain their share) were in contradiction with the only thing that such a party could have supplied for people who had reservations about the very idea of a party – organisation with a minimum of control. Yet, it was precisely because its members had found in the Harakat the opposite of a party that they had joined it in the first place. Fundamentally, warfare demands a degree of politicisation and organisation which is at odds with the character of Afghan civil society.

The Harakat managed to retain its support in the south because the tribal nature of the local fronts corresponded to its "federal" structure. The basis of a front is tribal, and the leader is often a religious figure. The party has, in addition, some exemplary regional leaders. The *mawlawi* who had known Nabi remained faithful to him. Nevertheless, many local commanders of Kandahar, such as Mullah Malang or Obeydullah, joined Khalis, from whom they could get weapons more easily. Nevertheless, the shifts of allegiance, in this region also, did not happen just by chance: the *tulaba* and the orthodox *naqshbandi*, who in the north went over to the Jamiat, stayed in this region with the Harakat; Khalis' party seemed less favourably inclined towards Sufism than the Jamiat. And there was a schism amongst the Harakat in the region of Gardez and Ghazni, under the leadership of Nasrullah Mansur, who formed part of the "coalition of the seven".

The rise of the Jamiat party

There were two important factors in the rise of the Jamiat: one, static, was supplied by the networks, the other, dynamic, by the example of Massoud and two other commanders, Ismael Khan and Zabiullah.

The networks do not explain the way in which support drifted from one party to another, but they made it possible for this to occur; now, as we have seen, the Jamiat was well placed at the meeting-point of three of the four networks which went to make up the Afghan resistance movement: the Islamists, the Sufis and the *mawlawi*. With the fourth network (the tribes) its position was much weaker, which explains why it found it so difficult to establish itself in the south.

The progress made by the Jamiat was at the expense of the Harakat in the west and the Hizb in the north-east and south. People went from the Harakat to the Jamiat because they found the Harakat too soft, and from the Hizb to the Jamiat because they thought the Hizb too ruthless.

In the west and the north-west, the Sufi orders acted as a bridge between Harakat and Jamiat. Workers in Hizb and Jamiat belonged to the network of Islamist intellectuals which served to bridge the gap. It was, thus, in the north-east, where the militants of the two parties were largely products of the secular government schools, that the instances of people going over to the Jamiat were more frequent. (But this common background sometimes produced a mutual hatred which was even more violent.) In contrast, in the west, the Islamists of the Jamiat were usually the product of government *madrasa* while the members of the Hizb had had a secular education; in these instances people did not pass from one organisation to the other. As always, the Aymaq were the exception: here, it was the network of the *qawm* and the fact that people identified with other Aymaq which made it more likely that they would move from the Hizb to the Jamiat.

Nevertheless, there is a deeper reason for the transfer of support from one party to another and this is to be explained in terms of the dynamic of the resistance movement, a dynamic which was a consequence of the spread of more efficient politico-military systems in the north. The Jamiat provided a political framework which was more favourable to modern guerilla warfare than did the Harakat, without breaking with tradition as the Hizb did.

Jamiat influence in the north was closely linked with the local reputation of three commanders. Ismael Khan controlled the region from Herat to Maymana, Zabiullah, based at Mazar-i Sharif and killed in 1984, was responsible for the area from Maymana to Qunduz, and Massoud operated throughout the north-east. In these zones there was no institution (such as a tribe) between the state and the local *qawm* to provide intermediate units capable of functioning autonomously, and therefore of providing an obstacle to the spread of a dominant party. In these conditions, the commanders were able to set up a military organisation that could operate throughout the whole of the region. They were not limited to attacking a post that happened to be in the territory of the local *qawm*. A strategy of this kind presupposed that the region was politically homogeneous, that the commanders were able to coordinate their activities and that decision-making was centralised. In these circumstances, the growth of the party was the result of better military efficiency. The Jamiat was therefore greeted favourably by the people in general and by the resistance fighters, always providing that the commander was able to prove his worth. In the case of Massoud, the failure of the seven offensives carried out against Panjshir between 1980 and 1984 caught people's imaginations and turned him into a legendary leader. His personal prestige and the efficiency of his military organisation persuaded many local commanders to come and learn from him. Thus, the spread of the Jamiat in the north-east was first and foremost a general acceptance of a model of military organisation deemed to be efficient, and of experienced local commanders. Furthermore, there was nothing in the sociocultural structure of society in the north which hindered the swelling of the ranks of the Jamiat party.

Zabiullah's political astuteness seems to have led to the spread of Jamiat influence in Mazar-i Sharif, in that he adopted more and more fully the "Massoud model of military organisation". Zabiullah, a former teacher who had been educated in the Ibn Sina school, was, of the three, the one who saw things in an ideological light. After his death, his successor, mawlawi Alam, did not achieve such broad recognition. Under Ismael Khan the growth of Jamiat influence proceeded more by inertia, since it was the party which from the beginning had controlled the core of the Islamist, Sufi and *mawlawi* networks. In all three cases, it is noteworthy that the Jamiat originated in the suburban areas or areas where there were many families who had some contact with the town (like Panjshir), while the Harakat was more firmly rooted in the peasantry.

There remains the question of the degree of support the Jamiat had in the tribal areas, which at the beginning was very meagre indeed. Long before the Taraki's coup, Rabbani had understood the absolute necessity of not allowing oneself to be cut off from the tribes. The whole history of Afghanistan is linked to the tribes, and even if the war has redressed the balance a little as far as the other ethnic groups are concerned, no party could get very far without the support of the Pashtun. After 1982, when the north had settled down to a fairly high level of support for the Jamiat, Rabbani concentrated all his attentions on the south. This implied two interrelated conditions: the development of the tribal structures so that they were no longer incompatible with a party like the Jamiat; and a process of adaptation within the party so that it could accept the reality of the tribes. The first condition was realised when the great families deserted the resistance movement inside the country and thus enhanced the position of the *mawlawi* who generally supported the Harakat, and it also worked to the advantage of the military commanders. It was amongst this latter group that a movement of non-ideological support for Khalis and the Jamiat appeared. Nevertheless the drift away from the Harakat was always to the advantage of Khalis. An alliance between Rabbani and Khalis could have derived advantage from the sociological and political transformation of the tribal zones.

The Hizb-i islami

It now remains to be seen why the *Hizb-i islami* was unable to make the best use of its organisation and its general effectiveness to increase its influence.

The power base of the Hizb did not extend beyond the network of the Islamists. But its approach to politics was that of a true party in the modern sense of the word: the development of a party machine and an overall strategy directed towards the conquest of power within the resistance movement. It regarded the Islamic revolution as being more important than the war and thought that the struggle against the Soviets could only be successfully carried out when the party had gained control over the resistance movement. Its fatal error was in standing aloof and in overestimating its chances of expanding.

Thus, conflicts between the Hizb and the other parties date from the first year of the war. It was not a struggle between Islamists and moderates but between the Hizb and all other parties. At the beginning, the Hizb had a policy of great militancy, and its commandos were the first to leave their own territory to impose party authority on neighbouring territories. The Hizb disarmed the other parties and would not tolerate their presence in its own territory. Its first goal was to control the civilian population, and being well organised it succeeded in setting up a solid and diversified administration. The traditional influential families were brushed aside and even the *qazi* were only allowed to exert their influence within the framework of the party. The party was very highly centralised and homogeneous. The elite members were visionaries, dogmatic, and living their whole life for the party and devoted to Hekmatyar; they were thus more detached from the group solidarity of the *qawm* than was the case in the other groups.

From the very beginning, the structure of the Hizb was opposed to that of traditional society, and party organisation was to replace the traditional framework within which power was exercised. For this reason it was generally rejected by the people, except in particular instances.

Among those who supported it were peasants and those in extreme poverty. For these people, its opposition to traditional structures had a "revolutionary" flavour about it.

The strategy of the Hizb consisted in avoiding direct contact with Soviet troops and in establishing firm bases, like the famous camp of Allah Jirga, which was more or less an enclave in Pakistan territory. (Here the Hizb put on a display for the benefit of journalists who were short of time, and stored a formidable arsenal which might prove useful in any post-war conflict, since its present-day military involvement was nil.) Places where the Hizb has established a presence are, in general, situated on the main lines of communication of the resistance and not of the Soviet army (Laghman, Ghorband and Koh-i Safi), and at regular intervals the Hizb has organised a full blockade of Panjshir.

In the long run, the rejection of the Hizb by the people in general and by the other parties, combined with a twofold internal crisis. At Peshawar, a split involved Hekmatyar's second in command, and some local commanders inside the country swung their support behind the Jamiat. These two occurrences meant that the Hizb became of minor importance, although it was never a force to be overlooked.

On the international level the Hizb lost a lot of the considerable prestige that it had enjoyed in 1980. At that time, most foreign observers would agree with varying degrees of reluctance that the Hizb was the backbone of the resistance. It was the only party which understood the importance of the mass-media and knew how to manipulate journalists, providing them with distorted information which they would incorporate in their reports.[3] At the beginning the British and Chinese embassies treated the Hizb with much respect, and it was also supported by the Pakistan Jama'at and Arab fundamentalist circles, though the support of Iran was always very limited. Nevertheless, after 1981, the Hizb's policy of sabotage began to cause misgivings and it lost a good part of the support it had enjoyed from the West. Finally, the crisis between Sayyaf and Hekmatyar in the autumn of 1983 meant that the latter ceased to be the privileged mouthpiece of the Arab fundamentalists.

The parties of Gaylani and Mujaddidi

It is difficult to deal with these parties in a chapter entitled "the development of the parties", since their support did not fluctuate much and was based on the networks defined above. Gaylani was essentially in control of a number of clans, through the allegiance of *khan*. These group loyalties had been established either before the war (as with the non-Durrani Pashtun, which in effect means the *murid*), or after the war (the

Durrani Royalist aristocracy which used Gaylani as its political instrument). There was no party structure; the local *khan* had freedom of action and people obeyed a local influential leader and not the party. There was no political office, but a small court; weapons were distributed according to the recipient's personal relationship with Ahmad Gaylani. The degree of stability was due to the fact that the establishment had no other form of representation within the country, and therefore had an interest in keeping the party going; but it had, in fact, reached the limit of its capability.

The Mujaddidi network was even more scattered (it was the smallest of the six Peshawar parties), but more diversified. It consisted of a network identical with that of Gaylani, and in the same way had little chance of developing further. Gaylani was banking on the support of the *jirga* but the *jirga* by definition was antagonistic to any party structure. The present drift of affairs, as we have seen, is not favourable to the *jirga*. It is possible, but unlikely, that the King could be a focus for consensus; such a consensus would require a political format which neither of the parties can provide, and guerilla forces are not the same thing as electoral coalitions. Moreover, widespread corruption discredited both parties.

The evolution of tribalism is the key, not only to these two parties, but to the whole resistance movement. Such evolution tends towards the abolition of the *khan* and the strengthening of the position of the *mawlawi*; hence it is vitally important for Gaylani and Mujaddidi to keep going their alliance with the Harakat, the one providing the brains and the other the troops.

The forging of opportunistic alliances and the rise of Sayyaf

Our analysis tends to show that there is a logic at work in the making and breaking of alliances and the changing from one party to another which is not mere opportunism. This is always the case when party allegiance can be correlated with a specific stratum of society. But it is axiomatic that isolated armed groups, without any demographic basis, will develop within the context of a ruling party and join a different party for opportunistic reasons. It often applies to local commanders in conflict with their "superiors in the hierarchy" and seeking, by a switch of loyalties, to gain promotion which they could not get any other way. It might also involve individuals who formerly wielded influence but had now been elbowed out by newcomers from the dominant party, or very small ethnic groups seeking to preserve their identity. Finally, there are other much more dubious groups, who border on banditry, for whom it is essential to have weapons to avoid being brought to heel by the dominant party. In each case, the repercussions, as far as the local population is concerned, are limited to the family of the members of the group. The problem is that these groups have a firepower out of all proportion to their local support, and they are therefore capable of bringing disorder, or even of generating armed conflict.

After 1982, it was mainly Sayyaf who provided the weapons to these groups. His policy was clear: to spread his influence by means of armed groups who had no particular support amongst the people (except at Paghman, his birthplace). In Nangrahar, to the south of Kabul, to the north in the area of Shibergan, Sayyaf's supporters multiplied, all of them well armed both in terms of quality and quantity. The degree to which they were eager for combat varied a great deal, according to their motivation. But the operation was a negative one, in that it removed the strictly military activity from political control, which is a flaw in guerilla operations. Based entirely on interpersonal links, the groups loyal to Sayyaf, even though increasing in number, could never form a party – only an aggregation of isolated units; in addition, the spread of Sayyaf's influence was checked by his hostility towards the Sufis, without whose support no section of the resistance in Afghanistan can hope to succeed. The dissolution of the fundamentalist alliance in 1985 has edged Sayyaf out.

It is surprising that this custom of giving one's allegiance to a leader in exchange for a supply of weapons is not more widespread, given, on the one hand, the segmentation of Afghan society and, on the other, the traditional social importance of the gift involving the pledging of one's allegiance to another. Even though many members of the resistance will say that they only follow someone for the supply of weapons they get in return, the paradox is that these same people often complain that they have not received any weapons from the parties which, according to them, they joined for that reason and that reason alone. This fact, of course, makes their original reasons seem irrelevant – all the more so since, in theory, anyone could get on to Sayyaf's payroll, which clearly does not happen in practice. In particular, except at Kandahar the tribal areas have generally resisted disruptive forces, which are a consequence of the offer to supply arms.

This phenomenon of fragmentation is to be found in the multi-ethnic areas where, as ethnologists have noted, divisions even run through villages. Between the *qawm* (now reduced to an extended family) and the ethnic group in the larger sense of the word, there is no intermediate social unit such as the tribe.[4] This, for example, is the case in the foothills of north-central Afghanistan: Saripul, Shibergan, Sangcharak. The existence of isolated armed groups is not here a consequence of tribalism, but of divisions which exist at subtribal level, whether caused by detribalisation or the breakdown of the unity of ethnic groups for historical reasons.

In general, the great tribes belong to two different parties at the same time – although manifesting a bias to one of the two: one group is made up mainly of the *khan* (Mujaddidi and Gaylani), the other comprises the *mawlawi* (Harakat, Khalis and sometimes Jamiat). Here there are scarcely any isolated armed groups. This fact is an indication that the tribes have for the most part left behind their traditional tribalism and that now, built into their social structure, there is a political dimension, which is given concrete expression through the establishment of a political party. We disregard the frontier tribes (Mohmand, Tani) which cannot readily be included in the resistance movement.

Myth and reality of the independent fronts

In the first two years of the war a strange episode took place which had more to do with Europe than Afghanistan. The press and many pseudo-specialists on Afghanistan (but also, unfortunately, some genuine experts, like Richard Tapper)[5] systematically opposed the parties of Peshawar, labelled as "fanatical" for the Islamists, "corrupt" for the moderates, in favour of an internal resistance movement comprising "independent fronts", led by democratic intellectuals who were openly "progressive". The fronts singled out for special praise were those in Nuristan, Nimruz, Farah and Hazarajat. This kind of commentary raised two questions: the place of the leftist Maoists in the resistance movement and the sociological reality of the "independent" fronts. The list of fronts which had something more than an ephemeral existence and which were independent of the Peshawar parties is a very short one: Nimruz, Nuristan and the village of Kalakan. The remainder were either short-lived armed groups, generally led by a Maoist student and without support amongst the people, or they represented a "change of direction" of a committee nominally dependent on one of the Peshawar parties (generally the Harakat), but thought of by foreign commentators as being autonomous. This change of political direction was generally brought about by secret infiltration of the committee by Maoists connected with SAMA or the "Mujahidin fighters". Usually the Maoist intellectual was a member of a *khan* family, and he would make much of the division between the *khan*, usually secularised, and the clergy, in order to gain the support of the former.

Usually, the Maoists who had infiltrated the committees were expelled when they tried to strengthen the link between the local committee and the clandestine Maoist organisation (as occurred at Anardarrah and at Farah), not without creating an internal crisis in the Harakat (as at Herat in 1981). Sometimes this even led to killings between the factions, as occurred in March 1984,[6] because of the rivalry between splinter groups descended from the *shol'e-yi jawid*, some of whom had been infiltrated by secret police (the Khad). By 1984, the Maoists were no longer a force to be reckoned with in Afghanistan.

There are many reasons for the failure of the independent fronts. First, the intellectuals who were their driving force could only make progress so long as they worked under cover. There was, therefore, a gap between what was actually happening in the front and the rhetoric seized upon by foreign commentators. When members of the front and other leaders who were not left-wing realised what was going on, there was an immediate crisis, all the more acute because the intellectuals were manipulated by the well-established local families, rather than it being the other way round. Secondly, the semi-clandestine organisations which attempted to link these fronts could not call upon the resources to match their ambitious strategy and started fighting amongst themselves, adopting ideologies or political stances which had no connection with reality. Thirdly, these political disputes were often the expression of unspoken tribal and personal conflicts. Finally, many of the minor groupings had been penetrated by the Khad. The only well-established independent front is the *dawlat* of Nuristan, a Wahhabi republic under the leadership of Mawlawi Afzal.

Between the form of organisation which best takes into account the divisions existing within Afghan society (the juxtaposition of local fronts) and its opposite (modern political parties), we have seen a middle way developing, the success of the Jamiat in the north and of Khalis in the south. Both claim that the solution to the problem of social disunity lies in political Islam adapting to traditional society. However, this political development has no meaning unless it can be related to the underlying changes which Afghan society has experienced during the war and in relation to the specific organisational form the parties have developed as they have emerged from the matrix of civil society. It is to these two aspects that we shall now turn.

Chapter Nine

The role of the Shi'a in the resistance

The Hazara represent the core of the Shi'a movement in Afghanistan. As they are concentrated in the central mountains, they play a very important strategic role for the resistance movement, for Hazarajat is both an important junction in the communications network and an area of refuge untroubled by the battles being waged elsewhere. Since 1981 the Russians have abandoned any pretence of controlling this region. Deprived of the opportunity of waging war against them, Hazarajat has been plunged into a simmering civil war, punctuated by sudden outbreaks of violence. The Shi'a are very clearly distinguished from the Sunni majority by their bearing, their political allegiance and the structure of their organisations. Only one Shi'a party is really active against the Russians: the *Harakat-i islami*, which originated in the town (thus *qizilbash*), but is now well established along the borders of Hazarajat.

Hazarajat

The situation before the war

The origin of the Hazara and their social organisation prior to the twentieth century is obscure.[1] It seems that the tribal system, dominated by the *mir*, was the rule – a system that was much more hierarchical and rigid than Pashtun tribalism. Even today, the Hazara are marked by an absence of egalitarianism and by the harshness of their social relations, in which respect they are strikingly different from the other ethnic groups. At the end of the nineteenth century, the military occupation of Hazarajat by Abdurrahman and the invasion of the province by the Pashtun tribes, who seized land and pasture for the nomads,[2] brought about the disintegration of the traditional tribal system because of the exodus, the mixing of different groups and the decline in the political power of the *mir*. On the eve of the communist coup, Hazarajat was still a poor and isolated region, where village life was still dominated by the *mir*, *arbab*

139

and *bay*. However, a large number of people went away to Kabul and Iran to find work and as a result their level of education was improved. Four social categories have played an important role in the war.

(1) The *mir* retain local economic power and share political power with Pashtun officials. While Daoud was always opposed to the Hazara, Amanullah and later Zahir tried to integrate the old Hazara elite into the state machine. Thus, in the elections of 1965, most of the Hazara deputies were *mir* and members of the indigenous population.

(2) The Shi'a clergy have enjoyed a revival because of the influence of Iran, which continued to increase throughout the period from 1950 to 1985. The traditionalist village mullahs and the *shaykhs* educated at Najaf or at Qom have little in common. The *shaykhs* keep close contact with their Iranian or Iraqi teachers; their political allegiance within the resistance movement reflects the conflicts surrounding the Ayatullahs of Iran and Iraq. While many *shaykhs* are *sayyad* (and the latter are more traditionalist than the others), few are from the families of *mir*.

(3) In Hazarajat the *sayyad* form what may be described as an endogamous caste. Held to be descendants of the Prophet, they are particularly revered by the Shi'a, for the true line passes from the Prophet through his son-in-law 'Ali, the first Imam of the Shi'a. The *sayyad* do not consider themselves as Hazara but as Arabs. According to one account they arrived in Hazarajat towards the sixteenth century, in answer to the request of a local group who wished to enhance their standing in comparison with their Sunni neighbours who had many *sayyad*. It is customary for the *sayyad*'s hand to be kissed as a mark of respect. *Sayyads* readily accept gifts and wear a distinctive black turban, yet in spite of this they do not constitute a separate social class; they are to be found on all social levels. Due to the fact that their caste is powerfully associated with the idea of religion, they find it easy to become mullahs and *shaykhs*, but, on the other hand, few *mir* are *sayyad*.

(4) A new type appeared in the middle of the sixties: educated youth. Strongly politicised, progressive and Hazara nationalists, they turned to Maoism (Keshtmand, the present prime minister, is one of the few to be pro-Soviet) or became followers of Khumayni. The Maoists, often sons of *mir*, were strong in the most developed regions of Hazarajat. They founded organisations which were both Marxist and nationalist, such as the *Hizb-i moghol* (the Hazara nationalists traced their origins to the Mongols) and the *Tanzim-i nasl-i now-i hazara-yi moghol* (organisation of the new Mongol Hazara generation). This latter was founded at Quetta at the end of the sixties, in Hazara emigré circles (perhaps with the help of Pakistani agents) to counter the support which Kabul was giving to the Baluchi and Pathan separatists. The followers of Khumayni became

politicised under cover of cultural associations founded at Kabul and Kandahar, around Wa'ez and Muhseni, at Najaf and amongst those who had gone to live in Iran. Initially, they gained more recruits amongst the *qizilbash* than amongst the Hazara, for there is no Islamist religious leader of stature in Hazarajat.

The anti-communist uprising of 1979

In the spring of 1979 a number of local revolts occurred. It was not long before the various groups became aware of the need to coordinate their activities throughout Hazarajat. In September 1979, several hundred people, *mir, mullahs, sayyad, shaykhs* and intellectuals, met together at Waras. After a few preliminaries, the details of which are not known,[3] Sayyad Beheshti was elected president of the *Shura-yi inqilabi-yi ittifaqh-i islami-yi Afghanistan* ("Revolutionary Council of the Islamic Union of Afghanistan"). Military command was placed in the hands of Sayyad Muhammad "Jaglan" (major), son of a grandee from Khawat and one of the few Hazara to have made the army his career and become an officer. These two people, Beheshti and Jaglan, were now in command of the *shura*.

The military situation very soon became stabilised. The government had only one post in the whole of Hazarajat (at Bamyan) and the Russians stopped their military operations in the region in 1981. This was a signal for internal schisms to appear. The *shura* was split three ways. At one extreme there were the secularists, which included the *mir* and the left (the alliance of Maoists and families of influence is an underlying theme in the Afghan resistance movement, the former often being the sons of the latter). This group had its own organisation, known as *tanzim*, based at Quetta. Another extreme group comprised the radical Islamists and included *shaykhs* who supported the Iranian revolution, and who accused the *mir* of "feudalism" and the *sayyads* of corruption and nepotism (a charge which was not far from the truth). There was also a traditionalist and clerical centre dominated by the *sayyad*. It was this centre, at first in the majority, which was the dominant force until 1983, a position which was achieved by supporting first one and then the other of the two extremes.

Conflicts up to 1983

Until the summer of 1982, the centre supported the radicals to destroy the political power of the *mir*: the principal leaders of the *mir* were arrested then banished to Pakistan. But in that summer the radicals of the *shura*, supported by the pro-Iranian Hazara party, Nasr (which until then had remained outside the *shura*), attempted a coup against Beheshti. Half the *wali* (local governors) of the *shura* and the second-in-command to Beheshti formed an alliance with the Nasr and attempted to capture Waras. The uprising narrowly failed thanks to Jaglan, who mobilised the Nahur peasants, formed an alliance with the *mir* whom he had formerly disparaged, and proceeded to recapture most of the land which the Nasr had held, causing them to fall back upon their strongholds of Daykundi, Turkman and Darrah-yi Suf. The situation remained stable until 1984 and the *shura* was able to establish its administrative system.

The government of the shura

The *shura* adopted all the trappings of the state machine of the old order: the same buildings, obligatory conscription, forced labour, taxes and uniforms. This was the only political tendency within the Afghan resistance movement which, instead of making a clean break with statism, took pleasure in reshaping itself in the mould of a state which, however, was more make-believe than real. Parenthetically, this statism is not easy to explain: how is it that Shi'ism, traditionally presented as rebellious by its very nature, has been able, in Iran as in Hazarajat, to come to terms with the state in the way that it has? What has become of Shi'ism and the Iranian tradition? Of course, Hazara society has a somewhat different structure from the other Afghan ethnic groups. It has less communal solidarity, and places greater emphasis on individualism. Family links are not so strong: in Hazarajat you find nuclear families, with – the inevitable corollary – widows bringing up their children alone, something which would be unthinkable in other parts of the country. In the same way you come across outcasts, such as lepers. The state is stronger to the extent that the idea of the *qawm* has a weaker hold on people's minds. In its place, there is a strong emphasis on the importance of social hierarchy, which almost amounts to a caste system.

Hazarajat is divided into nine *wilayat* (provinces): Jaghori, Nahur, Behsud, Waras, Lal, Yakaolang, Balkhab, Darrah-yi Suf and Daykundi. Each *wilayat* is under the control of a *wali* (governor), assisted by a commander who is responsible for security. The small towns are run by a nominated *shahrwal* (mayor), and the villages are organised according to their traditional system. There are four military fronts whose areas border on Hazarajat: Jaghori, Nahur, Behsud and Bamyan, each of which has its own independent military commander. Unlike the remainder of the resistance movement this administration is far removed from the people and has developed into a petty bureaucracy, complete with red tape, inefficiency and often corruption, specific office opening hours, official stamps and so on. All the *wali* are *sayyad* and the educated youth are kept well away from positions of power. (We shall discuss the military organisation in chapter 11.) Until 1983 the people accepted this system for two reasons. First of all, the peasants who live well within the interior of Hazarajat, which is where the strongholds of the *shura* are, are conservative in outlook and used to living in a strict hierarchy. Secondly, the authority of the *shura* rests upon two foundations: religion – through the respect enjoyed by the *sayyad* – and the nation. In people's minds the *shura* stands for Hazara independence, which has long been their goal; and the fact that the *shura* mimics the state is not seen as a fault but as proof that Hazarajat has attained political status: we, the Hazara, have our own officials and their corruption is no more than visible proof that they exist, for, in any case, there isn't very much administering to be done.

There was a real transfer of power, both political and economic, from the *mir* to the *sayyad*. Nevertheless, the *shura* was finally to collapse, more from its own internal weaknesses than because of the rival attractions of its enemies. The great problem was its corruption. The tax system the *shura* established was harsher than any other which I have come across in Afghanistan. First, it seems that the principles of Shi'ite law are more rigorous than those of Hanafite law; secondly, tax collectors interpreted the law broadly and often did not hesitate to take 20 per cent of the total turnover instead of 20 per cent of net revenue; finally, they used force, and took bribes as part of their levy. (We should remember that one of the first measures taken by the *shura* was to disarm the population, an extraordinary action to be taken within a resistance movement.) The consciousness that the *sayyad* had of their caste, combined with the sense of social hierarchy which distinguishes Afghan Shi'a from Sunni, caused the *shura* to be cut off from the people.

Opposition centred around Khumayni's followers

The Nasr is a pro-Khumayni organisation set up in Iran after the communist coup by a merger of activist groups originally founded at Kabul in the seventies (for example, the *geruh-i mustazafin*) with an association of religious activists from Najaf (*ruhaniyyat-i mubariz*, "the militant clergy"), whose teacher was Khumayni. The Nasr gained its recruits amongst the Hazara living in Iran. There is no evidence that the Nasr is linked to the Tudeh or to the *mujahidin-i khalq*. Nothing is known about the leaders of the Nasr and it seems that it was an amorphous group, organised in Afghanistan on the basis of a certain amount of local support, rather than a party in the true sense of the word. This is confirmed by the different attitudes that characterised Nasr members inside the country: those of Turkmen are sectarian, those of Behsud and Jaghori more loosely organised. Nasr, which was an intellectuals' organisation, could only hope to achieve a breakthrough in alliance with the local clergy. It received aid from Iran.

About 1983, a new name appeared on the scene: the Sejah-yi Pasdaran (army of the guardians (of the revolution)). It seems that the formation of this organisation was directly encouraged by the Iranian Pasdaran who considered that they had the right to control the Afghan Shi'a. The Afghan Pasdaran were led by people who had seceded from the *shura*; at the beginning, they were in close alliance with the Nasr, but tensions arose because of the Nasr's desire to remain independent of Iran and thus not to be integrated into the Pasdaran; the latter received weapons from Iran (in very limited quantities) and were joined by young Hazara living in Iran. In positions of leadership were young *shaykhs* who had been educated in Iran but who were very much opposed to the *sayyad*. Until 1983, in spite of an annual summer offensive, Nasr and Pasdaran were incapable of making any inroads into the virtual monopoly enjoyed by the *shura*. However, in the spring of 1984, they drove Beheshti from his capital, Waras, and took control of two-thirds of Hazarajat. The *shura* fell back on Nahur, which was Jaglan's stronghold, and Behsud became a no-man's land. What was the reason for this sudden success of the pro-Khumayni forces? First of all, the people had in many instances had enough of *shura* excesses. The only other alternative was the pro-Khumayni group or the *mir* who had set about organising themselves on a political basis inside the *shura-yi arbabha*, which was fated to remain impotent because of traditional rivalries. The *mir* of the regions close to Kabul, which were more closely connected with the *shura*, had been removed from the political scene during the two successive offensives carried out by Nasr in 1983 and 1984. The others could not come to an agreement, which left the field open for Khumayni's followers. However, people were by no means ideologically committed to the Khumayni line and very few peasants enrolled in the new forces, made up mainly of young people who had just returned from Iran. It is therefore possible that the situation might change, for what is particularly striking in Hazarajat is the number of times that people suddenly switch sides and the situation is turned on its head, in contrast to the stability of the resistance in Sunni areas.

As we have seen, the Khumayni movement is far from being unified. Moreover, parties, such as the *Harakat-i islami*, which pursued the

Khumayni line in 1980, are now opposed to it. Disillusion with Iran has spread to Afghanistan. However, what is striking is that the young mullahs who have lived through the Islamist revolution in Iran and who studied at Qom have returned to Hazarajat. Young, well educated, dynamic and having an awareness of the importance of organisation whatever their political loyalties, they are having a marked effect on traditional society. Thus, schools and libraries are being opened in the villages under their control, whereas the *shura* did nothing. At *nihzat* schools at Anguri a hundred children are receiving education, the Nasr library at Khujur has a section for children and even for women, and new *madrasa* are appearing everywhere. Hazarajat is experiencing its own mini-revolution.

Soviet policy

There can be no doubt that it is more in the Soviet interest to allow the situation in Hazarajat to continue to get worse than to intervene militarily. Nevertheless, there are two points worthy of note. First, the conflicts in Hazarajat can be explained without resorting to underhand manipulation of events by the Khad or the KGB. There is a social question to be resolved in Hazarajat, which either does not exist or has been resolved in the other regions. Hazarajat is a society whose evolution has met with an impasse and the Shi'a contribution (clericalism, hierarchical structure, respect for authority) has made divisions worse. There is no doubt that the Russians are exploiting these contradictions, but these problems did not start with them.

Next, in spite of the fact that people are weary of internal conflict, there is no discernible drift towards the government which, more than ever before, is regarded by the Hazara as foreign. The communist ascendancy seems to them to be a rebirth of Pashtun power. In the resistance movement, the Hazara have regained control over their own land: the Pashtun nomads have disappeared or are forced to deal with the Hazara administration on an equal footing. The resistance has meant that the Hazara have achieved what they dearly wanted to achieve for more than a century: to be self-contained and independent. The government has never given the slightest indication that it is willing to accept this state of affairs. Apart from the Maoists, there are very few Hazara communists (and those there are come from urban backgrounds). The Hazara prefer to live with their own internal conflicts rather than to see a return of Pashtun dominance. If a crisis should arise, it is more likely that there would be a mass exodus to Iran than a rallying to the government side.

It is possible that the government hopes to derive some advantage from the presence of small groups of ex-Maoists, such as the *tanzim*, who in 1980 were giving out copies of a work entitled *Hazarajat*, which advocated a "greater Hazarajat". This book was in fact no more than the translation of *Khazarejtsi* by the Soviet author L. Temirkhanov.[4] But in order to take advantage of such propaganda activities it would be necessary for the Russians to establish a definite internal policy. At present they waver between the creation of a great number of different nationalities (which would work to the disadvantage of the Pashtun, who provide the major source of communist support) and support for a Greater Pashtunistan (which would mean running the risk of antagonising the other ethnic groups, who today are more militant in their opposition than the Pashtun).

The other incalculable element is what role Iran will play. Logically, if Iran gains firmer control over Hazarajat, it will either be forced to accept a modus vivendi with the Russians (who would agree not to interfere in Hazarajat, in exchange for Iranian neutrality with regard to the Sunni groups), or become more involved with Afghanistan, through the intermediary of the Shi'a, which latter outcome is clearly one that the USSR most fears.

Harakat-i islami

Although it is allied with the *shura*, the Shi'ite *Harakat-i islami* (not to be confused with the traditionalist *Harakat-i inqilab*) has been inspired by Islamist ideas; they are few in numbers, but militarily very effective, and they play a pivotal role in the resistance movement. Founded by Shaykh Assef Muhseni Kandahari, who himself speaks Pashtu as his first language, the movement did not originate with the Hazara and has recruited its members from amongst the educated and politicised Shi'a, whatever their ethnic group may be. The movement is strongest in the border areas of Hazarajat, for its members are townspeople who have withdrawn to the countryside: south of Mazar-i Sharif, at Charkent, west of Kabul, at Paghman and Dahan-e Syasang, Jaghori and without doubt also in the suburbs of Kandahar. It is the only Shi'a party which really fights against the Russians. Places where its fronts are most solid are at Mazar, on the hill of Unai (near Behsud) and to the south-west of Ghazni; the movement also has clandestine networks in the towns. It has in its ranks officers of great worth and well-trained commandos. From the ideological point of view, it espouses moderate Islamism. It has good relations with the hierarchy of the Iranian Ayatullahs, but its relations with the Pasdaran and the Khumayni circle are somewhat fraught. Shaykh Muhseni is a former pupil of Ayatullah Khuy (an old Iraqi rival of Khumayni who refused to go into exile in Iran during the Gulf war), and is held in suspicion by those close to the Imam, although he has lived at Qom since 1979. In 1984 the party was considering withdrawing to Quetta and allying itself politically with the Jamiat, which is its Sunni equivalent with regard to its ideological stance and its recruitment. In fact, the Harakat formed an alliance with the *shura* after having been attacked by Nasr during the summer of 1983.

Apart from Hazarajat and its border areas, Shi'a resistance is insignificant; nevertheless, especially at the Iranian frontier, small local groups have taken the name of *hizbullah*, in general to try and go one better than the followers of Khumayni. The town of Herat, the majority of whose citizens are Sunni, has a strong *hizbullah* group, led by a young man of secular background, Qari Yekdast ("the one-armed man"). They are a disciplined and well-armed force and are placed directly under the command of the Iranian Pasdaran, for which they act as a communication line into the Afghan interior. Their political importance is greater than their military importance, for they serve as an intermediary between the resistance (here Jamiat) and the Iranian authorities. The Russians have conducted an intense propaganda campaign against this group after the Iranian Tudeh were outlawed.[5]

All along the frontier between Iran and Afghanistan there are other small Shi'a groups which, in general, profess allegiance to a small pro-Khumayni group (*nihzat* or *reja*, the latter led by Shaykh Naghavi in Seistan). Most of the Shi'a at Nimruz are secular in outlook and follow the leader of the Nimruz front, Parwiz, who, it seems, has recently moved into the Iranian fold, to ensure that he receives adequate supplies.

While relations between Shi'a and Sunni have clearly improved because of their participation in the resistance movement, and the strategic interest of Hazarajat has led the Sunni parties to follow closely what is happening there, there is no means by which the Shi'a parties (established at Quetta) and the Sunni (at Peshawar) can coordinate their activities. Only the Jamiat has agreed to the main demand of all the Shi'a: that Shi'ite law (the Jaffarite rite) should be applied to Shi'a. Khalis, whose communication lines with Pakistan are regularly cut by the Shi'ite Pashtun tribes Orakzay and Turi, remains mistrustful of the Shi'a. Nevertheless, those Shi'a who fought, especially at the beginning of the war, have made their political existence felt. But only if a move towards unity patches the existing Sunni rifts will unity be able to spread to the Shi'a. On the local level Shi'a and Sunni are linked or separated by numerous agreements and conflicts. The rifts are, therefore, political and have nothing to do with religion: the Hizb of Hekmatyar has joined with Nasr against the *shura* and the latter has allied itself with the *Harakat-i inqilab* against the Hizb and Nasr. There is the same polarisation between moderates and radicals, but it is more acute in the case of the Shi'a because there is no viable centre (the *Harakat-i islami* is too weak). The violence of the internal conflicts in Hazarajat makes the evolution of the Shi'ite situation a key to the outcome of the war.

Chapter Ten

Society and the war

The war has brought about profound changes in society. But before studying the economic and demographic problems, we should first consider the ideological and social developments. The three important aspects of this change are the emergence of the young Islamists, the way in which the *'ulama* have managed to reassert their control of civil society, and the diminishing power of the influential families. These aspects correspond to the distinction between an ideal centred around the concept of the state (the Islamists), a universal authority which did not allow any place for the state (the *'ulama*) and an amorphous civil society (the network of the *qawm*) (see chapter 1).

Unlike most Third World countries, the advent of modernism is a recent phenomenon in Afghanistan.[1] There has been no uprooting of the population and no sudden loss of traditional culture. Peasant society still retains its memory of the past and its identity. The fact that there has been no crisis of identity explains the absence of fanaticism. The Islamist intellectuals are part of the first generation to be confronted by the problem of cultural alienation. They all have close links with traditional society, such as a family in the countryside or parents for whom tradition is important, and they have all been taught the Qur'an in their childhood. The Islamists are much more in tune with society than the communists, and they have retained the *adab* (which is not only the traditional politeness but also the culture of the past). They have also retained the style of dress and the gestures which characterise the peasant. Though they now wear beards, this does not mean that they have embarked upon that false search for tradition which is so often found in Iran, the Maghrib and Egypt (the invention of a new style of clothes, called "islamic", and the development of a new symbolism involving one's behaviour and general bearing). Not surprisingly there is change: denims are popular in the bush and Western terms are frequently to be heard in everyday speech. But these changes are taking place *in situ* and are an example of the mutations undergone by traditional society in time of war.

The refusal on the part of the *'ulama* to accept responsibility for the political leadership of the resistance (it goes without saying that they consider themselves to be the *heart* of the resistance) is completely consistent with their view of politics. The body of the *'ulama* are happy to allow their authority to be used to legitimate political power in exchange for two things, both of which are quite compatible with the views held by the Islamists: the management of civil society and the recognition that religion is pre-eminent in society. Thus, the *'ulama* concede the political arena to the Islamists (except in the south), and the latter acknowledge the supremacy of the *'ulama* in civil affairs, that is to say in matters concerned with law. Previously the Islamists held theories which sought to embrace the totality of the social order, but the war has brought them face to face with the reality of the social sphere (see chapter 3). Law cannot be reduced to politics. Thus the Islamists' ideology is quite different from the other revolutionary systems. With the rest, law and politics are held ultimately to coincide, rooted as they are in the openness of social experience, and any failure to connect is seen as a form of alienation, all of which being the best way to introduce totalitarianism in the name of openness. This assertion, indeed this reinforcement of the concept that civil society has its own independent existence is the point where the Afghan resistance is most original.

At the same time, it has to be said that this system has not yet been translated into reality. The *'ulama*, lacking any institutionalised clergy, have never attempted to assume the political leadership of the resistance (they have not even succeeded in bringing about an alliance between various parties); the party structure is often as undermined by the *qawm* network as the central state has always been, and traditional society is more tantalisingly out of reach than ever it was.

New directions in traditional society

The decline of the khan *and the rise of the* 'ulama

The war has brought in its train a weakening of the power of families which previously enjoyed a degree of local influence, and at the same time the *'ulama* have reasserted their control over civil affairs. These two trends have affected the whole of Afghanistan in varying degrees, including the tribal areas and Hazarajat. The category of notables is not homogeneous: the local power of the *malik* and the *arbab* in the villages has been less diminished than that of the *khan*, if only because there is usually no *'alim* on their level, but only mullahs. Appointed by vote, they continue to represent their village, but this time in the context of the resistance; when the resistance movement established a system of elected representatives (the *namayanda*), the *malik* were frequently chosen to fulfil that function. Their power has not really diminished except in those places close enough to the firing line for the local "committee" of the resistance to assume great importance, in which case the resistance leaders often take over some of the functions of the *malik*. The *khan*, on the other hand, have almost disappeared from the political scene in non-tribal areas. The decline of the economy, in particular the market economy in which many of them were engaged, has deprived them of a great part of their power. Above all, the traditional link between the *khan* and the government administration has worked against them at a time when the state has suffered overwhelming rejection. Strangely, the *khan* did not at first see the new regime as being communist and, at least in the more remote areas, seem to have believed until the agrarian reform that they could continue to work hand in glove with the authorities. It is not usual for them to be the ones who call for revolt – that is usually instigated by the clergy and the *malik*. Many *khan*, especially in the west, have opted for exile. Finally, the *khan* have found themselves in a dilemma between ideology and the types of organisation of the *jihad*. In the old social order, the *khan*'s politics were, on the whole, secular. Moreover, their individualism and the fact that by tradition they are engaged in a competition for power have rendered them ill-suited to the task of organising inside a party structure. It would be incorrect to speak of the *khan* as being opposed to the resistance, but rather they can be described as being rendered politically impotent within the movement. In many cases, their only involvement has been to provide food for guerilla groups as they passed through. And it is clear that the Khad's pacification policy has as its main goal the winning of the support of the notables, considered by the regime as the weak link in the resistance. The presidents of the provincial sections of the patriotic front are very often influential *khan* (and, in particular, former deputies from the period of the monarchy). Hazarajat provides one example of the way in which the *khan* has systematically been removed from the centre of power. The Shi'ite clergy, a very tightly knit body, has involved itself in the process of disarming the *khan* and has robbed them of the political power that they enjoy at village level by weighing them down with taxes and dues. The *khan* have tried to counter-attack by creating a *shura-yi arbabha* (council of *arbab*), but the principal leaders were imprisoned and exiled by the *shura*.

Nevertheless, in the north it is not unusual to find that local *khan* have family ties uniting them with the emerging officer class of the resistance (both *mawlawi* and Islamist), a circumstance which makes for good personal relations. But the very great families have disappeared, in general having chosen exile.

In the tribal areas, as we have seen, the rivalry between *khan* and *'ulama* was much more acute. When, as sometimes happens, a *khan* has retained a certain amount of political power, the section of the tribe under his control is generally much more restricted (in terms of actual numbers of people as well as geographical area) than is the case with the *mawlawi*, who control the major part of the great fronts. The Nurzay of Anardarrah (Farah) follow a *mawlawi*, while the Acheqzay and the Barakzay of Sharafat Koh are led by a mullah. The most famous instance is that of Jallaluddin Haqani, commander of Paktya, representing Khalis' party, who has ousted the Babrakzay family from their position of influence in the powerful Jadran tribe. Overall, the *khan* who remain in positions of influence rarely belong to the establishment of the old order; the great families, like the Karzay and the Babrakzay, having at first attempted to lead the resistance movement in their own tribe, have all now left the country. No member of the Muhammadzay establishment, or even the Durrani, has returned to the country. The *khan* who have stayed are better described as the small landed gentry rather than the aristocrats.

The power of the *khan* is in decline amongst the Pashtun and the Nuristani. By contrast, amongst the Brahui and the nomadic Baluchi it has remained intact. The power of influential families has not been affected in areas where social differences are not very noticeable and where there are not many *'ulama* or intellectuals, as amongst the nomads in general and the Aymaq. Thus the north and the south are becoming more alike, since the disappearance of the aristocracy and the most powerful *khan* has left behind individuals of moderate but not excessive influence, unaffected by these changes, and has made it possible for the *mawlawi* to gain greater prominence.

As we have seen, in spite of their previous decline, the network of *'ulama* is still very active in resistance campaigns. The *'ulama* have often led anti-government revolts, and it is their ideologies (the *shari'at*, *umma*) that the insurgents are using to oppose the reforms the regime is attempting to carry out. The *'ulama* have retained political and military power in those places where there are few Islamist intellectuals. They are to be found as provincial Amirs at Kabul, Faryab, Paktya, Zabul, and in Hazarajat. But what interests them mostly is not military or political power, but the power to shape civil society. The resistance movement has brought with it a strengthening of Islam's role in shaping the social order: everywhere the *shari'at* has been superseding common law and some-times even the legislation enacted by the parties, who in any case are careful to leave civil law well alone. Muslim law, which is complex and intentionally casuistic, requires lengthy study: only the *'ulama* have mastered this law, whose authority is now accepted by the whole resistance movement. On the other hand, the fragility of party political structures has meant that it has not been possible in every corner of the country to rise above the disunity which affects traditional society. By their preaching of universalist doctrines and because they have in common an identical educational background, the body of *'ulama* points the way forward for traditional society in its quest for unity and freedom from petty factionalism. Even though they themselves are not generally involved in politics, they have created an atmosphere more favourable to the growth of political parties, or at least to a growth in the political awareness of society. However, all the *'ulama* whom I met during the course of my investigation belonged to one of the parties of the resistance movement.

The fact that the *'ulama* have developed as a significant social force does not mean that all the clergy have played a key role in the campaigns; the village mullahs have only shared in the rise in status if their competence transcends the mere ability to carry out religious rites. The ordinary mullahs have not improved their standing to any great extent during the war. The rise in influence of the *'ulama* does not mean that Afghan society is under the thumb of the clergy.

A society based on law

With the exception of those tribes where the concept of *pashtunwali* has retained its hold (Tani, Mohmand), the *shari'at* has become the ultimate legal authority. Justice is dispensed by *'ulama* who have specialized in law (when fulfilling this function they are known as *qazi*) and who generally form a *shura*, or council, at least when dealing with important matters. Their party membership is generally of no importance in this context, though the Hizb only recognises the *qazi* who are members of their party. In the regions where there are many *'ulama* (Panjshir, Herat), there is a preliminary court and a court of appeal. The articles of law, procedure and jurisprudence are all those of the Hanafite rite. While the military authorities of the resistance movement may take a certain number of decisions whose sanction does not directly derive from the *shari'at* (concerning discipline, the control of weapons, the circulation of goods and the movement of people), it is clear that obedience to the *shari'at* is incumbent even on the political parties and the military leaders. Naturally, the degree to which the *'ulama* or the local political leaders are able to impose their will depends on their degree of influence vis-à-vis one another. In areas where a strong political personality has emerged, the role of the *'ulama* has been reduced to responsibility for civil law, but in the areas where no leader has emerged, the *'ulama* have won political control of the resistance movement.

Everything which has to do with personal matters, such as marriage, or inheritance, lies within the jurisdiction of the *qazi*, as do civil crimes. The trouble is that in a country at war, it is sometimes difficult to make a distinction between a civil and a political crime, especially in the Muslim perspective which does not recognise the distinction between the temporal and the religious spheres. When a communist is taken prisoner, should he be treated as a political enemy or as an apostate? This question is not purely hypothetical: many prisoners have declared their intention to make honourable amends and to return to the practice of religion. The *qazi* would be likely to make them undergo some kind of religious examination, while the military commander would be more aware of the dangers of seeing the prisoner return to the enemy camp. What of a government informer who has infiltrated the resistance? The military would be likely to execute him on the spot, while the *qazi* would probably insist that the case made against him should be in confirmity with Hanafite law. The decision actually taken would depend, as it always does, on the relative influence of the military and the religious leaders in the local resistance movement. The author witnessed a particular instance in October 1982 at Herat. The resistance had arrested a man whom they suspected of being a government agent. He attempted to escape one night, was recaptured and beaten up. His family made a complaint to the *qazi* against the resistance movement, accusing the Mujahidin of torture. The very next day, a commission of enquiry descended on the committee, gathered evidence, including that provided by the accused, and solemnly reminded the resistance fighters that any form of torture was totally inadmissible. The preliminary investigations lasted a fortnight, and were conducted by a council of four *qazi*; the family of the accused man (who lived in the government section of the town) contributed to his defence. The accused was finally condemned as a traitor and was executed.

The local people always have the right to make a complaint to the *qazi* against any abuse of power, such as theft or brutality on the part of the resistance. Few resistance leaders would be willing to defy the judgement of a *mawlawi*. The parties forming the resistance movement have no power to nominate *qazi*, who are co-opted from among the *'ulama* who have received legal training in a *madrasa*. The Afghan resistance probably takes more care than any other comparable movement to ensure that the civilian population receives fair treatment, a policy which has contributed to the considerable degree of support they enjoy. While seasoned fighters do not need to be reminded of the importance of treating the population in an honourable fashion, the same cannot be said for young people aged between fifteen and twenty, who are forming an ever larger proportion of the fighting force and who tend to believe that they can do anything once they have a gun in their hands. As far as this latter group is concerned the control exercised by the *qazi* provides a necessary constraint. In this context Shaykh Assef Muhseni has written a booklet entitled "The problems of war" (*masa'il-i jangi*), which is not a guerilla manual but a statement of a large number of legal problems which the guerilla fighter might be confronted with, together with the solution of these problems.

The limitations on the rule of law which this system has achieved are due to the fact that there are not many Afghan *'ulama* and those that there are are often of advanced age. The network of non-government *madrasa* ceased to attract young people after the fifties. In many areas, the resistance *qazi* is no more than a mere mullah whose knowledge of law is somewhat rudimentary; in other areas the resistance has recruited government *qazi* who resigned under the previous government in protest against the secularisation of the law. The *madrasa* are not evenly spread throughout the country and some areas do not have any at all. Nevertheless, after the blow dealt the system by the first few years of the war, we are now witnessing a revival of the *madrasa*: in particular at Peshawar, where hundreds of mullahs are being educated to go back to the tribal zones; and in the interior, where for the *madrasa*, connected with the Sufi brotherhoods of the north, the goal of sending out fighter-priests has always been a historical mission. But in the south, most of the *madrasa* have closed.

In some cases, the legalism of the *qazi* and their excessive preoccupation with formalities may hinder the military effort of the resistance movement. The commendable refusal to proceed with summary executions leaves at liberty people who are clearly government agents. The insistence on the importance of the religious and ethical dimension often obscures urgent political choices: for example, when choosing between rival leaders, should one choose the candidate thought to be the "best Muslim", irrespective of his military ability; and should one require that in the name of Muslim fraternity candidates should give the appearance of settling their differences – a dilemma which is likely to paralyse the whole enterprise. Nevertheless, the legalism of the Afghan resistance is an important asset in a long war where the support of the population is vital.

The attitude of the people towards the *'ulama* is very positive. The *shari'at* has at least one advantage: it places before the people the ideal of a society based on law which they can respect. Secondly, in a country which is at war, crimes are much rarer, excluding, of course, violent deaths due to conflicts within the movement, which are settled by political agreement and not by the application of the penal law according to the *shari'at*. Cutting off a thief's hand, or stoning couples caught in adultery are very rare events. In addition, the return to the *shari'at* has many advantages for the peasant: its norms are in harmony with his religious view of the world; the *qazi* of the resistance movement is more accessible than its government equivalent and is not often corrupt; proceedings both in civil and in criminal cases are conducted orally in a way that is understood by all and, above all, are quickly dealt with. Finally, Qur'anic law is well suited to rural society. In particular, the refusal to countenance usury and the security of ownership for property which has been honestly acquired are fundamental issues very popular with the peasants. Also, the *shari'at* outlines a taxation system which is clear and moderate (*'ushr*, tax of between 5 and 10 per cent on agricultural products; *zakat*, tax of 2.5 per cent on capital). State monopolies, such as the mines of Badakhshan, are abolished, collective rights over water, waste land and pasture, which are under threat from the proposed introduction of a land register, are preserved. The *qazi* are more independent of the powers that be than they were before (except, of course, in Hazarajat). In the same way, the principle enunciated in the *shari'at* that uncultivated land should be made productive allows people to derive profit from cultivating the land left by refugee or absentee landowners. The return to the *shari'at* is, thus, generally seen as a restoration of Islamic justice and a means of putting an end to the tyranny of the powerful. When they are dissatisfied, the peasants mainly complain that certain injustices continue to be practised and that those in positions of responsibility often act in an authoritarian manner, not about the necessity of extending the application of the *shari'at*, except in areas where tribalism is still strong.

Another restriction on the activity of the *'ulama* is that their authority only extends to civil affairs, and they have no power to sort out conflicts between different groups of Mujahidin who belong to different *qawm*.

Tradition and modernisation

The systematic return to the *shari'at* has created the necessary conditions for one kind of political modernity, by transcending the traditional division of society into *qawm*, even though the activities of the *'ulama* are never sufficient in themselves to guarantee this transition to a political system. This is why the Islamist parties support this development, while attempting to control it politically. The concept of tradition is somewhat ambiguous: for the *'ulama* it is the *sunnat* and thus an ethical ideal, but in the minds of many of the older generation tradition is equated with the way things have always been done as long as they can remember. The modernist leaders of the resistance movement have therefore attended the *fatwa* (consultations about legal matters) of the *'ulama* to see how best they might introduce up-to-date practices which the traditionalists consider to be detrimental to religion, although they are not in actual contradiction with the teaching of the *shari'at*. For example, modern schools are often considered to be one of the sources of communism and people are very reluctant to support their reopening. In Panjshir, as in Wardak, young intellectuals who wish to open the schools again have attended *fatwa* to obtain pronouncements from the *'ulama* in favour of re-establishing a modern educational system. By leaving the *qazi* to settle private conflicts, resistance leaders avoid getting involved in such affairs, where they might be suspected of not acting impartially but of favouring the group to which they happen to belong (which is, moreover, often the case when – in spite of everything – they finally do intervene).

The major problem for the resistance is still the survival of *qawm* membership. Even though the rhetoric used now makes constant reference to such universal themes as *jihad*, membership of a *qawm* involves a harking back to local organisation, group membership, loyalties and enmities. While private conflicts can easily be resolved by having recourse to the *qazi*, group conflicts all too easily turn into vendettas and can only be settled by negotiations at the highest level. Although such vendettas hopefully end in a peace treaty, this has no legal basis other than the fact that it was agreed between the two parties. In these circumstances *malik* and village elders regain the esteem that was theirs in the past. It is, therefore, a political necessity to the resistance to keep the balance between the *qawm* and to avoid vendettas at the price of making compromises which sometimes diminish the military effectiveness of the movement. For example, weapons are distributed according to the communal allegiances of a particular group and not according to the strategic needs of the situation; certain leaders are where they are only because they belong to a *qawm* which the resistance wishes to absorb into the movement. Or again, a *qawm* will not take kindly to one of its members, who happens to be a government sympathiser, being killed by someone outside the group. From this stems the conflicts that involve killings within the resistance movement, because they have taken on the aspect of a struggle between *qawm*. This contrasts with the care, indeed even the tolerance, shown by the movement towards government supporters, to avoid giving the impression that an act of political terrorism is in reality the waging of a vendetta. This is why it is always unsafe to execute someone who is suspected of being a government agent without his case being first heard in a *fatwa* convened by a respected *mawlawi*. The legality of the afghan resistance is politically necessary to avoid the movement collapsing under the weight of its sociological contradictions. But it is quite clear that while the *'ulama* succeeded in extending the area in which the *shari'at* was applied and setting up a society based upon their concept of law in those places where they were numerous and well organised, they never succeeded, nor even really attempted, to create a national structure over and above the *qawm* and above the parties. The political parties, therefore, remained the only alternative to the social fragmentation signified by the *qawm*, but they could only be established with assistance from the *'ulama* network. The conditions for the modernising of traditional society are therefore present in the resistance movement but the fragmentation into *qawm* seems to be much more than a mere survival of the past.

Another element which suggests that the process of modernisation has begun is, quite simply, the fact that the Mujahidin are beginning to acquire professional skills. When young people gain positions of responsibility, this always has an effect on traditional society. The arrival of radios and weapons, necessitating technical skills, creates favourable conditions for the emergence of technicians in the resistance movement. Another symbolic item is clothing; in the past there was a clear distinction between the modern and the traditional. This has now changed – most forward-looking members of the military resistance now wear battle fatigues and the *pawkul*, the beret which originated in Chitral and which has become the symbol of Panjshir. The war has also uprooted a great number of people and created a greater social mix. People are more interested in what is going on abroad because they know that the aid they receive depends on this. For this, the BBC is the principal source of information. The countryside is ceasing to be a mere provincial backwater.

The organisation of society

The spirit of jihad *and people's morale*

The war of resistance has introduced a spiritual dimension into individual behaviour. True, there is the rhetoric of the *jihad*, just as there is the rhetoric of Islamic justice, but the proximity of danger and the necessity of choosing between flight and personal involvement in combat have given an authentic resonance to the desire for *jihad*. This is indeed desire, for, although a fighter does not display that thirst for martyrdom which one finds in Iran, he is nevertheless motivated by a profound belief that he will go to Paradise, either because he has killed an enemy (and become a *ghazi*), or because he himself has been killed in combat (and has therefore become a *shahid*, martyr). The preaching of the mullahs and the *'ulama* falls upon fertile soil. Collective prayers and preaching in the mosques have reached an intensity unlike anything that was ever witnessed before the war. The sacrifices which the war imposes are easily borne, providing that their purpose is clear. People accept Islamic taxes, are willing to provide lodgings for the Mujahidin and even suffer the bombardments which come as reprisals, provided that the resistance acts in a honourable way towards them, fights effectively instead of living on the country and gains a modicum of success. The government, and more especially the Russians, have never been thought of as protagonists in a civil war, but as standing for a diabolical reality in a universe apart.

The resistance has more volunteers than it has weapons. Often, attempts to rationalise the military organisation and professionalise combatant groups have met with strong opposition: why should one make the *jihad* the monopoly of the young? Throughout the country there is no shortage of willing guides, people who will lend out their horses, provide shelter, education and finance, without any coercion. To anyone who knew the old Afghanistan where, apart from individual hospitality, everything had to be paid for, the spiritual growth of the people is a striking phenomenon. Of course, the resistance has its share of collaborators, its shirkers, its braggarts and its profiteers, but, when all is said and done, they are a tiny minority. As a general rule, the number of "spineless people" is directly proportional to their distance from the fighting. The morale of the fighters is at a high level everywhere. That of the civilian population who have been tested much more severely varies a great deal and bears no relation to the intensity of the fighting that they experience: the people of Panjshir, who have been attacked seven times and finally driven out of their valley, are still firm in their support for the resistance. On the other hand, many of the tribespeople left their areas at the first sign of an attack. Morale is very high amongst the old, who see in the war an opportunity to end their days with some sense of uplift, the very young, who are fascinated by the idea of heroic action, and women, who are always the first to speak up against the suggestion that people should emigrate. Morale is low amongst middle-aged men and amongst the *khan*, who still harbour a nostalgia for the golden age of the Royalist period and who would welcome any chance of a compromise making possible a return to the status quo ante. The religious leaders, like the Islamist intellectuals, are, of course, amongst the most obdurate. There has been a decline in morale in a few areas where conflicts between members of the resistance have led to settlings of accounts and extortion of money or goods from the people, which has caused the latter to begin to doubt the usefulness of supporting combatants who have become parasites.

One is struck by the significance people attach to ethical values.

Individuals will do a great deal, even putting their lives in danger, without any kind of external pressure beyond invoking the *jihad*. And here I am not speaking about combatants, who have chosen this way of life; simple shepherds, or nomads that one comes across in a moment of danger, will agree to escort the stranger through enemy patrols or under low-flying helicopters, and yet refuse any payment whatsoever.

Bases and administration

The further away you get from combat zones or from densely populated areas, the more tenuous becomes the parties' hold over the population and the more robust the traditional system of the *malik* and the councils of village elders.

Every time a party takes root, even if it does not enjoy total control it organises itself at provincial level. In control of the province there is an "Amir" in whom is vested civilian and military power. He is usually elected by party members and his nomination is confirmed by Peshawar. The Amir is assisted by a deputy, a military commander, someone who is responsible for finance and a *qazi*, to whom are added, in the case of the Hizb and the Jamiat, someone who is responsible for cultural affairs and another delegate who is in charge of organisation and propaganda (the "political commissioner"); the Amir ratifies the elections of presidents of local committees and if there is a dispute his decision is final. As an example, Massoud, Amir of the provinces of Parwan and Kapisa, was in 1981 assisted by seven committee members representing the following "ministerial departments": war, supplies, finance, intelligence, culture, preaching and organisation and health; and a department for external relations, responsible for contacts with officials who were secretly members of the resistance. The authority of the Amir extended only to the local committee members of his own party, but in those cases where one party more or less enjoyed absolute control of a province (as with Ismael Khan at Herat, and Massoud in the north-east), he is seen by the civilian population as being the governor of the whole resistance movement in that area. The real power of the Amir depends on his personality, but also on his relations with the *qawm* networks. He will only be the undisputed leader if he is clearly seen to have risen above the restrictions imposed by membership of a particular *qawm*.

The fundamental unit of the Afghan resistance movement is the local "committee" (*komite*), known also as *qarargah* ("the base", in Panjshir), *markaz* ("the centre", amongst the Pashtun), *paygah* ("the base"), *hawza* ("district", by the Hizb) (henceforth called the base). Whether this base is subordinate or not to an Amir, depending on the party's influence at provincial level, it is always affiliated to a party; the area for which it is responsible is generally a district (*uluswal*), but it is also possible to find a single base responsible for a village, indeed several if the village has different *qawm* or several parties. Istalif had six bases (one per party), Panjshir valley forty *qarargah*, all Jamiat; on the other hand, in the desert areas of Farah or on the Ghor plateau you can travel up to two days on horseback without encountering a resistance base. Thus, there are three things necessary if a base is to come into being: a geographical area, a network of *qawm* and membership of a political party. The base is installed in a precise spot: often the *qala'a* (fortified farm) of an influential family which has swung its support behind the government and whose goods have been confiscated by the resistance. In contrast to the outposts of the former regime, bases are generally located actually inside the villages, in spite of the risks involved. Only the Hazara have taken over administrative buildings of previous governments. In very exposed areas the base is always on the move. In 1984, it became usual to keep them away from inhabited villages.

At the head of the base there is a "director" (*ra'is* or *mudir*), with his assistant (*mu'avin*), a treasurer (*amir-i mali*) and a military commander. Large bases have a *qazi*. The base has a double task: military and political. One or more armed groups reside there, each one led by a "group leader" (*sar-i grup*) who has no political power. The Jamiat and Hizb bases usually have a section devoted to cultural affairs, propaganda (*da'wat-o tanzim*) and sometimes health. Whether this is the case or not depends on the degree of influence exercised by the Islamist intellectuals in the base. It is the base which receives the taxes paid by the peasants, which deals with their complaints and their requests; and it is with the bases that the *malik* discuss affairs having to do with their fellow citizens. The base controls the movement of the population. It provides passes for deserters, controls the corntrade (to avoid it being seized by the government), provides an escort for journalists, receives groups from other parties who find it necessary to cross their area of jurisdiction, and provides hospitality for groups belonging to their own party. The place where the base is located also serves as a prison for people who have committed felonies and the supporters of the regime; it is in the base's rooms that the *qazi* meet and have discussions with people of local influence. Questions of law and order are dealt with directly by the *ra'is*, who also sometimes intervene to establish certain price controls and to avoid speculation. Generally this is where military operations are planned.

The military activity undertaken by the base varies a great deal, as we shall see; many are no more than garrisons lost in some sleepy backwater.

The bases are always made up of militants who are natives of the place. It is true that they represent a new political force, but they are still the representatives of the local community; sometimes the base may be no more than the mouthpiece of a local *qawm*, but if so you can be sure that the other *qawm* will, sooner or later, set up their own base belonging to the same party or to another one. The village of Esfarz, in Herat, has got two Jamiat bases in this way, each base having twenty-five members who are all active combatants, one for each of two *qawm*, both of them being Persian-speaking. At the same time, because it belongs to a party, the base also represents a form of centralised power which is now established at the heart, and no longer at the periphery, of the village community.

A liberal society and economy

Social life in the liberated zones is far from being completely occupied with the political affairs of the resistance. Everywhere the *'ulama* maintain institutions concerned with the upholding of the law which parallel the local resistance committees. Even if the base has become the centre of political activity in the liberated zones, there are other public places which are outside its sphere of influence. The mosques, for example, are the places where strangers passing through the village usually stay. This group includes fighting men from other regions, refugees and deserters. At the mosque anyone can get bread and tea provided by the villagers. The mosque does not belong to any party and anyone can enter it. In Hazarajat and Paktya, the private inns still function as before. In addition, the better-off families continue to have a guest room available and do not consider themselves bound to account to the base for those to whom they provide hospitality. The private home is an inviolable sanctuary and the members of the resistance never carry out a house search. Even a group involved in a military operation will always ask permission from the master of the house before intruding into a private home. Terrorist activity is always carried on outside the house of the man who is to be gunned down: the inviolability of private property is a rule which applies even to the enemy.

The economy of the liberated zones is still a liberal economy. Prices and contracts are negotiated directly between the parties concerned. The resistance only intervenes to control the movement of corn and certain prices (such as the cost of transport). The government tries to buy corn at bargain prices just after the harvest, when, of course, the prices are lowest, using nomads as go-betweens. For example, in the autumn of 1982, some Samanzay nomads from Badghis offered the Aymaq of Ghor more than a hundred *afghanis* per *sir* (7 kg) of corn, whereas the local price was thirty-five *afghanis*. The corn was transported as far as Qala-yi Naw and given to the Russians. The aim of this operation was twofold: to supply Russian troops and to cause prices in the liberated zones to rise. The resistance countered by imposing on the nomads a quota of corn estimated according to their needs, and a number of armed skirmishes took place. At Herat, it is not possible to transport corn without written authorisation from the resistance. In the same way, the prices of certain services are also controlled, for example transport costs which have risen a great deal because of the danger and the lack of petrol. But the drivers' organisations prefer to regulate the market themselves; they are powerful bodies and negotiate directly with the resistance bases. Thus at Jaghori, in the south of Hazarajat, the point of departure for vehicles going to Pakistan, there are two "corporations" (*ittihadiyya*), one Sunni and the other Shi'ite. After competing against each other for several months, they decided to share the market: departures for each group take place on alternate days and the cost of the journey is paid at the confederation's office.

Certain regions have undergone a considerable economic decline, but in others there has been a boom, although it is not very soundly based. In Hazarajat, the number of bazaars has multiplied and it is possible to get basic essentials from them. Traders usually have a shop at Kabul, looked after by an old man who runs no risk of being conscripted; while in the liberated zone young people look after the shops. Traders solve the problem of transport by grouping together. The resistance is satisfied with just having a post to control the bazaar and, of course, to collect the taxes, which are very high in Hazarajat. The resistance has never bothered to organise supply networks for the civilian population. In areas cut off by the fighting which have no bazaar, each family organises its own regular trip to the bazaar in the nearest resistance area. The Aymaq, for example, walk five days on end to go either to the bazaar at Del-e Takht in Herat, or to the one at Garmao in Hazarajat. The trader who takes the risk of transporting goods into isolated zones can then name his price. The resistance, whose logistics are none too good, knows that it cannot take the place of private initiative, and that a too harsh control of economic activities would paralyse the markets. In any case the ideology of the resistance favours the notion of private property and free enterprise. Nevertheless, there can be no doubt that the resistance has underestimated the political importance of the economy and of supplies. Even the transport of weapons is mostly organised by the private sector: a group of Mujahidin hires the services of a camel driver, or buys horses. It is rare for requisitioning to occur, and when it does it is temporary and frowned upon. The positive side of this executive weakness is that it is more difficult for the Russians to break up a communications network which is run by a number of different individuals and which is, moreover, profitable. The traders who benefit from deals with the resistance are influential at Kabul; as soon as the Russians cut a communication route it is usual to see small entrepreneurs, enticed by the idea of profit, trying to open up a new channel. Finally, there is no black market: the economy and the commercial networks used by the resistance are those in use throughout the country. Any move to block them would ruin the economy of the whole country, something which the Russians cannot allow to happen, so long as they are not in a position to provide food in the areas which they control. So, apart from temporary blockades in certain areas and large-scale but very selective disruption, the economy of the resistance will survive. Since it makes less demand on available resources and is less regulated, it is more soundly based than the government economy.

As prices are regulated by the law of supply and demand, the market fluctuates wildly: it is possible for the price of corn to increase five times between the period immediately after the harvest and the shortfall which occurs in the spring. The prices of agricultural produce are noticeably lower in the liberated zones than they are in the capital; but on the other hand pharmaceutical and industrial products are more expensive in the countryside. However, the general level of poverty and the insufficient supply of food is a situation not fundamentally different from that which obtained before the war, even if foodstuffs such as sugar are often in short supply.

The contracts for share-croppers and for wage-earners are always freely entered into. If these contracts are fairer than they were before, it is less as a result of the preaching of the *'ulama* than because of a shortage of labour due to emigration, in particular of young people who have gone to look for work in Iran or in the Arabian Gulf. The seasonal workers, who used to travel round, planning their route to fit in with the dates of the various harvests, have all but disappeared, because of the difficulties involved in going round the country. Young people have left the outskirts of the town for fear of being drafted, and other potential workers have joined the resistance. Reports from Hazarajat state that there is a dearth of agricultural workers in the province.

The *qazi* of the resistance have brought in measures against usury, a practice which more than any other undermines the economic well-being of the peasants; at least they have been able to do this in those places where the *qazi* can count on the support of a large number of resistance bases against the richer, more influential families of the neighbourhood. Nevertheless, the departure of the great *khan* and the troubles the war has brought have reduced social inequality, in so far as the simple peasants who make up the great battalions of the resistance are now in possession of weapons and have acquired some political clout. Neither the parties of the resistance, nor the local resistance committees are in any way under the power of the *khan*, whose political decline has already been described.

It has to be said that there are some cases of corruption: in Hazarajat these are frequent, as they are in certain committees which in remote areas are left to themselves. A number of instances of banditry have occurred in the frontier areas (rackets involving the convoy of arms). Nevertheless, the resistance cadres are for the most part honourable and, wherever possible, the resistance through the *qazi* is working to ensure that ethical values play a substantial part in the formation of contracts and economic exchange; but its chief weapon tends to be exhortation and the levelling of accusations against a few well-heeled individuals guilty of corruption, rather than the setting up of a system of economic checks and controls generally associated with the communist government. For the Afghans, the concept of liberty includes economic liberty.

Migrations and the reclassification of ethnic groups

Refugees who have fled to Pakistan or Iran fall outside the scope of this study;[2] a refugee ceases to be a member of a resistance movement. What is more relevant is why people decide to leave, and the changes brought about in the class system by large-scale migration. A mass exodus from the countryside does not necessarily follow intense fighting in the area. Sometimes, as in Panjshir, the civilian population will cling on in territory which has been devastated or, in other instances, will anticipate an approaching combat and leave before battle has commenced, as in Helmand, or again they will sometimes flee after a single small-scale operation, for example in Kunar in 1980. Sometimes people will flee abroad, but on other occasions they will make their way to the capital. Cultural factors are involved in this decision.

The protest exodus or hijrat

To leave Muslim territory occupied by infidels, without fighting, is, while not actually recommended by the Qur'an, at least permitted: "Those who believed and left their homes and strove for the cause of Allah . . . these are the believers in truth"; "'We were oppressed in the land'. [Then the Angels] will say: 'Was not Allah's earth spacious that ye could have migrated therein?'"[3] Following the example of Muhammad leaving Mecca for Medina, many Muslims believe that their religion obliges them to leave a territory which has ceased to be Islamic, in order to dwell in another Muslim land. *Mohajir*, "refugee", according to its aetimology, means one who has experienced *hijrat*, or Hegira. When an exodus of protest occurs in Afghanistan it is always a collective phenomenon, instigated and organised by those families who have traditionally been influential; to be classified as such a migration involves the journey of an organised group to a foreign country, usually Pakistan, where it retains its cohesion for a certain period. The event which finally sparks off this movement in not always the gravity of the military or economic situation; sometimes it may be caused by a very limited local threat. The protest exodus nearly always involves tribes. An exceptional instance of *hijrat* to the interior of the country is provided by the *cheshtiyya* brotherhood of Chesht-i Sharif (Herat): following the preaching of their *'ulama*, who took as their text those passages in the Qur'an which deal with *hijrat*, three hundred of the four hundred families left the town in a single day (11 April 1981) to take refuge in the surrounding mountains, where they continued to fight until they retook the town two years later.

Flight from the combat zone

In certain areas, the regular Soviet offensives with armoured vehicles and air support, the intensity of the fighting, the destruction of harvests and reprisals against the civilian population have made survival difficult. In these cases the flight from home and land does not involve the community as such but individuals and it is usually somewhat chaotic. The decision is taken by each family separately. First people take refuge in the neighbouring valleys and then they either go to Kabul or they go to Pakistan. When the families arrive in their place of exile, the larger social units to which they belonged previously do not re-form. This type of exodus, therefore, breaks down social bonds; for this reason many families are loath to leave their homes and attempt to stay, even under very difficult conditions. This is frequently found in non-tribal areas. A protest exodus, on the other hand, essentially involves structured groups, in particular tribes, and is carried out at the instigation of influential people in the community; while in the non-tribal areas, the tendency is for the leaders of the community to discourage the movement.

Not all refugees end up in Pakistan or Iran. As a result of the war a new kind of exodus from the countryside has occurred. Previously bachelors left the country to work in the towns, while their families remained in the countryside. Now it is the other way round: the families take refuge at Kabul, while the young people keep well away from the towns for fear of being forced to join the army. The Persian-speaking population (for example the Panjshiri) prefer flight to the town to emigration. This flocking of people to the town only applies to Kabul, for in the other towns sporadic fighting takes place even inside the urban boundaries. The population of Kabul has multiplied two- or threefold, and people are crowded into lodgings. When city people decide to run away, they go to Pakistan and not to the countryside, except for those young people who join the resistance.

Changes in the nomadic way of life

Nomadism has not died out but there are fewer people involved now and the journeys they take are shorter. But certain groups, especially stock-breeders, have started to live as nomads again, to try to get away from the fighting. When this occurs, however, the journeys they make are only short ones. The semi-nomadism of the Aymaq still continues, for their summer camps are safer. Before the war, two Pashtun tribal confederations, the Ghilzay and Durrani, used to make the journey each summer from the borders of their territory towards central Afghanistan. One major snag was that their winter quarters, which generally comprised desert plains, were easily accessible to Soviet armoured vehicles on patrol, which controlled and pillaged the area and forcibly conscripted young men into the army. The tribes which were most under threat were those which remained between Herat and Nimruz to pass the winter (the Nurzay, Alizay, Sarzay and Brahui). Only the Taraki and the Samanzay of Badghis and Faryab, ironically living on the Soviet border, were left in peace. Secondly, it was difficult to cross the tarmac roads which separated the winter quarters from the summer pastures; these roads were constantly patrolled and the nomads were subjected to all kinds of harassment. Although the summer pastures in the Hindu-Kush were safe, the rigours of winter meant that they were not a practical proposition. Finally, the traditional system of bargaining between nomads and agriculturalists was breaking down. The Russians forced some of the nomads to buy corn in order that they themselves could purchase it from them; in the medium term, the rise in corn prices was against the interest of the nomads as a whole, since meat prices in the countryside have not changed very much and the trade in animal hides is in decline. Whenever the Soviets interfered with road traffic, as occurred when motor vehicles travelling between Herat and Nimruz were machine-gunned by helicopters at the beginning of 1982, the traditional exchange of goods between villagers and nomads (corn in exchange for meat, skins and brushwood for fires) was interrupted, with grievous consequences for the nomads in particular.

For many nomads this was their last journey; they decided not to leave their winter pastures any more. In many cases they went off to Pakistan. Thus, the Pashtun tribes of Baghlan and Takhar began to change their route in 1980, crossing the Hindu-Kush southwards into Pakistan. For the present, such changes are considered to be temporary; the tribes are waiting in their winter quarters for the situation to get better, but little by little the camp is becoming a village of urban dwellings and there is not much prospect of them returning. In 1985 most of the remaining Pashtun nomads north of Afghanistan left for Pakistan.

Where the nomads have attempted to continue their traditional wanderings, they have changed their routine. They choose a different route and destination, the group has not the same cohesion as it had before, and the rhythm of their life has been disrupted. Their journeys are now shorter: there are no longer any nomads to be found between Behsud and Chakhcharan, and their bazaars have disappeared.[4] Since they run the risk of having their goods looted by the Russians, the nomads have no incentive to transport merchandise intended for customers who in any case are now poverty-stricken. But nomadism continues to flourish on the borders of the central massif of the Hindu-Kush and the plain of Nahur is still an important meeting place for nomads in summer.

Finally, there has been a modification of the nomadic cycle; some nomads spend one or two years in safe areas, without leaving in the springtime. The Ghilzay, for instance, used to spend the summer in the Nahur region; because of Taraki's blockade of Hazarajat in 1979, they did not return until two years later, and when they did they found a new situation, in which the Hazara peasants, by tradition somewhat subservient, were now well-armed and organised.

On the whole, the nomads have adapted well to the new balance of power vis-à-vis sedentary people who now have weapons and are organised, in spite of the disappearance of the Pashtun administration which favoured them. In many cases they have joined one of the resistance parties (Harakat or *Mahaz-i islami*). The nomads of the southwest are very much involved in the resistance movement; those who live in the east and the north are more opportunistic.

Changes in the classification of ethnic groups

Migrations have not affected all the ethnic groups equally. Highly structured groups (the tribes) tend to react as a whole; when the decision to move is taken, it is always to Pakistan that they decide to go, for the social structures in the frontier areas of Pakistan are very similar to those of Afghanistan and the people living there are Pashtun. The proportion of Pashtun amongst the refugees, including those who have gone to Iran, is greater than the proportion of those who remain in Afghanistan. There has, therefore, been a demographic shift within Afghanistan away from the Pashtun, and this has had political repercussions. Some small ethnic groups have almost completely disappeared, while the relative strength of the Tajik, the Hazara and the Uzbek has considerably increased, all the more so because the people who have crowded into Kabul tend to be Persian-speakers.

In the many regions where an ethnic minority was surrounded by other larger groups, this group has often gone back to its original region, especially if it is of recent origin or is composed of people sharing a common trade (seasonal workers, tradesmen, etc.). Apart from the nomads, there are no longer Pashtun in Hazarajat or on the borders of Nuristan; and the Hazara have left Kabul and Ghazni. Only the north still has what may truly be called a mosaic of ethnic groups, but in 1984 the Pashtun who settled in the north in the twenties left massively towards Pakistan.

In conclusion, the socio-political consequences of these population movements have involved a decline in the influence of Pashtun, the tribes and the nomads, in relation to settled and non-Pashtun people. But it would be more accurate to speak of a restoration of equilibrium rather than a new dominance by Persian-speakers.

Changes in the geography of the country – the communications network and the economy

The movement of people around the country has not come to a halt with the war, though people now use new routes or the old paths that the opening of modern roads had caused to fall into disuse. Regions which declined in importance because of the opening of these roads have once again become transit areas for men and materials – such regions are Hazarajat, Paktya and the Anjuman and Wulf passes until they were reoccupied by the Russians. Some mountain massifs, difficult of access, now play their part, for they provide shelter from bombardment. In certain places, the fact that routes have been opened up for members of the resistance, refugees and deserters has brought in its wake economic prosperity for that region with the opening of inns, bazaars and "roadside stations" (Paktya, and Hazarajat, where Jaghori is the prototype of this kind of economic boom). Smuggling is more frequent than ever amongst the Mohmand, Jaji, Mangal and Baluchi (there is even a "smugglers front" at Robat, in Baluchistan).

Bazaars have been established at road terminuses in valley floors which are accessible to vehicles and relatively safe; the lower slopes of the valleys, which used to be suitable market-places, (Hari-rud between Obe and Herat, Andarab, and Panjshir) are now unsafe and have no bazaar. Some erstwhile channels for the transport of goods have totally disappeared and whole regions have been cut off from the national economy. The province of Ghor was previously provisioned by Chakhcharan bazaar, but this has now been transformed into a Soviet base and is inaccessible.

While it is true that the road network has been transformed and there are now new economic centres, this situation is unstable, for at any moment the new bazaars may be destroyed and the communications network cut by the Russians. Moreover, the bazaars set up by the resistance have become political (and financial) prizes to be fought over between the parties. In particular, the Hizb and the Jamiat fight for the bazaars in the north, in places like the mountain valley of Andarab and Gorziwan in Faryab. Disputes of this kind, discreetly encouraged by the Russians, sometimes mean that whole regions which would otherwise be inaccessible to the occupation troops have been neutralised.

The strategic consequences of the changes in population structure

It is possible that the Russians may succeed in taking advantage of all these developments to formulate a counter-guerilla strategy. Migration from the countryside, in all its forms, has deprived the resistance movement of its demographic base. A certain number of contradictions have come to the fore; the nomads and the villagers strongly disagree on the question of the free movement of grain; the people who run the bazaars controlled by the resistance oppose the military activity of the latter which might upset the status quo; the smugglers, also, would like to achieve a modus vivendi with the Russians and of course this kind of smuggling involves the whole tribe. Finally, the refugees are a destabilising influence in Pakistan.

However, the Russians are having difficulty in controlling all these phenomena. The harsh reality of the refugees pouring into Kabul has brought about a level of inflation and of poverty in the capital that they cannot control; and people in general are still hostile to them. The goods for which the government provides subsidies disappear into the countryside, where, apart from some shortages, corn, wood and fruit are already cheaper. The Russians have not been able to isolate the capital, for if they are going to feed the population, there must be access to the country for food production and distribution. There is, therefore, a contradiction between the two aims of their policy: to isolate the countryside, and to normalise everyday life in the town. Private enterprise is still flourishing in the Soviet-controlled areas, and the resistance profits from it.

The influx of refugees into Pakistan has created sharp tensions between them and the local population, but international aid has enriched the frontier zones. Up to now the Afghan refugees have been tightly controlled politically by their parties, and they have integrated into local life quite well. There is no parallel here with the plight of the Palestinians. There have even been some partial returns of refugees to their homeland.

On the other hand, it seems that for some time to come the resistance will have a sufficiently large demographic base to enable it to gain an adequate number of recruits.[5] Moreover, the flight from the countryside has brought some advantages. First, the increase in population, which was leading to a shortage of land, is no longer a problem, and thus the social pressures have diminished. Then, the people who left first were the ones "without backbone". Thirdly, relations between nomads and villagers have got back to an even keel, since with fewer nomads there is less pressure on the summer pastures. The fact that population levels have found a new equilibrium has brought about a new political balance between the ethnic groups, which augurs well for greater cohesion within the Afghanistan resistance movement. For example, the Hazara have, by joining the resistance, gained greater autonomy than they could have hoped for from a central government that was both Pashtun and communist. They are collaborating with and assisting the other ethnic groups in the resistance all the more willingly because they are now dealing with them on an equal footing. The coming and going of Mujahidin and refugees brought diverse populations into contact with each other, and this created a nationalist outlook.

The question arises as to whether the replacement of the central state by autonomous groups will not end in the dismembering of Afghanistan, which in turn would mean that the Russians would be able to take over the country piecemeal. It is true that the first phase of the revolt has resulted in the break-up of the country. But, while there can be no doubt that individual characteristics will persist, the forces working for unity within the resistance will triumph over disruption. The elements which contribute to unity are political (parties organised on a national scale), cultural (the same vision of the war as *jihad*) and sociological (the increased prominence of the *'ulama*). The demographic changes are not likely to effect the underlying unity of civil society.

Chapter Eleven

From freedom fighter to guerilla

Who are the Mujahidin? It is possible to distinguish between three categories of fighters. The armed resistance, men who have enrolled permanently (*maslaki*: "professionals", *nizami*: "soldiers", *mutaharek* or *sayyar*: "mobile troops"), number some 150,000 for the whole of Afghanistan, that is to say as many as the Russians had in 1983. Next come the part-time soldiers (*mahalli*: "locals", *molki*: "civilian forces"), generally belonging to one of the parties and organised by a local base, but who are only mobilised in a crisis and who meanwhile cultivate the land. Finally, every Afghan who has a weapon and lives in the liberated zones is potentially a *mujahid*. It is the first category which we shall concentrate on here.

The active members of the resistance are always organised at a local level by bases which are much alike in all parts of the country, whether they are functioning in tribal zones or not and whichever party they represent. Nevertheless, whenever it is a question of engaging in a higher level of combat, divergences begin to appear in the way of thinking, the outlook and in organisational structure.

The general characteristics of the military organisation

Bases, networks and areas

To plan a military strategy, it is necessary to go beyond the purely local level and to be able to operate on a regional, or even on a national, scale, and this means facing up to the problem of the *qawm* with all its potential for creating division. For example, misunderstandings are apt to arise when an armed group operates in a region other than its own. The local people might well prefer to be ruled by a power which although communist is at least far away (a situation which leaves them with a considerable amount of autonomy) to being controlled by an armed group which they see more as the representatives of a rival *qawm* than of the *umma*. The situation in the tribal areas is different from that in the north. Tribal territory is often clearly demarcated; there is therefore a tendency here for relatively homogeneous tribal fronts to be created. Armed groups do not go outside their tribal land unless they are attacking "detribalised" targets, such as large bazaars which are not situated in any specific tribal territory, and which are not run by any clearly recognisable group. Most bazaars in the tribal areas have a mixed population – often people whose native tongue is Persian. The neighbouring tribes will therefore jointly organise a series of sudden swoops on these bazaars. Even though each tribal front may belong to a different party, this does not play any significant part in the military organisation or the strategy of the tribes. In the Kandahar region, it is not unusual for a front to be split into two parts: the base camp is in the mountain, but the groups operate on the edge of the town at a distance of two or three days' march away. Such fronts often contain from fifty to a thousand members – the number varies according to tribe and the prestige of the leader. If there is good understanding between the various groups, there is no need for any specific coordination and a dozen different fronts will coexist in the same region, all representing different parties.

In contrast, in the north the *qawm* are much less clearly associated with specific units of territory and the only means of achieving any kind of unity is through the structure of the political parties. But at the same time, the rivalry between the parties is stronger here than in the south. We have the paradoxical situation that the potential for conflict and disunity is greater but, consequently, there is a greater chance that a military structure may evolve, making the coordination of activities possible. In the north, a base represents a network rather than a geographical area. On the other hand, the fact that the *qawm* and the parties are less clearly associated with a specific unit of territory makes it easier for armed groups to move around, or at least it makes it easier to assemble mobile groups whose members have different affiliations. Thus, Massoud has been able to set up garrisons of Panjshiri troops at Ashawa (to the west of Salang) and at Andarab. The Herat regiment (*ghund*) has a number of members on active service and even officers who are natives of Shamali, Badakhshan and Faryab, including some Uzbek. That is why it is in the north that a resistance army will first come into being, while the south will find it hard to get past the stage of local bases and short-lived coalitions.

Permanent combat groups

Permanent combat groups are closely linked to the local bases. The composition of these groups and their daily life is much the same throughout the whole country. One group has between twenty and fifty men. The men live permanently in the base headquarters, but they are allowed to go and visit their families from time to time, or, as frequently happens in the tribal areas, they have an arrangement whereby their brothers are allowed to substitute for them. In general, they are young and from a poor peasant background. In the base headquarters, their lifestyle is superior to that enjoyed by their family (for example, they often eat meat). Discipline is strict, although there is a very good-natured atmosphere. Everyone is responsible for looking after his weapons and the ammunition which has been entrusted to him; in certain bases, there is an ammunition check every evening and any individual who cannot satisfactorily account for all his supply is forced to pay for what is missing. The group leader has only a military role: he is a lieutenant in charge of the section and he is usually older than the soldiers under his command, having usually had a certain amount of education. Nevertheless, there is not much difference between officers and ordinary privates (except amongst the Shi'a, who, as usual, are keen on hierarchy). They eat the same food and sleep in the same room. They are always together and there is not much opportunity for privacy. The base usually has a cook. In their quarters, the base president, who exercises political power, works in a reception room to which ordinary members have free access. Everything is public. "Secret" matters are communicated by whispering in someone's ear. Each day is punctuated by collective prayer; many bases run politico-religious classes, which, of course, are more strongly emphasised amongst the Islamists.

The patience and endurance shown during long periods of inactivity marked by unvarying routine are astonishing. In one sense, the fact that most of the enlisted men have a better standard of living than they did as civilians is a powerful antidote to the boredom. Although it is possible to see a "garrison mentality" developing in the bases located far from the combat zones and those unable to fight outside their own communal territory, they are always ready and their morale is high. There is never any shortage of recruits, and they are forced to refuse some volunteers because there are not enough weapons to go round.

The military activity of the local bases

The level of activity varies according to how close to the enemy they are. In those areas where they are quite close, especially in the immediate locality of the towns, there is something happening every day (patrols, routine ambushes), even though skirmishes, in the proper sense of the word, are rare. As the fighting becomes more intense a gap is opening up between the Mujahidin who have had a lot of experience in the war zones, and who are becoming more and more professional, and those based in more tranquil areas, whose approach is still rather amateurish.

But for most bases military operations are the exception rather than the rule and much of their day is spent in routine. The most important event is the selection of night sentries. There is scarcely any training, though former army sergeants try to teach the privates how to march in step, an activity whose usefulness is not very much appreciated by those involved. Target practice is by means of shooting competitions. There are no attempts to rehearse attacks, and no demonstrations involving the use of plans or models.

The base will launch attacks against government posts or on vehicles travelling along the roads within its territory. The operation is decided upon at the last moment and in a democratic way. Since the group knows the land very well, there is no need for any preliminary instructions. The most recent information provided by the "agents" of the resistance are passed to the group leaders. Improvisation is the order of the day.

The groups just outside the towns are more active and have a wider range of targets: police posts, government groups, administrative buildings, enemy patrols. In contrast, groups in the countryside have, in many cases, established a modus vivendi with government posts: the latter provide food and ammunition and are very careful not to get involved in any sorties. For their part, the members of the resistance movement content themselves with making symbolic attacks which make it possible for the commander of the post to justify the expenditure of ammunition which he has, in fact, handed over to the resistance. Things are very different when the Russians mount an offensive. Generally, the resistance groups avoid any confrontation at first and just harass the enemy; but sometimes, as at Kandahar, Paktya and Panjshir, there is a real exchange of fire from fixed positions.

The Russians rarely take the risk of using helicopters in order to flush out a particular base but prefer either to use precision bombing, or to engage in a massive operation. This means that the bases, on a strictly military level, scarcely ever suffer Soviet counter-attacks. In the exposed areas, they are well protected in the mountains and sometimes have the advantage of anti-aircraft fire which dissuades the pilots from coming too low. When there is a big offensive, the bases, which are on the alert day and night, swiftly evacuate the threatened position. It is, therefore, the civilians who bear the brunt of Soviet counter-attacks. The military losses suffered by the resistance are low: for example, during the biggest Soviet offensive on Panjshir in May 1982 (Panjshir V), Massoud lost no more than 10 per cent of his fighters in a two-month period.

The network of local bases is very close-knit. There is at least one for each of the 325 districts (a district like Panjway at Kandahar has several dozen of them). There must be at least 4,000 bases, each having on average thirty to fifty permanent fighting members, with a reserve double the size that can be mobilised at a moment's notice, but the differences are enormous. Several bases belonging to the same party constitute a front (*jabha*). It is the ubiquity of these bases wherein lies the true strength of the resistance movement in the country. Military success and political importance are not directly linked. The bases are politically indispensable, they are the visible symbol of the resistance for the local people, even when they are militarily insignificant.

While the bases are the backbone of the resistance and the essential link between those who are fighting and the people in general, as also between military and civilian structures, they are, nevertheless, static and relatively inactive in comparison with the fighting men that they are able to call upon. Does the resistance have any other more dynamic combat structures?

The models on which guerilla activity is based

The outlook of the guerillas, like the organisational forms which have emerged from the resistance, may be divided into three ideal types: traditional tribal warfare (especially in the south), imitation of the regular army (Hazarajat and the north-west) and adherence to the theories of Mao and Giap (the north-east quarter of the country). These ideal types have each undergone a certain degree of evolution and have met with varying degrees of success as they have been tested in the real world.

Tribal warfare

The first chapter provided an account of the traditional conception of war among the Pashtun tribes. The initial uprisings and the present organisational forms exhibit many of the characteristics of tribal warfare. It is a people's war in which every adult is an active member and the framework of military activity is that of civil society. It is a war fought by part-time soldiers, in which people go back to their villages at harvest time, for if all the guerillas were mobilised for too long, agricultural activity would come to a halt. This explains the explosive nature of tribal warfare; a sudden flare-up of violence is followed by the break-up of the battle formations (*lashkhar*) as the troops disappear back into the countryside. Tribal warfare is carried on within a precise space-time framework: there is a time for war and there is a time for peace, there is a place for combat (the *sangar*, or "trenches") and a place of sanctuary (the village). It is symbolic warfare, where the goal is to show one's valour and not to achieve a strategic objective – which is the reason for those bizarre displays in front of military objectives (taking pot-shots at a post that one is not actually trying to capture); or mobilising dozens of men for another kind of shooting – a photographic kind. The purpose of military activity is booty, but the purpose of warfare is to obtain glory and the recognition of the prorogatives of the tribal group; military activity, properly speaking, is secondary. Tribal warfare is, above all, a means of dissuasion and is carried out against a background of constant negotiation. Finally, it presupposes that civil society will continue without hinderance: villages are not burnt down, the fighting is carried on well away from the places where people live, women and children are left alone, farming and trading continue as if nothing has happened.[1] It is a war between equals.

How has this model fared in the face of the offensives carried out by government forces and the Russians? Each intrusion by the communist forces has been met with a mass uprising of fighting men that the government army has been quite unable to deal with. Where the government troops have directed their offensive at specific targets they have always been defeated by a tribal *lashkar*. Two examples of this which occurred just before the Soviet invasion were the conflict in Nuristan in the summer of 1978 and the offensive against Paktya in October 1979. In the first instance, the government's use of tribal militia enabled them to defeat the Nuristani tribes, who, nevertheless, turned the tables when they were only faced with the government battalions in the winter of 1979–80. In the other case, the elite of the Khalq troops were massacred by a Jadran *lashkar*. But the space-time framework of tribal warfare is not well-suited to modern warfare and methods of counter-insurgence, where there is no such thing as a dichotomy between two kinds of time and two kinds of space, one for war, the other for peace. It is impossible to maintain a tribal army for very long under arms; the troops tend to disband as soon as the action is finished, because this is when the traditional rivalries between *qawm* and between different leaders reappear on the surface. Next, the war can only continue if village life goes on more or less normally. Any attack on the village has a catastrophic effect on the provision of supplies and the morale of the troops. This is something which the British understood when they fought their great campaigns against the Mohmand in 1916, 1933 and 1935; by the use of blockades, the systematic destruction of harvests and through the bombardment of villages they were able to subdue the revolt.[2]

It would be surprising if the Russians had played the game according to the ethics of tribal warfare, even though the Khad has made great use of the tradition of negotiating. War as waged by the occupiers is total warfare: there is no intermezzo, and no place of sanctuary. Villages have been bombed and harvests burnt. The tribes have moved out, to a much greater extent than other groups within the country, because they have been unable to adapt to total warfare. But the ideology of the *jihad*, which is close to the heart of every individual guerilla, has been very successful in preventing the system of tribal relations (the rivalry of the *qawm*) from being manipulated at will by the Khad. The emergence of the *'ulama* as a force to be reckoned with in a number of tribal sectors has brought with it a decline in the rivalry between the *khan*, which was the primary channel by which government influence was able to penetrate the tribe. The ideology of tribal warfare (the emphasis being upon "appearances", whether this be booty or individual action) is now being replaced by the ideology of *jihad*. Egalitarian sentiment, very strong amongst the tribes, has been strengthened by the fact that the *lashkar* has become more democratic; the *khan* has yielded in importance to the *'alim* and weapons, provided through the party, no longer depend on the personal wealth of the individual guerilla.

The spread of professionalism is occurring in the tribal zones just as it is elsewhere in those places (such as Kandahar) where combat takes place every day. The number of men on active service tends to accord with the maintenance of a much reduced level of agricultural activity. General mobilisation is replaced by a kind of rotation: one brother is at the front, another in the fields, the third works in Pakistan or in the Gulf. In order to spare the villages, the guerillas often withdraw into the *sangar* where they mount guard for long periods. The *sangar* soon became an archetype of Afghan resistance, except in the case of Massoud and his followers. Armed groups, comprising a varying number of guerillas, hold the small mountain massifs, which exist in great number but are often separated in the south by plains which are accessible to armoured vehicles. In spite of the development of many "*tulaba* fronts" which go beyond the level of the tribe, both in ideology and in their area of recruitment, the political influence of the parties is less than it is in the north. In Paktya political affiliation is now superseding tribal affiliations but this is a very new trend.

Tribal habits have reappeared in fighting tactics and in the behaviour of the individual soldier; but here we see, once again, one of the basic realities of Afghan society, the only difference being that it is more noticeable in the south.

The sudden eruption of violence which has always characterised tribal warfare is very striking. Periods of semi-apathy follow waves of furious activity. Thus, from August to November 1983, hoards of guerillas attacked the garrisons at Urgun and Khost – although the latter was not actually captured. When the government forces counter-attacked in December, they were able to reopen the road without much opposition: the fighting had taken place between harvest time and winter, then everyone departed to his own affairs. For those entrusted with the task of holding the road there was an additional reason why they preferred to return home; they might not get their share of the booty if Urgun was captured without their help. There is no such thing as strategy when it comes to tribal fighting; you fight in order to make immediate and tangible gains.

The *sangar* is still best described as a tribal front, comprising a number of guerillas from the same *qawm*, who do not move outside their own immediate communal area. This close connection between fighting men and the civilian population is balanced by a clear separation of tasks: those who fight do not attempt to exercise undue influence in social matters, and when the soldier returns to his village it is as a member of his family and not as a representative of the resistance movement. The degree of separation which exists in the minds of the tribespeople between civil activities and war means that the parties do not concern themselves with the task of organising the people. In a time of crisis, the people are therefore left to themselves, which explains their panic when the Russians mount an offensive, like the one at Logar in January 1983. This is all the more so because a number of *sangar* operating in the same area but lacking coordination is incapable of providing any kind of viable defence against an offensive comprising the combined operations of armoured vehicles and helicopters. Tribespeople under arms are all too ready to disband, but they regroup just as readily once the offensive is over, since the military and political structures have not been destroyed, precisely because there are no such structures. Regrouping occurs on the basis of family ties and not political allegiance, and the local front revives quite unaided after the storm, however disorganised the region as a whole or the political parties may be. The very weakness of the tribal fronts, paradoxically, constitutes their strong point. For the Russians, trying to bring order to the tribal zones is like trying to iron out the creases in an eiderdown – the task is never done. Social divisions such as the *qawm* and the tribe (*qabila*) make it easy to cut existing social ties, but difficult to fill the vacuum with a state machine.

Nevertheless, formidable strongholds have gradually been created in, for instance, Anardarrah, Jadran, Sharafat Koh and Kandahar, places where gifted leaders, generally *'ulama*, have been able to take advantage both of the spirit of *jihad* (politicisation and escape from petty divisions) and the force of tribal loyalty, which ensures the armed groups work extremely well together. Thus, the main issues and the problems are no different from those one finds in the other regions of Afghanistan.

The attempt to create a professional army

In Hazarajat with the *shura* and in the north-west provinces at the instigation of the Jamiat, the method of waging war is modelled closely on that of the government army. The *shura* has gone far in imitating the state model: obligatory conscription of the young at twenty-two, the disarming of the population and the monopolising of weapons by the public authorities, and the setting up of a guard around Beheshti, whose members are nearly all sons of *sayyad*. The army of the *shura*, which lacks mobility, is spread out in garrisons in the interior of the country and along fronts near the enemy. The imitation of the government army even extends to the level of detail (ceremonial marches, the wearing of uniforms, etc.), and a permanent officer corps, for the most part quite incompetent. Jaglan has tried to create a corps of fully-mobilised soldiers, on the basis of one soldier for every eight families, who are supposed to provide him with food and pay for his weapons and ammunition; but the system is very unpopular. This monopolising of the *jihad* by the major party in the province has brought about a total demilitarisation of the people, who play no part in the war. The other Shi'ite parties (Nasr and *Harakat-e islami*), who are more flexible, have only called up their militants. The *shura* army has shown itself to be inefficient.

In the north-west, the Jamiat has a body of excellent former career officers. While maintaining recruitment on a voluntary basis, their aim is to establish more powerful units. They have taken the regiment (*ghund*) as the basis of their military organisation, and in theory this unit contains 600–900 men, divided into three battalions (*kundak*) of three companies (*tulay*) each. In fact, as always, the basic unit is still the group (twenty-five men). The *ghund* have garrisons near Herat, far away from the combat zone in Faryab; operations are carried out on the level of the *kundak*, and, therefore, involve about 200 men. The task of the bases is to ensure local security, while the *ghund* fight anywhere within the provincial territory. On paper, the organisation into *ghund* may seem to be well suited for concentrating troops to attack objectives beyond the reach of the local bases, but, in fact, the system is too heavy. The *ghund* are not sufficiently mobile to carry out surprise attacks; their weapons, which are all too similar to those used by the local bases, are not sufficiently powerful to allow a real concentration of firepower: the *ghund* of Alla'uddin, the largest in Herat, in 1982 had only six 12.7 machine-guns, three recoilless guns and four mortars; those at Lawlash had a dozen 12.7's, a mortar and two recoilless guns. The troops were immobilised inside garrisons located in one specific place and therefore easily open to attack. Efficiently operating *ghunds* could be counted on the fingers of one hand.

While the idea of using mobile groups in addition to the local bases is a good one, the organisation into *ghunds* has resulted in a lack of flexibility and is clearly far too premature for the level of military development that the resistance has attained. Sooner or later the Jamiat leaders will have to break the *ghund* down into smaller units and adopt a form of organisation closer to that of Massoud. Nevertheless, the system adopted by Ismael Khan works well on the political level and makes for good contacts between civilians, local groups and "professionals". The *ghund* and the general staff are run by Islamist intellectuals and *'ulama* who come from the towns; the local committees at Herat are generally organised by Sufis; the more distant villages keep their traditional structure. In the Jamiat and the province of Herat, the three levels function well together: there is no clear distinction between an aristocracy of leaders and their followers, which is such a marked feature in Hazarajat, and neither does it suffer from the latent militarisation of Massoud's system. Once again we see that, as far as the resistance is concerned, there is no automatic link between military and political efficiency.

Massoud's strategy

Massoud is the foremost military leader of the resistance movement. He is fully aware that the counter-insurgency strategy of the Russians seeks to isolate territories from each other and that the only way to strike back is to coordinate simultaneous attacks on the main axes of communication. To carry out his strategy, he needs a military instrument and a political organisation. We have already seen how the structure adopted by the Jamiat has enabled them to resolve the problem posed by the divisions within society; on this count what Massoud is doing is nothing new. On the level of military activity, he has created self-sufficient mobile groups capable of carrying out raids far from their bases, but which, because they travel light, are able to escape capture.

The system is founded on the base, in Panjshir called the *qarargah*. The *qarargah* comprises two types of guerillas: the "locals" (*mahalli*), and the "mobile groups" (*grup-i mutaharek*). The *mahalli* ensure the security and defence of the territory in case of attack; there are several groups in each *qarargah* and they carry on their everyday activities only lightly armed. The *mahalli* elite are gathered together in the *grup-i zarbati* ("shock troops", one for each base, each of 33 men), which is better armed and has undergone regular training. These provide the first line of defence if the area is under attack, and allow time for the others to counter-attack or to withdraw. The *grup-i mutaharek* are professional soldiers, well trained, well armed and provided with uniforms; in each group there are 33 men, usually divided into three sub-groups each with its own commander, his deputy and someone to link with the other groups. Unlike the permanent groups of the bases in the other zones, Massoud's mobile group has no territorial base. Unlike the *ghund*, it is organised as a commando group; the men, unhampered by a lot of equipment, can get around quickly and do not need more logistical support than the resistance can provide. Massoud's groups have proved their usefulness by taking part in fighting some 100 km from their base in Shamali, Andarab, Salang and in Badakhshan. From a strictly military point of view, this is an effective compromise between the lack of mobility of traditional bases and the heavily equipped *ghund*.

Nevertheless, Massoud's model of guerilla warfare has a side-effect on the life of society. This has been the first time since the resistance movement began (except for a few attempts made by the Hizb) that guerillas have carried out operations outside their communal territory. If this development is accepted by the local people, the resistance will have made a great step forward; if not, Soviet methods of pacifying the countryside, which are based upon the assumption that local people, torn between loyalty to a distant government and allegiance to a rival group nearer home will choose the former, will have proved to be well-founded. Everything hinges on whether Massoud (assuming of course that he is not killed in the meantime) can demonstrate that his political astuteness is as great as his ability to organise military campaigns. He has internal as well as external problems. The people of Andarab, traditional rivals of Massoud's Panjshiri, automatically joined the Hizb. In the spring of 1983, Massoud, who was tired of seeing the Andarabi blocking the road from Panjshir each time he carried out an offensive or tried to buy grain, decided to conquer the valley and to disarm the Hizb. The operation was carried out without bloodshed, but when the Soviet offensive took place in 1984, the former members of the Hizb decided to support the government, in revenge for their defeat at the hands of Massoud. A test for Massoud will be the attitude of the people of Panjshir who, so far, have remained very loyal to him, but whom he tends to regard as merely one element in a general equation. Massoud subordinates all other considerations to the logic of military operations, quite unlike certain other leaders, such as Ismael Khan.

Massoud's military organisation has proved its worth, but the other methods mentioned above are closer to traditional Afghan society, which is at one and the same time the source of their strength and their limitations.

Tactics, weapons and communications

Tactics

The resistance has avoided set-piece battles and prefers the tactics of ambush, harassing government posts and political terrorism. Ambushes involve one or two groups; most of the group members provide cover, while those who are carrying RPG7 anti-tank rocket-launchers (rarely more than two on each operation) move forward until they are within a range of less than 100 m, for they rarely use sighting gear. The road has been mined in advance, and the attack is directed at the head of the convoy or at the rear. When the first vehicle has been blown up, each man carrying a rocket-launcher fires off one or two rockets and then withdraws. As soon as the forward unit has rejoined the unit providing cover everyone withdraws in no particular order and without taking many precautions. Usually these ambushes are successful, principally because of the cumbersome nature of Soviet weaponry and the reluctance of Soviet soldiers to take any military initiative, preferring to wait inside their transport vehicles until reinforcements arrive.

Attacks on government posts are noticeably less successful. The Mujahidin never attack in waves, a method which is quite contrary to their spirit of individualism. They usually prefer to get one of their commandos in as near as possible so that he can open fire on any targets that present themselves and then withdraw straight away. The resistance are not very good at handling mortars, nor indeed high-angle weapons, which are mainly used for show. They pepper the post with anti-tank rockets and shells from recoilless guns, which are quite useless against trenches. Because they have no artillery or 120 mm mortars, the guerillas are not in a position to attack Soviet bases, except when the government troops turn a blind eye so that they can infiltrate commandos, which was what happened at Bagram and Jellalabad.

The resistance have few properly-trained commandos to carry out sabotage, or experts who can infiltrate enemy lines and place explosives on strategic objectives, such as electricity power stations. The objectives are attacked in a classical fashion using rockets. Terrorist operations (*terur*) are basically carried out in the towns; in the country attacks can only be directed at those representatives of the government who have no links with the local people, for fear of causing a vendetta, unless a *qazi* has delivered a *fatwa* condemning that person. In short, there is, within combat groups, no attempt to apportion tasks or to specialise in the pursuit of certain objectives. The resistance is short of officers with technical training, or of sergeants who could provide instruction; there is little provision for training recruits and its democratic attitude assumes that everyone is capable of carrying out any task. By Afghan thinking, it is better to have twelve groups fighting once a year than one group fighting once a month. This is the reason why the local bases are so inactive.

For the most part the *sangar* offer extraordinarily little protection. Until 1984, the Afghans did not attempt to dig trenches, although now there are trenches and air raid shelters in the zones where bombing is heaviest. Elsewhere, the best protection is provided by natural caves. Although some bases are better organised than others, on the whole the dominant impression one gets is of a reliance upon improvisation and a generally relaxed attitude.

Nevertheless, it would be a mistake to conclude from all this that the whole military effort is ineffective. Massoud's and 'Abdul Haqq's groups, for instance, are noticeably more efficent (pp. 199 and 192). Secondly, success often comes through the enemy's general ineptness, in that they commit errors or fail to take advantage of opportunities. Finally, and above all, the numbers within the resistance movement and their close links with the people make it possible for them to engage in routine military activities in order to pin down the Russians and the government forces in their bases, which means that the resistance enjoys uncontested political control over the greater part of the country. If one accepts that all guerilla warfare is first and foremost political warfare, it is in these terms that one should assess the strength and the success of the Afghan resistance.

Weapons

The first revolts against the communist government were carried out with an amazing medley of weapons which were already to hand. These included weapons for hand-to-hand fighting, flint rifles and breech-loaders, with Martini-Henris and Lee-Enfields dating from the British colonial period, Nagants from the Czarist period, Soviet weapons and a few Lebels dating from 1886. However, the resistance is much better armed now than it was at the beginning. Indeed, by 1985 striking progress had been made in weaponry, training and organisation. The new weapons come from two sources: some have been captured from the enemy and others have come from outside the country. In both cases they are of Soviet make, manufactured in Russia, China or elsewhere. The proportion of those weapons coming from outside the country and those captured from the enemy varies considerably according to how near the frontier you are, so much so that there is a great difference in the quality of weapons in different areas.

Individual weapons

The basic weapon is still the English Lee-Enfield 303 from the last war, and its American equivalent the Garant, known as "11 shots" (*yazdah-taka* or *yazdah-tir*). These are well-liked for their reliability and their accuracy at long range. The drawback is the cost of the ammunition which can only be obtained from abroad. There are also semi-automatic rifles dating from the fifties: the Simonof rifle made in China, which the Afghans call the "10 shots" (*da-taka*), and the American rifle M-1 (*m-yek*) usually in the possession of the Shi'a, since it comes from Iranian army equipment. The Soviet assault rifle, AK-47, has become the standard weapon of the resistance, at least as far as long-term guerilla fighters are concerned. Known as the *kalashinkof*, it is very well-liked; the ammunition (7.62 calibre), captured from the enemy or sold on the black market by the Russians, is in good supply. A new version, which causes much severer wounds because of its 5.45 calibre, has appeared and is referred to as AK-74, which the Afghans call *kalakof*: it is chiefly found in Panjshir, because it can only be obtained when captured in the fighting against Soviet troops. Those resistance groups which are really short of weapons still carry PPsh (*papasha*): a somewhat rough and ready sub-machine-gun which gained renown at Stalingrad. Some G3 assault rifles come from Iran, where they are manufactured under German licence.

One also finds grenades F1, RDG-5, RG 42, RKG-3M (known as *farashuti*, anti-tank grenade); a grenade is known as *garnet* or *bomb-i dasti*. The revolvers are the Makarov and the Takarev (known as *titi*). All the above have been captured from the enemy.

Collective weapons

First, we have a whole range of machine-guns of 7.62 calibre: RPK, RPD (called *sad-taka*, the "hundred shots") and the Goryunov (known as *gurnuf*). These weapons have been captured either from infantry men, or have been dismantled from destroyed tanks. Finally the standard anti-tank weapon of the Afghan resistance is the rocket-launcher RPG-7, and the simplified version RPG-2; this is easy to manoeuvre, and is now obtained from abroad because the front line Afghan and Soviet units no longer use it.

"Heavy" weapons

In this category we have, first, the famous 12.7 machine-gun DshK, known as *dashaka*; this is relatively light, is easy to take to pieces, does not require a great deal of technical knowledge, and is therefore the prime anti-aircraft weapon. It is not particularly effective in itself, but represents a great threat if it is used to provide concentrated fire, for the Soviet pilots prefer to remain at a high altitude when they know that they are faced with this weapon. But the ammunition is very expensive. The DshK are obtained either from tanks or brought in from abroad (in which case they are Chinese). The Afghans use them in fixed positions and do not take them with them on operations. With the RPG and the AK-47, the DshK is the standard weapon of the resistance movement. Next, especially in the east, come the heavy 14.5 mm KPV /ZPU anti-aircraft machine-guns, with one, two or four barrels (Soviet or Chinese) which the Afghans call *zigo-yek*. However, because they are heavy, difficult to move around and require specialised technical knowledge, these weapons are only useful in those areas where the resistance is well-organised.

The resistance has also a few 82 mm or 81 mm mortars (*hawan*), which are not much used because there is a shortage of ammunition for them and not many people know how to handle them. There are also some 75 mm (Chinese) and 73 and 82 mm (Soviet) recoilless guns (*tup-i bi paslagad*); in this case, too, ammunition is in short supply. In 1985, the Afghans obtained 107 mm ground-to-ground missiles.

SAM-7 (portable anti-aircraft missiles) and 120 mm mortars are rare and once again there is a shortage of people with the necessary technical qualifications. Thus, in terms of quality, the military hardware that the Afghan resistance can call upon is of 14.5 mm calibre for machine-guns and 82 mm for mortars and recoilless guns. This is not enough to endanger the Soviet bases. The decision to stay within these limits is quite clearly a political one. Nevertheless in 1985 there was a big improvement in the military supplies of the resistance.

Transport and communications

All supplies coming from abroad, whether weapons, ammunition or medical supplies, pass through Pakistan. The actual amount received is still extraordinarily low. For example, the Panjshir front receives only six convoys per year. The Panjshir convoys are amongst the largest run by the resistance: from fifty to a hundred horses, carrying a maximum of ten tons on each journey. An ordinary resistance group of twenty men may spend six months at Peshawar, which is the time required to get together their consignment of a dozen AK-47s, an RPG with a dozen rounds and some Lee-Enfield rifles. To bring a DshK back is a major task reserved for highly regarded local commanders. Generally speaking, the parties are not able to handle the logistics by themselves, except for the important fronts like the Jamiat and the Hizb: the commanders have to go in person to the place where the supply of arms is.

In every case, the fronts and the bases have to finance the movement of arms themselves. As we have seen, there is scarcely ever any requisitioning of goods and everything depends upon people's generosity. To take an example, it costs 80,000 *afghanis*, or 1,500 dollars, for a group of twenty Mujahidin, travelling on foot, to transport a DshK with its ammunition from Pakistan to Maymana. The weapons are delivered either to the party headquarters or to the Afghan frontier. Then the group fends for itself. The only problems they face are Soviet helicopters and ambushes, and Hekmatyar's Hizb groups, who specialise in confiscating weapons. The other parties allow all the groups to pass freely through their territory, although a few local chiefs insist on a small payment. Usually the routes they follow are the traditional paths used by nomads and by merchants before the main roads were made up.

It is somewhat of a paradox that the precautions taken are very elementary. Only particular regions, like Logar, are crossed quickly and by night. This is because the Russians, although they have increased their pressure on the communication network of the resistance, have insufficient soldiers to be able to close the tracks completely. In any case, the nature of the countryside makes any effective blockade impossible. There is no Ho-chi-minh trail as far as the resistance is concerned, especially as one travels further south, where the desert makes the very idea of a track unthinkable. When the Russians carry out military operations against a specific route the only result is that they interrupt the convoy traffic for a few days or a few weeks. It is not a catastrophe for the resistance: their weaponry is so unsophisticated that the fact that the supply network is disorganised does not seem to bother them. The Russians were only able to blockade the direct route to Badakhshan by occupying Koran-o Munjan in 1982, for here the altitude makes it difficult to find other routes. Finally, Afghans are never in a hurry: if the journey takes one or two weeks longer that is not really a problem. In short, if they are ever to get a stranglehold on the resistance, which consists mainly of groups which are a law unto themselves, the USSR must pour in many more men and improve the quality of their techniques of detection, and this, at the moment, they show no sign of doing, although the possibility cannot be ruled out for the future.

News travels in the form of rumour, written reports (duly stamped, dated and signed) and through BBC broadcasts, which still represent the main source of news for the resistance. There is no resistance radio. Radio Free-Kabul was on the air for a while and was very popular, but did not last for long: technical and staff problems were too complex.

The different fronts of the resistance are still very much isolated, not on account of danger, but merely of time. You can only travel in Afghanistan if you are willing to take your time about it. Everything takes a long time to decide and to get going. Even though in the south and the centre there are motor vehicles, journeys on horseback and on foot are still the most usual ways of getting about. It is a slow war. The Afghan resistance is still one of the least well equipped in the world, especially considering the political stakes that are involved. As for weapons, their levels of supplies are far below that of the Palestinians, the Eritreans and the anti-Sandinistas. It is a resistance organised by poor people in a war waged by the poor.

Chapter Twelve

Military operations

The war map

For the Russians there are three Afghanistans: strategic Afghanistan, the Iranian glacis and the areas in which they have no interest. As we know, the resistance has not deployed its troops in line with strategic considerations. Soviet disposition of troops and strategy determines the military activity of the resistance, who only become involved in fighting when Soviet units appear inside their territory. When there are only government troops, a modus vivendi is soon established between the two sides.

Strategic Afghanistan

That part of Afghanistan which is of strategic importance is shaped somewhat like an hour-glass in which the Salang Pass is the neck. It includes the northern plains from Shibergan to Kunduz, the strategic road from Termez to Kabul and from Kabul to Jellalabad, the capital and its immediate environs as far as Logar. It is a rich, well-populated area, which has the only geological resources in the country that could be exploited in the immediate future by the Russians (gas and oil fields at Shibergan and copper mines at Aynak in Logar). This is where the main urban centres are (except for Herat and Kandahar). Finally, it is the main route to India.

The Russians have built two of their three major bases there (Bagram and Kilagay). This is the only region in Afghanistan where they have established a series of small military posts along the road, and most of their troops are concentrated in this area. Their tasks are to ensure the safety of the capital, to keep the road open, and to carry out clearing-up operations in order to contain or destroy the resistance strongholds.

This strategic area is bordered by resistance strongholds, mostly belonging to the Jamiat but also to the Hizb, whose general staff are often placed quite near the Soviet positions. At Mazar-i Sharif the Zabiullah front controls the gorges which overlook the town. In Badakhshan the

Qazi Islamuddin and Basir fronts are located at Iskamesh and Yaftal, and they control, and indeed regularly cut, the road from Kunduz to Fayzabad, and thus the mountainous area of Badakhshan remains outside the Soviet strategic zone. Then there is Baghlan (Hizb, with Sayyad Mansur) and Andarab, which alternates between the Hizb and the Jamiat. To the south of Salang, we have, of course, the Panjshir front, whose mobile groups were, at the end of 1983, developing without hinderance in Shamali, Salang and Andarab. They were responsible for most of the ambushes of convoys carried out at that time. In the western sector of the road, the Ghorband valley is firmly held by the Hizb. Kohestan has been paralysed by rivalry between the two parties, but Shamali, which is mostly controlled by the Jamiat, is a very active zone.

The fronts to the south and the east of the capital belong to another resistance area. The region of Kabul has groups belonging to all the parties; the most active being Khalis' Hizb led by 'Abdul Haqq, whom we shall refer to again in connection with urban terrorism (p. 192). Nangrahar is Khalis' stronghold, and it is well-organised, militant and active. The general staff is at Tora-Bora, in the "White Mountain" on the frontier with Pakistan. This is bombed regularly, and it was here that the first Soviet pilot was captured in July 1981. Khalis maintains a constant pressure on the area and on Jellalabad.

The situation is more complex in Logar, which is the last sector within the strategic part of Afghanistan. The Russians have a base at Pul-i Alam, in the Logar plain. They regularly carry out large operations designed to clear the guerillas out of the area. The political situation in the resistance is marked by fragmentation, but generally relations between the parties are good. Nevertheless, the resistance has not been able to agree upon a common military commander; the main Mujahidin tactic is to withdraw while the Soviet offensive is going on and then reoccupy the territory immediately afterwards. Paktya became one of the fiercest battlefields in 1985.

The Iranian glacis

In the west of Afghanistan, along the Herat–Kandahar axis, the Soviets have a large number of troops based at Shindand, but these are much less mobile than those in the east of the country. The aim here is not to hold the territory, but to establish a buffer zone between Afghanistan and Iran and to protect the airfield at the Shindand base, which directly threatens the Persian Gulf. The fear of a long-term Iranian threat can clearly be seen by the sensitivity of the Soviet press since the banning of the Tudeh in April 1983.[1] While Pakistan could never represent a threat to the

Soviet Union, Iran, a centralised state, which has a long-established national tradition, aspires to be a great regional power. The Russians have a division at Herat, Shindand and Kandahar and airborne battalions at Bost, Girishk and Lashkargah. The large numbers of airborne troops and airstrips bears no relation to the level of Afghan resistance here, which, although active, is not a threat to Soviet bases. The Russians in this region carry out local cleaning-up operations in the area around their base. They do not, as in Panjshir, seek to dislodge the resistance from its strongholds, nor to nibble away at their territory, but to get a stranglehold on the resistance, which is all the more vulnerable because it is fighting in the plain. There are many government supporters at Adraskan and Lashkargah.

Between Kandahar and Herat geography and tribalism combine to enable local fronts to consist of distinct, homogeneous strongholds, mostly Harakat, and separated by semi-desert areas. A large number of parties are represented in the oasis of Kandahar, the second most important town in the country, but amongst the multitude of bases there a few Khalis and Jamiat fronts are emerging. The resistance is very active at Herat (a Jamiat stronghold) and Kandahar, where they regularly control more than half the town. In 1984, the Russians set about systematically destroying the approaches to Herat and Kandahar and every day sees new fighting which is just as intense as that in Panjshir.

Unaffected areas

Large tracts of the country have never seen Soviet incursions. Most of this area is in the central massif, except for Chakhcharan and Bamyan. The last time the Russians tried to cross Hazarajat was in the summer of 1980, and they tried to get to Chakhcharan from Shindand the following year. In the centre, there are government posts, only in the two places mentioned above and Tulak, Tirinkot, Darrah-yi Souf and Obe. Chesht was recaptured by the resistance in December 1983. Nuristan, Upper-Laghman, and two-thirds of Badakhshan have only experienced occasional bombing. Finally, the frontier in the south (from Urgun) and west of Afghanistan as far as Shindand has only experienced intermittent patrols by helicopters and armoured vehicles: only the frontier post of Spin Buldak (between Kandahar and Quetta) and Kang, the regional capital of Nimruz, are firmly under Soviet control.

These regions, which are vast and thinly populated, are considered to be of no strategic value; it is better to leave them alone rather than to pin down large numbers of troops who would be very exposed because the lines of communication would be over-stretched. As a result, since there is no enemy, the network of resistance bases is much weaker there than elsewhere and the most able-bodied men often mount guard at the "frontier", waiting for an offensive which never comes. The drawback for the Russians is that these regions provide the resistance with long but safe lines of communication, a place to fall back to and a source of supplies in case of hardship. Furthermore, the fact that they control a certain amount of territory adds to their credibility.

Individual cases

Kabul and guerilla warfare

Kabul is the only area where the Russians exercise satisfactory control, the Khad is well organised and has its informers in every social circle. The Afghans know next to nothing about underground resistance and are ill-suited to this kind of combat, being somewhat indiscreet. In the autumn of 1982, the Russians seized a list of 600 members of the underground networks run by Massoud, and as a result he had to spend a year reorganising these groups. The presence of rough country only a few kilometres from the capital acts as a magnet to the militants who are more at ease in open action, and this has proved an obstacle to the setting up of a real underground network. Next, a section of the urban intelligentsia was linked to SAMA, the organisation which developed from the Maoist movement. The execution of its charismatic leader, Majid Kalakani, in the spring of 1980, was a grievous blow to the organisation, and led to a political crisis, involving many splits, old scores being settled and many people going over to the government side. As a result many underground networks disappeared. This is not to say that there is no armed opposition at Kabul, but when there is it comes from the resistance bases just outside the town. In fact, underground activity, a section of the resistance controlled by 'Abdul Haqq in the south, greatly increased in and around Kabul in 1984. Usually their operations involve small groups acting at night on information received; their objectives are government patrols, but especially officers and party members, or well-known government sympathisers (singers who perform on the radio, *'ulama* and people who hold honorary posts). 'Abdul Haqq, based at Shiwaki, has been carrying out operations actually inside the town on a much higher level of activity: attacks on police stations, factories, military posts and ministries, including even the Russian Embassy, using groups of up to fifty men. A coordinated assault which took place during the night of the 13–14 August 1983 had as its target Radio-Kabul, Mikrorayon (the Russian quarter) and the Bala-Hissar garrison. At the same time, SAM-7 missiles and rockets began to appear, and there was nightly shelling in the summer of 1985.

Such pressure exerted against the town is possible because the resistance has well-protected strongholds just a few kilometres away: Paghman, a former summer resort in the mountains, held by supporters of Sayyaf (a native of Paghman); Shiwaki, the southern suburb, and the Koh-i Safi, a mountain massif in the north-east. The Russians have been unable to make much impression on these strongholds, in spite of the severity that they have consistently shown towards the Paghman area, where a series of military posts defended by artillery and helicopters has been set up. The cordoning off of Kabul has not been successfully achieved, and their control over the hinterland is correspondingly more insecure. The resistance has many sympathisers in the urban population, the army and the administration, perhaps because, on the whole, fighters find indiscriminate terrorism distasteful. No bombs are left to go off in crowded places and no bursts of random machine-gun fire take place, except in places such as the cinema or airport which are almost always only frequented by government agents.

Paktya
Paktya is the only region where intense fighting has taken place without the Russians being directly involved. Until 1984, the Russians avoided engaging in operations along the frontier of Pakistan. While they do not hesitate any longer to create pressure in the frontier zone, they do not need to be present in force in Paktya, the only region where the government army is effective, for its elite is bogged down there. The best soldiers in the Khalq come from the tribal areas, particularly from Paktya, so the government troops there are well-motivated and know the countryside in great detail. On the resistance side, the most formidable force is the Jadran tribe, organised militarily by Khalis' Hizb and led by Jallaluddin Haqani. The government forces hold Urgun, Khost and Jaji Maydan, where they have many supporters amongst the population. The resistance has blockaded the roads (including the famous road from Gardez to Khost which was strewn with broken-down tanks) and only just failed to capture two towns in a siege which lasted from August to October 1983. Increasing pressure on Khost forced the Russians to launch a strong but unsuccessful offensive in August 1985.

Chakhcharan
Chakhcharan is the only example of a Soviet base isolated in the heart of resistance territory; it is the capital of Ghur province, and has a bazaar

and an airport where a number of armoured helicopters are stationed, as well as a motorised battalion. In addition it has 1,500 civilians and a government battalion. People are forbidden to go in or out of the base and it is permanently besieged by groups of Aymaq Hizb, who are poorly armed but very active. The method chosen to defend the base is to bomb the villages within a radius of 30 km, and although the civilian population has suffered grievous losses it has remained where it is.

Soviet strategy and the history of military operations

The aim of Soviet policy is to draw Afghanistan little by little into the Soviet orbit by playing on the war-weariness of the people and by strengthening, slowly but surely, the state machine at Kabul. To go beyond this level of hostilities would oblige the USSR to increase its manpower commitment drastically, and would cause regional tension to mount to an uncontrollable degree. The Soviet strategy is to employ a classical army with a strong firepower, and the Afghan political police, the Khad, which is directly answerable to the KGB. Its task is to encourage the Afghan tradition of warring factions, in order to exacerbate quarrels in the resistance movement and to swing groups behind the government, not on an ideological basis but on the basis of local rivalries between *qawm* and *khan*. The army's and the Khad's tactics have gone hand-in-hand from the very beginning. Parallel to this strategy, the government has attempted to get the support of influential people and certain sections of the tribes; the first offers of truces and individual peace treaties made to tribal leaders date from the autumn of 1980.

It is possible to distinguish four phases in the evolution of the fighting, which correspond to the regimes of Brezhnev, Andropov, Tchernenko and Gorbatchev. Not that these regimes represented radically different policies, for the phases were complementary. At the most, there was a difference in emphasis. The Brezhnev period involved classical operations in which the enemy was underestimated, the Andropov era saw the rise of politics and policing, and the Tchernenko period was marked by the harshness of its military operations and by its lack of subtlety. Gorbatchev's era is a combination of both military showdown and political manipulation.

The Soviet army

The 40th Soviet army stationed in Afghanistan had in 1983 about 110,000 men, in addition to military advisors and at least three divisions based in Soviet territory but taking part in the fighting in Afghanistan.

This army has more than eight mechanised divisions and two parachute divisions reinforced by several brigades. The army committed to Afghanistan does not differ in any way from the other Soviet armies: it has the same multi-ethnic policy of recruitment, the same kind of weapons, and the same training. Since the Soviet forces undergo rigorous but very stereotyped and mechanical training to fit them for a classical war in Europe, it is not surprising that they are not well prepared for guerilla warfare. The main weaknesses of the Soviet army are its over-centralisation, the absence of initiative, the weight of its armour, the low level of logistics, poor relations between soldiers and officers (and between war recruits and veterans) and the prevalence of generally irresponsible attitudes. The soldier is unwilling to fight far from his armoured vehicle (in a mountainous area), there are few commandos and no foot patrols. The black market flourishes and morale is low, except in the parachute brigade, which is much more willing to engage in combat.

On the other hand, the Soviet army has very great firepower and has progressively learnt to make use of its technical superiority in a more intelligent and coordinated fashion, although this does not mean that it has effected a sudden revolution in combat tactics, or military strategy, nor has it modified its military structure. Routine activity is patrolling; the regiment moves slowly along roads which are likely to be attacked but does not deviate from them. As reprisals the airforce bombs and the artillery bombards villages suspected of harbouring Mujahidin, although they do not always show a willingness to follow up this operation by an attack on the ground. Finally, the typical offensive operation of the Soviet army is a combined land-air attack, which links the massive transport of troops by helicopter to the rear of the guerilla forces with a slow advance of armoured vehicles to try to trap the guerillas in their net.

The tactical improvements have to do with the speed in which the operation is able to get underway, an increased transport capacity for the troops travelling by helicopter and fighting without the support of the armoured vehicles, the use of high altitude bombers (TU 16) and slow bombers (SU 25), the greater use of ambushes by day and by night, and a greater ability to carry out operations in very different areas, that is to say a more rational use of combatant troops. The elite troops (paratroopers) are now used extensively.

The policy of pacification

This policy is carried out by the secret police, the Khad. Far from being the usual type of communist subversion, it involves an attempt to gain influential support by making use of traditional tribal rivalries, a policy in a direct line of descent from those followed by the British in the nineteenth century. The people whose support they hope to get are offered sinecures and honorary posts; they are gathered into the patriotic front (*jabha-yi padarwatan*), and guerillas who belong to their *qawm* are transformed into government militia. The Khad usually make contact with someone of local importance who belongs to the resistance and whose rivalry with some other leader in the resistance is well known; the contact is usually made through the intermediary of a pro-government member of the same *qawm*. The Khad then proposes a mutual "non-aggression treaty". The person in question is confirmed as leader of the *qawm*, and he receives weapons and subsidies without having to agree to any ideological conditions. All he has to do is to prevent the Mujahidin from using his territory and allow the government to re-establish the state machine there. The goal, therefore, is not to carry revolution into the countryside, but simply to "pacify" the area, in the strict sense of the term: to bring the hostilities to an end.

This policy only applies to the countryside and not to Kabul, where, on the contrary, the people are the object of a campaign of sovietisation: this involves cutting them off from their cultural roots and inducing a sharp break with traditional society. Propaganda campaigns and long stays in the USSR are directed not at people of influence but at young people who it is hoped will, in the long term, provide the social base for the new government. Soviet policy has intentionally broadened the gap between town and country.

Classical war and counter-insurgency

The fact that the Russians are having only limited success is due to the contradiction in the two aspects of their strategy. Everything that happens indicates that the Khad's activities and the military operations are planned without coordination. For example, militia groups raised locally with great difficulty are decimated within rifle shot of the Soviet base without any reaction from the troops; and a Soviet offensive is carried out as if it were a training exercise, without any consideration of the complexity of the local situation. Nevertheless, the Russians are very well informed about the positions and movements of the guerilla forces, who have no idea what secrecy and caution mean. It seems, nevertheless, that the Russians find it difficult to take advantage of this information by getting active combat groups into the field immediately, because of the slowness which is a traditional feature of Soviet troop movements, and because the command is too highly centralised, so that it is always necessary to have a programme worked out in advance.

The Soviet press quotes examples of officers speaking local languages, living close to the people and engaging in social work, but we have found no confirmation of this. It seems, on the contrary, that the army as such is there in a purely technical capacity and takes no interest in the civilian population.

On the other hand, any anti-guerilla strategy presupposes the raising of an independent native army and militia. But the goal of handing over responsibility for the fighting to the Afghans themselves is far from being reached. Due to the number of deserters, the government army has scarcely ever topped 30,000 men, in comparison with the 100,000 which were planned for; it is still not very reliable, in spite of the fact that there are a few competent brigades. Obligatory call-up has alienated thousands of young people, who had no particular liking for the resistance but who desert as soon as they are able. The local militia remain static, and, while they are able to prevent the resistance making headway locally, they are not the stuff of which mobile units are made.

The timing of the large-scale offensives

While there is always some fighting going on everywhere, large-scale Soviet offensives always take place from May to June and from September to October in the "strategic area" and between Herat and Kandahar. In 1980, the only large-scale operations were designed to free the main roads from guerilla activity, without the use of helicopters to convey the troops. Convoys of soldiers attempted to reopen the main arteries through the country; Kunar in February, Paktya in March, the route from the interior to Hazarajat in July–August, Logar and, with great regularity, the tarmac road from Kabul to Kandahar, but they were unable to spread out away from the main routes. The Russians also tried to clear the area around their bases: the region round Ghazni was attacked in May and the first two offensives against Panjshir took place shortly afterwards (April and October); in November it was the turn of Nangrahar, and the region of Surkhrud was destroyed. In July the Russians dropped a massive quantity of small anti-personnel plastic mines along the tracks leading to Pakistan: the main victims of this activity were children and animals.

In 1981, the Russians reduced the level of their activity and concentrated on clearing the strategic zones. Troop units transported by helicopters made an appearance but only played a minor role; in contrast, aerial bombing became regular and intensive. The targets were the same as in the previous year: Logar, the Kabul region, with extremely violent fighting at Paghman, Kandahar and Nangrahar. Panjshir experienced the third and fourth offensives in April and the beginning of September. The results for the Russians were disappointing, but there was widespread destruction and the number of people pouring into Pakistan as refugees increased.

In the winter of 1981–2 bombing became even more intense, and this was accompanied by the cordoning off of the target zone by mechanised units which gradually advanced to try and overwhelm the resistance. This tactic was used at Kandahar, Herat and in Shamali. There were many civilian losses. In the spring the resistance regained the initiative on most fronts. There were two offensives against Panjshir in 1982 (May and August), which exceeded anything which the Russians had attempted up to that time. For the first time, the essence of the strategy was to land helicopter-borne units within a period of a few hours on the mountain ridges; the armoured vehicles only occupied the valley after this had been carried out and there were fewer of them than on preceding occasions. These offensives met with a rebuff and the Soviet troops withdrew in December to the entrance of the Rokha valley. In August the resistance massacred some government sympathisers who had come to celebrate the "liberation" of Paghman. In contrast, Logar suffered an offensive in June which produced a high casualty rate amongst the civilian population whom the resistance were unable to protect.

In 1983, no large-scale Soviet offensives took place. A number of clearing operations occurred in Logar (January) at Herat (April), and Ghazni (June). Shamali was heavily bombed in May and in October. At Kandahar, the Russians recaptured the government post at Khakrez, 50 km to the north of the town. Also in 1983 a truce was declared between Massoud and the Russians, and the resistance in Paktya, still led by Jellaluddin Haqani, laid siege to the two towns of Khost and Urgun at the end of July. A new element now appeared: the Mangal, Jaji, Tani and Waziri tribes which had, until then, been passive, took an active part in the fighting, the first three under the flag of Gaylani and the Waziri for the Jamiat. This sudden uprush of activity coincided with the King Zahir's appeal on 22 June for a united front, and rumours went round that the Royalists intended to set up a provisional government in a liberated Khost; it is certain that Gaylani was receiving great quantities of arms at that time. Khost was not captured and the local militia threw their support behind the resistance, in word if not in deed. But by October the Tani had withdrawn from the coalition because of a tribal rivalry with the Jadran, and, as winter came on, many guerillas went back home. At the end of December the government army, which had arrived from Gardez, raised the siege of the two towns and recaptured Jaji-Maydan. The newly active tribes followed the usual pattern of tribal warfare in every detail, periods of fierce fighting alternating with movements of withdrawal. The Russians did not intervene directly in the battle for Khost but the policy of penetrating the resistance in order to syphon off support reached its high point in 1983.

In contrast, 1984 represented a return to a purely military conception of the war, but this time with a more seasoned army, more troops and a clear intention to fight with no holds barred. The Russians, with their Panjshir offensive of 21 April, brought about an escalation in the level of fighting. Was this because of the failure of the pacification programme? Was it a by-product of the generally aggressive nature of Soviet policy in the world? Or a return to well-tried remedies through inertia? It is too early to be sure. 1985 saw two big but ineffective offensives against Panjshir in June and Paktya in August.

The offensives against Panjshir

The first four offensives carried out in Panjshir were classical ones and only involved a single column of armoured vehicles preceded by aerial bombing; the operations were very much like those carried out elsewhere in Afghanistan. The three other offensives (May–July, August–September 1982; 21 April 1984) showed by the scale of the attack, the number of soldiers involved and the tactics employed that Massoud's Panjshir had become the prime target. The three offensives were all planned in the same way: the operation relied upon troops flown in by helicopter, and often some paratroopers as well, taking up positions right behind the enemy lines on the crest of the valleys, in the villages and along the mountain tracks; shortly afterwards these troops received support from an armoured column. On each of these three occasions, Massoud's strategy consisted in withdrawing his troops into the neighbouring valleys, allowing the Russians to spread out, then recapturing their positions one by one, mostly after they had been handed over to the government army.

In January 1983, the Russians offered Massoud a truce. No doubt they thought that in exchange for being left in control of his own region he would be content to remain there, an attitude usually adopted in the Afghan resistance. But Massoud realised that there was no point in having strongholds if they did not threaten Soviet strategy, and there was no hope of exerting political or military pressure if he was not prepared to operate outside his own territory and create a supra-regional organisation. Constant pressure from Soviet troops prevented Massoud from breaking out, but the truce offered him the opportunity to do so. While scrupulously observing the truce in Panjshir, he organised fronts in the north-east, disarmed the Hizb in Andarab, got Sayyed Mansur's group in Baghlan behind him, tried to make an alliance with Niyazi's group in Kohestan, and persuaded the Jamiat commanders in Baghlan to adopt his military tactics.

The Soviet generals realised their error (unless it was the KGB that forced the truce upon them): it was now urgent to "crush" Massoud. Moreover, this military necessity coincided with a general hardening of the Soviet attitude which led to increased pressure on Pakistan and a return to the earlier attitude which saw the solution to the conflict in purely military terms.

The Soviet offensive in Panjshir in 1984 was the largest since the beginning of the war. At the end of the offensive, the Russians occupied one-third of Panjshir valley up to and including the villages of Astana and Barak, as well as the lower Andarab valley. But Massoud was still alive and for the most part his guerilla force was intact. The civilian population of Panjshir had left the main valley. The methods used were noticeably more effective than hitherto and makes it seem likely that the offensive was decided upon at the highest level in the Kremlin. TU 16 medium-altitude bombers (8,000 m) engaged in blanket bombing over the whole of Panjshir. Their attack was but the beginning. About 20,000 Soviet soldiers were involved and 5,000–6,000 government troops. At the beginning of April, a group of commandos specially selected from the Khad failed in an attempt to assassinate Massoud.

The full offensive was launched on 21 April. Troops were transported by helicopter to the ridges of the valleys at the same time as an armoured column made its way up the Andarab and Panjshir valleys. Other troops were transported by helicopter to the Anjuman pass, in the depths of the Panjshir valley and to Khost-i Fering, which was where the Russians thought the guerillas intended to withdraw to. The armoured column reached Banu in Andarab and Astana in Panjshir without any difficulty. But when the Russians attacked the neighbouring valleys, where Massoud's mobile groups had withdrawn, they suffered heavy losses. In May they abandoned Khost-i Fering, but strengthened their position in lower Panjshir. The journalists who later visited Panjshir saw a valley which had been destroyed and emptied of its population, but two-thirds of which was still held by Massoud's men, who had become hardened in combat and were now even more ready to fight than before. The Russians then adopted a new tactic. In the morning, units of up to five hundred soldiers were transported by helicopter to encircle a village, without the support of armoured vehicles; the village was searched and the members of the resistance, a list of whose names was in the possession of the Russians, were arrested; the unit withdrew before nightfall. It became more difficult for the resistance to concentrate its troops and to prepare ambushes against troops who were as mobile as this.

The Soviet goal was not to occupy the territory, but to destroy, or at least to get a stranglehold on, the enemy forces. Their plan was to cut the lines of communication and block the escape routes. Next they would attack the heart of the enemy position, and pursue them into the neighbouring valleys. There the resistance would have to turn and fight, or to retreat further, where a larger contingent was waiting for them on the outer limits of the region. What did the Russians achieve from this policy? The end result was nothing more nor less than a return to the status quo of autumn 1982, on the eve of the truce, and to achieve this they suffered heavy losses. As it turned out it was a setback for the Russians.

How was Massoud able to avoid this trap? He had a general idea of how the Russians intended to proceed and he knew more or less the date when the offensive was going to begin, but he underestimated the scale of the attack. What he had to do was obvious: he had to completely evacuate Panjshir, establish a base for his men in the north-east sector of the territory and avoid any outright clashes; he also realised that he must focus his attacks on the Soviet lines of communication, that is to say on the main road from Kabul to Termez. He had always been aware that his men might be trapped in the Panjshir valley. There was no purpose to be served in defending a stronghold; people tend to forget that guerilla warfare is not at all the same as trench warfare and there is not much point in capturing territory. In November Massoud began to evacuate the civilian population (about 30,000 of the 100,000 people who had lived in the valley before the war). In February, he evacuated his troops, although a small detachment remained close to the Soviet base of Anawa, at the entrance to the valley. On 20 April, the day before the offensive began, mobile guerilla groups wiped out a whole convoy at the foot of Salang. When the Russians attacked, there was scarcely anybody left in Panjshir. Massoud delayed his counter-attack until the Soviet forces had dispersed and their lines of communication were over-stretched.

Even though the quantity of men and materials involved in the attack had taken Massoud by surprise, he was able to withdraw and preserve the core of his forces. In any case, Massoud spreading his influence throughout the north-east was a greater danger to the Russians than when he was shut up in his stronghold in Panjshir. Moreover, the closing of the supply lines was not an insurmountable problem, in that the resistance's unsophisticated weapons makes it less dependant on supplies from outside and also because other lines of communication – longer, it is true, but just as dependable – can be opened up. When the truce was agreed, Panjshir was only receiving six convoys per year. Finally, the outcome of this offensive revealed just how reliable Massoud's information sources were.

In 1985 Massoud's military organisation was the best in Afghanistan. He took the government base of Pushghur in half an hour with fifty men, and the Soviet commandos were unable to rescue the 126 officers made prisoner.

The resistance and Soviet prisoners

When the invasion occurred, the Mujahidin considered every Soviet soldier as a militant communist and took no prisoners. Since then the attitude of the guerillas has changed, as has their perception of the USSR. Discussions with Soviet soldiers who are also Muslims, and the distinctly unwarlike attitude of most of the soldiers (lack of enthusiasm for the war and unwillingness to fight, their participation in the black market) has convinced the Afghans that the Soviet soldiers are not well-motivated, have been tricked into fighting and couldn't really care less about spreading communism throughout the world. At the same time, the fact that they have no money, and that they are ready to steal military equipment in order to exchange it for goods, has persuaded the Afghans that the USSR, far from being a developed country, is, on the contrary, a poor one. The Soviet soldier is therefore usually thought of as an "unlucky beggar" rather than as an enemy. Deserters and even prisoners who have offered no resistance are almost immediately offered the chance of taking up arms again. Those who refuse are handed over, without much difficulty, to the Red Cross, which keeps them in Switzerland for two years before asking them to choose between political asylum and repatriation. The Afghans would like to be able to exchange prisoners, but the Russians are adamantly against this. The change of attitude on the part of the resistance dates from July 1981, when Khalis' guerillas captured a pilot who was handed over by the Pakistanis to the Soviet Embassy.

The Soviet prisoners are always well treated; only Hekmatyar's Hizb exert great pressure on them in order to try and convert them. Elsewhere they are not placed under close surveillance. The leaders of the resistance understand the political advantage to be derived from adopting a humanitarian attitude towards prisoners; such a policy improves the image of the resistance and encourages others to desert. But in any case the people are friendly by nature: one of the paradoxes of this war is that one often finds prisoners being treated as guests. Holding people in captivity is foreign both to Islamic law and to common law; you either get killed or you are treated as a guest.

The number of prisoners and deserters taken altogether during the period 1980 to 1984 is no more than a hundred; the proportion of Muslims amongst them is higher than the average number of Muslims in the expeditionary force, which indicates that Soviet Muslims are very much the Achilles heel of the USSR. It is probable that the resistance will increase this output of propaganda directed at Soviet soldiers, and more especially that beamed at the Muslim republics within the Soviet Union.

The long-term potential of the resistance

The military dimension

There is no possibility of the resistance being crushed by military might. The guerilla forces are never concentrated in one place, if only because of the factions within society. Even if the Russians get better at moving around quickly in search-and-destroy operations, they will not succeed in surrounding and wiping out the Mujahidin in any significant numbers. The very flimsiness of the military infrastructure of the resistance (lack of artillery, depots, training camps or centralised general staff) means that there are no military objectives. All that the Russians can hope to do is to carry out a war of attrition in which they would aim to drive a wedge between the civilian population and the resistance and then, once the latter have been forced to withdraw into the mountains, to slowly draw the noose tight around them. This policy envisages massive reprisals being taken against villagers who shelter the resistance and it also assumes that the Soviet troops will become sufficiently mobile so that the people will no longer feel secure in the protection provided by their sanctuary. The challenge for the Mujahidin is whether they can establish more flexible links between their military organisation and the civilian population, so that civilian morale does not suffer; and whether they will be able to withstand the pressure on them when the number of Soviet troops increases. Up to now, as we have seen, the guerillas mostly live amongst the people, although they do not have the means of protecting their fellow citizens when there is a full-scale attack. The existence of safe havens, like Hazarajat, is due to the fact that the Russians have no wish to occupy large tracts of territory, and is not a measure of the resistance's ability to keep Soviet troops out. These havens give the resistance the illusion that it is invincible and prevent it from coming to terms with the next stage of the fighting, which will inevitably be reached when the Russians pour in more troops. In these pseudo-havens the resistance lives quite openly and mingles with the civilian population. As there is no underground organisation they are incapable of providing a flexible response to the enemy; they fight and then they run away. Up to the present, because of limited Soviet operations, it has been possible to flee and return a few weeks later in order to carry on as before. But if the Russians adopt a higher profile, not by establishing themselves permanently in the locality, but by constantly sending out mobile patrols which only stay for a few days, or even for just a few hours, and which, acting on information received, systematically destroy the houses of the resistance leaders and take selective reprisals against the villages, then it will no longer be possible for civilian life to continue as if nothing was happening. Nevertheless, in Panjshir, as at Kandahar, the experiences of the armed guerilla groups living outside the populated areas have been encouraging.

The resistance should set up an underground organisation, so that when the Russians come to occupy the territory there are already underground groups in existence. The idea of going underground presupposes that the resistance has adopted purely political criteria which have little to do with the existing hierarchies within society, for it is impossible to imagine the *'ulama* or the *khan* operating secretly. But, although society has changed a good deal during the war, it has not changed that much. The degree of inflexibility which characterises traditional society helps to nullify the ideological influence of the communists, but it also means that it is very fragile in times of crisis. This is why the number of Afghan refugees exceeds that of any other nation on earth. There has been an overwhelming rejection of the present government, but the ability of society to adapt to the war is more limited, and so the only way of demonstrating this rejection is to emigrate. The second challenge is that it will be necessary for them to put into the field mobile patrols and professional soldiers, which will be the only way to counter the greater degree of mobility that the Soviet army now has. As we know, great tact is always necessary when guerillas seek to operate beyond the confines of their communal territory, for local rivalries may well result in the local population, cast in the roles of unwilling hosts, to rally behind the government – at least for a time – in order to get rid of the intruders. Even though these changes of allegiance on a local level are short-lived, they are sufficiently serious to make it impossible to set up a widely ranging liberation army. Thus, the military problems faced by the resistance are at root political problems.

In fact, on the strictly military level, the two weaknesses of the resistance are their lack of military supplies and the length of their lines of communication with Pakistan. Although heavy armaments are increasingly being supplied, these would only have a role to play if a genuine liberation army were established. As for the second, at their present troop levels, the Russians are nowhere near being able to exercise effective control over the lines of communication. If they brought many more troops in, the only way that the resistance could cope would be by coordinating – which in effect means centralising the control of – the activities of the mobile groups, again a political problem. Nevertheless, it will always be extremely difficult for the Russians to control the lines of communication, whatever the resistance's degree of effectiveness.

Thus, on the military level, the war could have two possible outcomes. Either the resistance will not achieve the vital step of creating mobile groups, in which case the war of attrition will continue for a number of years without any noticeable increase in the level of military activity – which situation will increasingly be to the advantage of the Russians. Or, the resistance will succeed in taking this step and the Russians will either have to intensify the war or negotiate.

The political dimension

A powerful factor influencing the outcome of the war will be whether or not the factionalism of the resistance (encouraged by the Khad) gains the upper hand over the forces making for a broader unity. Another key issue is whether the government will be more successful in consolidating its position than the resistance in maintaining its dynamism.

To what extent will the resistance be able to defend itself against the political infiltration of its ranks by the *qawm* network? The first line of defence is Islam itself, since the government is still seen by most people as being atheistic. Next, the very existence of factions provides a sturdy obstacle to such penetration: for example, an Afghan can only act within his *qawm*, thus a deserter, a potential infiltrator, will be sent back to his village, where he is known. The existence of factions can be double-edged: government agents infiltrating the resistance do so through the *qawm* network and not through the parties. The resistance also uses this network to penetrate the government. In short, while the existence of factions is an indubitable fact of Afghan political life, it is something which may be used for ulterior ends. Everything depends upon which way the wind is blowing. So long as the resistance is seen to be a dynamic force and so long as it is more dangerous to be a government agent than a member of the Mujahidin, so long will communal loyalties work, on the whole, in favour of the resistance. It is evident that the government has only been able to gain support in those places where the resistance was already in decline – a decline that cannot necessarily be put down to the activity of the Khad, but which can just as easily be explained by local feuds. If, therefore, the government is to successfully infiltrate the resistance, using the secret police and adopting political methods, it will first be necessary for it to have gained a firm hold on the local population.

The resistance is capable of offering a universal ideal which provides the only hope of overcoming its disunity: this ideal is represented by a common ideology (Islam) and political parties. It is hampered by the fact that it has few intellectuals, the *'ulama* are ageing and there is no clear party organisation. As we have seen, in some cases the character of the party can be entirely determined by the factions – the *qawm* – in its midst. Conversely, to press ahead too rapidly with the creation of parties and military structures on a national level may offend those groups which still cling to tradition and push them into the arms of the government, which is now seeking the support of influential families and playing the card of tradition for all it is worth. The resistance must take care not to disrupt the pattern of social life, as the communists did in 1978. The temptation to do this is particularly strong for Islamist intellectuals such as Massoud. In short, the resistance must chart a middle course between the Scylla of allowing itself to be submerged in a sea of petty local rivalries, and the Charybdis of prematurely identifying itself with another would-be state, which cannot be set up.

One thing is certain, and that is that the fighting will escalate. Such a conclusion accords with what we know of Soviet thinking, for their strategy is never to allow the civilian population a moment's respite, so that it will remain neutral through sheer war-weariness. It also accords with the outlook of the more active leaders, such as Massoud, who feel it encumbent upon themselves to widen the war in order to avoid being enclosed within their own strongholds, and who are now better equipped to do so.

The resistance can only hope to survive through the extension of a political organisation which is not weakened by its own internal divisions. At present the Jamiat is in the ascendant and needs to make an alliance with Khalis' party in order to make headway in the tribal areas. The spreading of Jamiat influence is closely linked to the extension of Massoud's military organisation, although in the north his progress has been blocked – at least for the moment. There are two obstacles in the way of this development, apart, of course, from the social segmentation which contradicts the very notion of the supremacy of a single party. One is the way in which the new thinking on military strategy is so dependent on the person of Massoud; should he disappear he would have no successor. Secondly, there is little international interest in fashioning the political parties of Peshawar into a more effective political instrument. The question of relations between the resistance and the outside world is now of crucial importance.

Chapter Thirteen

The conflict from 1986 to the Soviet withdrawal

The Afghan war reached a turning point in 1988, when Moscow decided to withdraw its troops from Afghanistan whatever the future course of the events. From that point, the Afghan war ceased to embody the conflict between East and West or between Islam and Communism. The ideological dimension of the war faded away, and the traditional domestic factors, mainly communal and ethnic, prevailed. Both the Mujahidin and the Kabul regime reverted to the traditional rules of the power game, although the changes brought by the war, mainly accumulation of modern weapons, emergence of a new leadership, politicisation of the society, massive emigration and urbanisation, undermined the traditional ways of regulating the conflicts which opposed communal groups to each other or to the state. Instead of providing an alternative model of modern state power, these changes plunged Afghanistan, just after the Soviet departure, into anarchy. On the same time, this creeping "lebanonisation" of Afghanistan became a stake in the regional game, where Pakistan, Iran, India, Saudi Arabia, but also the Soviet Union, are playing their regional cards, enhancing what they see as their national interests through what they see as their Afghan proxies. But, as usual, every foreign player who tries to impose his strategy on any Afghan player finds himself bogged down by the Afghan domestic factors.

The course of the war had led in 1986 to an increasingly obvious stalemate. Soviet and government troops had been unable not only to crush the Mujahidin or to win any local significant victory, but also to cut or reduce the Mujahidin supplies coming in greater volume from Pakistan. On the other hand, the Mujahidin had never been able to take any large city, or even to launch coordinated large-scale offensives against the regime. But this stalemate led also to an escalation in the fighting, both sides using a growing fire power.

1986: The difficult year

The decision to leave Afghanistan was apparently taken in 1986. But before leaving, the Soviets tried to strike some decisive blows against the

Mujahidin and pushed the Kabul regime to adopt a more subtle policy in order to attract disenchanted Mujahidin inside an acceptable political framework.

1986 saw an increase in fighting. The Soviet army, better equipped and using new tactics like night ambushes, made a better use of its huge fire power. Paktya, Herat and Kandahar were the main targets of the joint offensives waged by government and Soviet troops. In April, Haqqani's stronghold in Paktya, Jawar, was briefly overrun. In Herat, the Mujahidin, at the cost of heavy losses, undertook to destroy the security belts established west of Herat city.

Massoud began his methodical expansion out of Panjshir by combining military operations and political moves. For the first time in six years he was able to establish himself permanently outside the Panjshir valley. In August he cleared out the base of Farkhar, in Takhar province, and in November he overran the headquarters of the 20th Kabul division in Nahrin (Baghlan), the biggest victory ever won by Mujahidin.

But generally, Mujahidin morale sank lower during 1986. Increasingly, local groups accepted a cease-fire with the government and sometimes even joined government militias. The growing discrepancy between the Soviet fire power and the lack of efficient equipment among Mujahidin also contributed to undermine the morale of the Mujahidin.

At the same time, the regime began to give up most of its ideological commitments and outlooks. In May 1986, Babrak Karmal was removed as Secretary General of the Party, and, in November, as Chairman of the Revolutionary Council, i.e. head of state. He was replaced respectively by Najibullah, former head of the Secret Police (*khad*), and by Tsamkany, a traditional notable without a communist background. In December 1986, Najibullah launched the "national reconcilation" policy, the aim of which was to provide a political framework in order to attract traditional notables and defecting Mujahidin by offering them not only material incentives but also face-saving political and ideological concessions, without endangering the leading role of the PDPA.

1987: The Mujahidin on the move

But in 1987, the picture changed. Facing an impending evacuation, the Soviets were less eager to engage their troops in large-scale offensives. Secondly, the American decision to upgrade military assistance to the Mujahidin, taken earlier, began to be felt on the field, especially as far as the anti-aircraft weapons were concerned. And thirdly, the policy of "national reconciliation" did not achieve any significant results.

The military situation of the Afghan Mujahidin thus dramatically improved in 1987. Not only did the USA increase their military help (from $300 million in 1986 to $600 million in 1987), but they provided more sophisticated weapons, including the effective anti-aircraft missile Stinger, 120mm mortars and anti-minefield rockets. One has to add $60 million of "non-lethal" equipment, from boots and medicines to sleeping bags and Tennessee mules. Stingers were very efficient in combat, at least until mid-1988, when Soviet and government pilots succeeded in finding new anti-missile devices and tactics.

Despite some progress in the techniques of night ambushes, the Soviets have been unable to cut the supply roads of the Mujahidin to any significant degree. Notwithstanding the rugged landscape and the long distances to some of their bases, the Mujahidin were able to carry more than 50 per cent of the weapons and ammunition to their destination. Of the remaining 50 per cent, only one third was destroyed by Soviet air strikes or night ambushes: the remainder were in fact stolen by fellow Mujahidin from other groups. The Mujahidin were still suffering from the formidable Soviet fire power, but they could establish heavily protected strongholds in the mountains, because the Soviets, through fear of the Stingers, were relying more on artillery than on air power to protect their own bases.

Stingers and better weaponry also made it more costly for the Soviets to carry out routine operations, such as patrolling along supply roads or providing air support to besieged government outposts. In fact most of the Soviet operations carried out in 1987, including breaking the siege of Khost, were defensive, in order to keep the Mujahidin outside sensitive areas, and had only very limited success, although they took a heavy toll on the civilian population. In March, following a resistance foray into the USSR in the Pyandzh area, the Soviets tried to clean the area between their border and Kunduz. In April, they took the Mujahidin base south of Baghlan city, which was retaken from the government army by the Mujahidin of Ghayyur and Mollah Shams one month later. In May they mounted a first and unsuccessful counter-offensive around the besieged city of Khost. In June and July they launched two large-scale offensives around the city of Kandahar and went up along the Arghandab and Arghestan valleys. In August they heavily shelled and bombed the Shamali and Kohestan areas, north of Kabul, and, at the beginning of December, they started a big offensive to break, for the first time since the invasion, the siege of Khost, the provincial capital of Paktya, at the Pakistani border; that was the only large-scale offensive in 1987, using paratroopers and involving about one Soviet division.

But all these operations only gave a breathing space to Soviet and government troops: the suburbs of Kandahar and Herat remained in

Mujahidin control, Kabul came more regularly under direct fire in 1987 than in 1986 (perhaps because of the greater range of the ground-to-ground rockets): the capital was shelled in the midst of the opening speech of chairman Najibullah at the big *loyah jirgah* (tribal assembly) on 30 November. Most of the provincial capitals, including Kunduz, had only their centre controlled by the government. Moreover, the Soviets were obliged to evacuate some remote positions, for example, in Bamyan, not because of direct military pressure, but because logistics were more and more of a problem, due to the impact of the Stingers on air transportation. After each offensive, like the one in Baghlan, the Mujahidin were able to retake control of the lost ground once the Soviets left, because government troops could not hold their gains. The counter-offensive against Khost was costly and only a short-run success. Even worse, government posts in the north-east were falling one by one in the hands of Massoud: Nahrin was taken in November 1986, Kalafgan in July 1987, Keran, a key position, in October 1987, and Burqa in January 1988.

Eight years of war also provided good training for the Mujahidin, who learnt to use new weapons and new materials, like radio and even computers. But, except in the north-east, under Massoud's aegis, the Mujahidin were unable to upgrade their tactics and strategy to a modern guerilla warfare that could really threaten the cities and provide a potential state model to challenge the weakened Kabul regime. Thus, the Mujahidin advance was in fact hidding their weaknesses which were more political and organisational than purely military.

1988: The turning point

The Soviet withdrawal followed the patterns indicated by Gorbachev in his speech of 8 February and confirmed by the Geneva Agreements signed on 15 April: it has been "front-loaded" and rapid. The withdrawal began on 15 May 1988; on 15 August, half of the troops had been sent back to USSR; after a halt in the autumn, the withdrawal resumed at the end of January 1989 and was complete by 15 February, as scheduled.

From the first stage of the withdrawal, Mujahidin began to occupy the territory left not only by the Soviets, but also by the government forces, unable to resist without direct Soviet fire support, or needed more urgently to replace the departing Soviets in the most sensitive areas – the big cities. Dozens of outposts and small bases were abandoned, mainly in the south and in border areas, such as Barikot (Kunar province, April 1988). The situation deteriorated for the government forces in August, when the first provincial capitals fell into Mujahidin hands: Bamyan, Taloqan (Takhar) and, briefly, Kunduz, followed in November by

Asadabad, in Kunar. The Soviets gave up small towns (some provincial capitals are in fact merely "bazars"), but wanted to prevent at all costs the fall of the big cities, using heavy retaliation bombardments and artillery shellings to deter the Mujahidin from advancing: Kunduz was thus retaken after heavy civilian losses one week after its fall, and Kandahar and Herat were prevented from falling. The defence of Khost and Jellalabad was easier because the government had more supporters in these areas. Thus a new military balance was established by the end of 1988, but the lines of defence of the regime had shrunk considerably by comparison with a year before.

In February 1989, all the experts thought that the regime would crumble from inside in the following weeks or months. The Soviets were only trying to gain a "decent interval", by giving the regime a breathing space for some months. On the other hand, the Americans (under the aegis of the new hard-line ambassador in Islamabad, Robert Oakley) and the Pakistani military services (ISI, then headed by General Hamid Gul) decided to accelerate the fall of Kabul by inducing the Mujahidin to launch an offensive against Jellalabad. The strategy designed and implemented by the American and Pakistani administrations was two-fold: first to form an Afghan Interim Government (AIG) based on the Sunni Peshawar Alliance, then to put this government in power through a military offensive. The battle began in March and lasted for some weeks. The government forces were able to hold their ground. By the summer 1989, any hope for a prompt military victory for the Mujahidin had to be given up.

The Mujahidin failure

One can explain the failure of the Mujahidin both by the strategy imposed on them by their foreign supporters and by their own inability to create a viable political alternative.

The increase in foreign aid made the divided Mujahidin entirely dependent of the Pakistanis and the Americans for political and strategic decisions. The Americans and the Pakistanis made all the possible strategic and tactical mistakes, completely ignoring the real balance of power inside Afghanistan, and bypassing all the ethnic and sociological considerations. The US administration was involved as it has never been before. Too eager to make Kabul a Saigon for the Soviets, the American Embassy in Islamabad, discounting warnings from field commanders like Massoud and 'Abdul Haqq that Kabul would not fall, imposed the decision to attack.

The Americans were so sure of the Mujahidin victory, through the internal collapse of the regime, that they did not bother to provide the Mujahidin with heavy weapons. More than that, they publicly announced their intention to collect the remaining Stingers, in order to avoid them being sold to "unfriendly elements". Once it was obvious, in July 1989, that the offensive against Jellalabad was a failure, Washington decided to step up its military supplies, without questioning its political approach. There was a tendency among the Pakistani and American advisers to see the war from purely technical point of view. But *all* guerilla warfare is first of all political. Under-equipped guerilla armies, sometimes even defeated militarily, could win politically, as in Algeria. On the contrary, well equipped guerilla armies, like the Contras in Nicaragua and the Polisario in Western Sahara, have been unable to achieve any significant success.

The political side of the initiative was doomed to fail from the beginning. The American strategy completely bypassed the few effective Mujahidin commanders, and instead relied exclusively on the Peshawar Alliance. The greatest part of the supplies went to Hekmatyar's Hezb, which used it to fight against its fellow Mujahidin. The Afghan Interim Government, created in February to provide a political alternative to the Kabul regime, has never been able to provide a political alternative or an administrative body that could run Afghanistan after a Mujahidin victory. The fact that the bulk of the American aid has been channelled through the AIG, in order to legitimate it, helped only to create a bureaucracy. This government was drawn mainly from Pashtun Ghilzay. Persian-speakers from the north and Durrani Pashtun from the south were under-represented. There were no Shi'a at all, despite the conciliatory approach of Iran. At a time when the ethnic factors were prevailing upon the ideological dimension of the war, this lack of a broad ethnic base prevented any success for the AIG. Thus the discrepancy between it and the field commanders was growing.

Mujahidin field commanders, who had borne the brunt of the war for years, were left out of the plan for taking Kabul and were just asked to obey the new interim Defence Deputy Minister, "general" Yahya Noruz, who had no fighting record inside Afghanistan. But the field commanders simply refused to fight in order to establish a government they had not chosen and which was too narrowly based on ethnic terms. They almost went on strike when ordered by Peshawar to make diversionary attacks in order to obtain the fall of Jellalabad. In fact, it seems that there has been a systematic policy of bypassing and estranging the field commanders.

The Mujahidin failed to build an effective potential state and a professional army in the countryside. In fact, the process of modernisation through war and politicisation that we have analysed throughout this book had achieved significant results in only a few areas, and had been more thwarted than helped by external influences. As we shall see in the next chapter, the return of the traditional segmentation, the fact that the Peshawar Afghan Interim Government was no more than a conflict-ridden bureaucracy, and Hekmatyar's tendancy to stab in the back any efficient Mujahidin commanders undermined the effectiveness of the Afghan resistance.

From a military point of view, the drawbacks of the Afghan resistance have been the same from the beginning of the war: a segmentation of the military fronts, which is in accord with the traditional segmentation of the society; a prevalence of traditional warfare, except on the big military fronts (part-time warriors opposed to skilled commandos); a lack of strategic coordination, even if there is now a tactical cooperation on the battle-field; a taste for local feuds. Improvements are confined to specific areas, like the north-east.

But generally, most of the military fronts coincide with a sociological unit (clan, tribe, ethnic group, kinship of some notable . . .), and are usually carrying out operations only on their traditional communal territory. But the growing number of heavy weapons provided for the Mujahidin tends to make them jump directly from a traditional tribal warfare to a classical one, beyond their political and organisational capacities.

The government policy

In order to survive after the Soviet withdrawal, the regime followed a double-track policy: first to remove the ideological dimension of the war, then to play upon the ethnic rivalries revealed by the fading away of *jihad* spirit. The decision to go back to more traditional patterns of power and to give up revolutionnary rhetoric was taken in December 1986, when the policy of "national reconciliation" was launched. In the Constitution drafted in August 1987, the word "democratic" was dropped from the official appellation of the "Republic of Afghanistan". The Party was said to have never been communist. Islam was recognised as the official state religion and tribalism as a legitimate political pattern.

In its endeavour to break the Mujahidin fronts, the regime has been helped by some external elements. The withdrawal of the Soviet troops from the country, and of most of the regime garrisons from the countryside in order to defend the capital, created a sudden political vacuum that was not filled by the Mujahidin provisional government. So the old local feuds made a sudden come-back among the Mujahidin, at a time when fighting with their backs against the wall had forced the regime members to play down their own tribalism and ethnic rivalries.

Paradoxically, more local groups joined the government after the Soviet withdrawal than before. Having nothing to lose, the government gave heavy weapons to local militias, which were until this time considered as not reliable enough to be given too many weapons. Local militias could thus have a better fire-power than the Mujahidin. Growing feuds among Mujahidin enticed some defeated or threatened local communal groups to join the regime, at least on a temporary basis and never on a ideological one.

These militiamen usually keep their former leadership and organisation (or lack of organisation). They try to protect their village against their former fellow Mujahidin, sometimes making local deals with them, sometimes using the new fire power given by the government to settle old scores based more on traditional tribal feuds than on ideological differences, with the Mujahidin.

The evolution of the situation is more than ever linked to the sociological changes in the society.

Chapter Fourteen

Cultural patterns and changes in society: an assesment

The central issue we have addressed in this book has been the aptitude of the Islamist movement to carry out a modernisation of society. After ten years of war, we can assess to what extent, if at all, new political structures have been able to bypass traditional segmentation, and whether Islamic law might have provided an alternative to both tribal common law and a pervasive endemic violence. The final picture is contrasted, but suggests a global failure with some local breakthroughs. But the war has definitely altered the traditional fabric of the Afghan society.

The re-traditionalisation of the new political structures and leadership

The sudden withdrawal of the Soviets, as well as of the government troops in many areas, deprived the Mujahidin of both a common enemy and of a *raison d'être*. As we have seen the strategy of a *qawm* is to enhance its local power and to fight state encroachments. When the state withdraws, as has been largely the case in 1988, the main danger comes from the next *qawm*, even if the antagonism is expressed in political terms.

In fact, the Mujahidin have never been able to replace a traditional structure by a modern political one. The "de-ideologisation" of the Afghan war that followed the Soviet withdrawal entailed a process of "re-traditionalisation" of the Afghan resistance. The situation in Afghanistan is not, on both sides, a mere return to tradition. There have been considerable sociological and political changes, but these changes did not finally result in a new model for state and society. Traditional society has not been destroyed in Afghanistan, but expresses itself through the new political parties. Most of the Mujahidin commanders either use traditional patterns of power and thus became the new *khan* and *malek*, or try to adapt more modern political structures to the traditional society. Compromise between ideological commitment and traditional society is the rule.

The ambivalence of the process of politicisation in Afghanistan is obvious. On one hand it gave a new look to traditional segmentation, but on the other hand it introduced political references (for instance to a specific ideology, which in fact is very alien to traditional society) and new structures. Subordination of local notables and commanders to an *amir* (both a political and military leader) is possible only if the leader is a charismatic and/or religious figure, or if the level of politicisation is so high that discipline exists. On the contrary, it is not rare to see Mujahidin field commanders, mainly petty ones, behaving like former notables and using the political fragmentation in order to express and enhance the traditional *qawm* segmentation. They tend to play the new political game by the old rules. Political parties are used by them to enhance a local status, not to achieve a nation-wide, ideologically motivated project. Thus the traditional power status in Afghanistan is an incentive both to political affiliation and to political segmentation.[1]

Rooting of modern political party structures in Afghanistan could either bypass the traditional segmentation (with Massoud or Ismail Khan) or, on the contrary and more generally, give a new boost to infra-political, infra-ethnic, and even infra-tribal segmentation, that is, at the *qawm* level: a local petty notable, followed by some dozens of relations and tenants, could regain some power by joining a Mujahidin group (or even the Kabul regime) which is a rival of the dominant party and will provide him with enough weapons and money to act as an independent agent. These local petty notables would not have expressed themselves politically before the war, but they now find in political affiliation an access to weapons and a new self-assertion, making it more difficult for the dominant party and leaders to assert themselves as a political alternative above the traditional segmentation. Such petty notables do not necessarily have a territorial base (so they are neither feudal chiefs nor war-lords), but their simple presence as an independent network is enough to thwart the process of implementation of a would-be state structure. Such a behaviour is not necessarily linked with the sociological background of the local leaders. Some *'ulama* and even some Islamist intellectuals behave now like former *khân*, as we can see by the tendancy of dozens of them to add the term *khan* to their name (like Basir Khan from Jamiat, or Bashir Khan from Hezb). They tend to distribute wealth, to arrest and even kill rivals or to marry new spouses in a strategy of rising above their equals, not of challenging the existing central power in the name of a different ideology. In some particularly detribalised or depopulated areas, there is a process of transforming a political group which people joined not necessarily out of consideration for *qawm* affiliation into a *qawm* network, a "communal group", whose existence is simply a consequence of the war, but which will try to perpetuate itself by accumulating wealth and political power. This reminds us that *qawm* and ethnic affiliations are in Afghanistan a dynamic process and not a static taxonomia.[2] Such groups are generally headed by self-made new leaders, who, whatever their sociological background, would oppose both the traditional notables of the pre-war period and the establishing of any state structures. It is not rare to see these new groups indulging in smuggling and banditry.

The trend towards a new fragmentation is exacerbated by the fact that Afghanistan has been recently flooded with weapons, and, to a lesser extent, by cash, provided both by the Peshawar parties and by the Kabul regime, and sometimes also, to a lesser extent, by cultivation of drugs in the south-west, Badakhshan and Nangrahar. Humanitarian help distributed through both idealistic young members of private voluntary organizations or more seasoned international agencies added to the growing monetarisation of the Afghan economy. This "artificial" money superseded incomes provided by crops and even private trading, and benefited first the Peshawar bureaucracy and then the local field commanders, who generally distribute it (instead of putting it into a Swiss bank account), but through a personal patron/client network. Foreign help, as well as the Kabul policy of national reconciliation, contributed to the re-traditionalisation of Afghan society.

There is a definite change in leadership, but not so great a change in leadership patterns.

The re-traditionalisation of the resistance has also been favoured by the decrease in numbers of intellectuals among the field commanders. The losses suffered during the war have not been compensated. In the course of the war, none of the Afghan intellectuals studying abroad went back to Afghanistan for more than a few months, nor did any of them achieve any high-ranking position among fighting Mujahidin. That is also true of Kabul students. Lack of educational facilities among the Mujahidin meant that there is a decrease in literacy and education. New leaders promoted after the death of well-known commanders tended to be less educated and also less politically minded.

The war brought also an obvious psychological weariness among commanders. In 1989, most of the famous southern commanders mentioned in this book did not stay for more than a couple of months every year in Afghanistan (Haqani, 'Abdul Haqq, Mohammad Shah etc.).

But this process applies also to the Peshawar parties, which adopted the worst aspects of a central government – bureaucracy and clientelism – without providing a credible and viable political alternative to the Kabul regime. This trend, as we shall see, was encouraged both by Pakistan, not eager to see the rise of too independent-minded field commanders, and by the Americans, obsessed by the idea of establishing an Afghan Interim Government that could challenge the legitimacy of the Kabul regime.

From Islamism to fundamentalism

Two contradictory trends emerged afer the Soviet withdrawal: the decline of the *jihad* spirit and the emergence of a strong Wahhabi fundamentalist movement. After the Soviet withdrawal and the launching of the policy of "national reconciliation", the distinction between "infidels" and "Mujahidin" became blurred, specially among the more traditionalist elements. The fading away of the *jihad* spirit and the failure to provide a model for a would-be Islamic state deprived the Islamist movement of what was its main originality: the endeavour to conceive what could be a modern Islamic state and theory of an Islamic Revolution. Thus most of the former militants reverted either to a traditional perception of the political game, as we have seen above, or to a "fundamentalist" conception of religion. The first move was encouraged by the permanence of traditional political behaviour, the second by an active Wahhabi revival.

Wahhabi activity is not new in Afghanistan (see above, p. 42). But from 1984 onwards an increasing stream of Arab volunteers poured inside Afghanistan, while Saudi and Gulf money was available for building hundreds of religious schools to train Afghan mullahs in Pakistan. Scholarships were also offered for training in Saudi Arabia. These proposals came when there was a tragic dearth of educational facilities for Afghans. Western-sponsored training facilities in Pakistan did not provide religious training. Traditional Afghan Hanafi schools had a desperate shortage of funds, at a time when Saudi – sponsored *madrasa* provided full board and monthly allowances for young students. They tended to profess strong opposition to any form of sufism, destroying the *zyarat* and calling the Afghan Mujahidin to change their way of life. In fact they advocate a reform in personal behaviour, in order to follow as closely as possible the model of the Prophet, discarding classical and even religious literature. In this sense, they are true fundamentalists, preaching a strict return to the Qur'an and the behaviour of the archetypal Muslim. For them, political and military organisation is not the key to victory. Victory will come when Mujahidin behave as true Muslims. Thus they did not bring to the Mujahidin any modern knowledge of strategy and tactics. These fundamentalist volunteers were generally courageous, even fanatical fighters, but they were not only unable to achieve any significant victory, but also helped to undermine the popularity of the Mujahidin by treating government people as "kafirs", selling the women of government soldiers as slaves, and so one.

Their influence was important for two reasons. They generally controlled the newly built *madrasa* in Pakistan, thus educating a whole generation of Afghan mullahs. Second, they used to attract local petty commanders by offering them huge amounts of money, in exchange for destroying *zyarat*, joining the most radical parties (Hekmatyar and Sayyaf) or even establishing local Wahhabi republics, as in Nuristan, Pech valley in Kunar and Argo valley in Badakhshan. Thus they contributed to the segmentation of the Afghan resistance and the weakening of the traditional ways of settling feuds, without providing an alternative political model. In fact they follow the patterns of Saudi history, where a religious ideology that was supposed to ignore traditional segmentation fitted perfectly with a tribal society.

As we saw in the previous chapters, the Afghan *'ulama* have been unable to provide a political framework of their own to impose *shariat*. They are confronted with a generation gap: fewer young mullahs are educated in traditional *madrasa*; the Kabul state Faculty of Theology is seen as a tool of the government; the Wahhabi influence tend to corner them out of the educational field. The most outstanding *'ulama* fighting inside Afghanistan tend to behave like any of the field commanders and are losing their aura as "holy men". Finally, *shariat* is of no help when feuds oppose parties, clans or *qawm*. For all these reasons, even if everybody in Afghanistan claims to want implementation of *shariat*, the Islamic law does not have the power to bypass the traditional segmentation, except when it is used as a political tool by clever commanders like Massoud.

Does the weakening of Islam as a political model entailed a return of traditional tribal ideology and institutions, like *jirgah, pashtunwali* etc.? The answer is no. The tribal ideology remains a rallying flag among refugees, specially the Durrani and the former establishment, but has lost its efficiency to shape social relations among tribalised people inside Afghanistan. In this regard, the war also brought some definitive changes. Where de-ideologisation occurred, it led to a return not to traditional ideologies, but to wilderness and anarchy. The traditional ways of settling feuds between *qawm*, that is mediation of elders or holy men after a symbolic battle, has given way to interminable vendettas, waged with heavy machine-guns and rockets, instead of First World War rifles. Generally speaking, due to the fact that commanders and warriors are young, influence of elders has faded away. Bloody feuds are waged between local commanders, where torture is used, a very new pattern in the countryside.

Some local commanders went out of all control, and tended to impose exactions on a population which did not always see the necessity of a *jihad*, once the Soviets were out of the country and the government out of the communal territory.

The dominant values are thus violence and strict fundamentalism, except in areas where an outstanding personality has been able to instaure a would-be state model. Let us examine the best example: Massoud's system.

A case of a working would-be state model: Massoud

Massoud has been one of the few field commanders to bypass communal loyalties. He did so by using a military model and not by establishing an administration.

At the beginning Massoud's front was established according to traditional patterns. People of Panjshir joined him because he was a skilled warrior from the area. But his closest followers were young Panjshiris living in Kabul, and thus referring to a broader identity than *qawm* affiliation. They think themselves as "Panjshri" and Muslims. Massoud's two assets were to control an homogeneous "communal territory" and to command urbanised, skilled and sometimes educated young fighters, without breaking with the traditional society.

It took six years for Massoud to get out his original "communal territory" and to establish in 1986 a professional, even if small, army. Ethnic and *qawm* factors did not disappear, but are not the main explanatory factor. Massoud's groups are now above communal loyalties, but still remain predominantly Tajik and Uzbek. Some local Pashtun commanders joined him, like Aref in Kunduz. The *qawm* factor, by contrast, is dominant among Massoud's opponents, as shown by the fact that some local Persian-speaking or Uzbek *qawm* joined Hezb-i Islami or the government to oppose the imposition of a centralised model. By contrast Massoud is seen as a Tajik hero, not as a proponent of his own *qawm* ("nuruzkheyl", which, incidentally, nobody seems to know outside his village).

In addition to the system we described in Chapter 11, Masud established a further level in his military organisation: "central units" (*qateha-ye markazi*) were created without consideration of *qawm* affiliation and are both the elite units and the military academy of Massoud. They constitute the hard core of a "Liberation Army" that Massoud undertook to build up in 1988.

But Massoud became soon aware of the danger of relying too much on the military. In 1985, he established a "supervisory council of the North" (shura-ye nazar) to give a political framework to his expansion outside his original "communal territory". This body was designed to attract the largest possible number of local commanders, bypassing Peshawar's bureaucracy, including that of Jamiat. He refers to the *shura* concept, giving a Qur'anic framework to what is a political step. Massoud became the "amir", that is both political and military commander, who is neither a *khan* nor a purely military commander. He is thought to be above traditional segmentation, so that a *khan* or an *alim* could pay respect to him, a younger man from a middle-class family, without being humiliated. It was only by giving an Islamic terminology and legitimation to what was an adaption to modern guerilla warfare that Massoud was able to establish such a system in most of the north-east of Afghanistan.

But if Massoud has been able to bypass the *qawm* segmentation, it is only to jump to a further level of segmentation: ethnic affiliation. Any further progress is linked with the evolution of the ethnic balance in Afghanistan and to Massoud's ability to make concessions to the Pashtun.

The evolution of the political map

The political map of Afghanistan, as we have described in the previous chapters, has been rather stable all along the war. In ten years, most Mujahidin commanders have remained loyal to their initial political party.

The Harakat-i enqelab party remains the party of the traditional clerics. Although its influence has decreased among the persian speakers, it is still strong among the Pashtun, both Durrani and Ghilzay, and the Northern Uzbek. Totally lacking central leadership, the Harakat is a collection of local fronts. We have noticed that it tended to be infiltrated by former Maoists. As the Maoists generally joined the Kabul regime from 1986, through the policy of "national reconciliation", Harakat's fronts in the north tend to turn more and more into local pro-government militias, like Pahlawan Ghaffur in Sar-i Pol area, Jauzjan province. Some new organisations, like "Gerûh-i kâr", a former leftist organisation turned into an avowed Uzbek-nationalist group, or "Ittihâd-i Samt-i Shamali", a "pan-Turkic" organisation, headed by Azad Beg and created by the Pakistani services, infiltrated most of the Harakat Uzbek fronts in the north, encroaching on Jamiat. These groups are more or less openly penetrated by Khad agents.

Khales' party did not broaden its bases after 1986, and remains mainly a tribal Pashtun party. Obviously, the young intellectuals, who were numerous in the party at the beginning, gave way to more traditional clerics and even to Wahhabi trained cadres. The Hezb of Khales, which was the bridge between the new Islamist ideas and the traditional society, embodies the general shift of the Islamist movement towards fundamentalism in the second part of the war. Strict application of *shariat* and an absolute lack of political perspective characterises the party. Young educated commanders, like Abdul Haqq, tended to distance themselves from the party.

The Jamiat succeeded to establish some bridge-heads among the Pashtun tribes, through Naqibullah, an Alikozay, in Kandahar, and Fazlullah, from the Mojaddidi family, in South Logar. But the party is still considered as mainly Persian-speaking by most of the Pashtun. After ten years of war, it is now obvious that the Jamiat includes the best field commanders in Afghanistan. But this apparent asset has also engendered a rivalry between the Jamiat bureaucracy abroad and these field commanders. The bureaucracy, headed by Rabbani's deputy, Nurullah Emmat, and the head of the military committee of Peshawar, Ingineer Ayub, overtly supports internal opponents of Massoud and Ismail Khan, like the "Afzali Front" in Herat. This bureaucracy remains radical, is closer to Hezb-I Islami and benefits from Wahhabi funds, but the field commanders and Rabbani himself can now be considered as moderates. These internal feuds prevent Rabbani from capitalising on the military strength of Jamiat to play a bigger political role.

Mojaddidi's party did not extend its influence, although it attracted one of the best of Hekmatyar's commanders in Kabul, Billal, a move which is not in line with the patterns of political affiliations we have underlined in this book. Gaylani's Islamic Front is still the party of the Pashtun tribal establishment.

The big question remains the Hezb of Gulbuddin Hekmatyar. The influence of Hezb has decreased all over Afghanistan. It has almost no representatives in the West. If the Hezb is still mainly made up of de-tribalised Ghilzay Pashtun, it retains some non-Pashtun followers in the north-east, mainly Tajik, like Farid in Kohestan and Nehzatyar in Baghlan, or recruited among isolated local *qawm*, like the Persian-speaking "Baluchis" around Keshm (headed by Abdul Wadud), and the Uzbek "mohajer" (who emigrated from the Soviet Union in the 1920s) around Burqa.

The Hezb pursued a double-track policy. On one side it upheld an hard-line Islamist policy, condemning any political concessions and exerting considerable influence in Arab circles, while still getting the biggest share of Pakistani and American support. On the other hand, it systematically undermined the military efforts inside Afghanistan. Most of Hezb commanders either openly joined the government militias or fought bitterly, with excessive savagery, against the other Mujahidin. In

Herat, Keshm, Kohestan and Lashkargah, for example, the local Hezb commanders made local agreements with the regime. During the battle of Jellalabad, the Hezb troops remained conspicuously absent, despite the fact that they were the better equipped. In addition, the Hezb launched a campaign of assassination against Massoud's commanders, killing for example Tariq of Laghman, in the summer of 1988. The worst incident occurred in July 1989, when thirty Jamiat Mujahidin, including seven commanders (among them the Uzbek Qazi Islamuddin) were arrested, tortured and executed by order of the Peshawar party headquarters. These incidents, in contrast to most of the internecine killings among Mujahidin, are more politically motivated than due to local *qawm* rivalries: Sayyad Jamal, the killer, is himself a Persian-speaker. Massoud is the arch-enemy for Hekmatyar, whose strategy is to seize power at any cost and whose priority is to eliminate rivals. Hezb used blockades and assassinations, including those of foreigners (like the British film-maker Andy Skrzypkowiak, killed in September 1987) to prevent Massoud getting of the Panjshir valley. Links between Hezb and some government circles (like the former Minister of the Interior, Gulabzoy) became more and more obvious.

The continuous American support that the Hezb enjoyed until September 1989 raised some doubts about American intelligence gathering (or the ability to convert information into a coherent policy) and about the real goals of some Arab circles, who had constantly supported Hekmatyar. The permanent feud between Hezb and Jamiat will be one of the keys of the evolution of the political situation in Afghanistan.

As far as the Shi'a are concerned, the trends that we have noticed in this book remain valid. The Shura-i ettefagh lost ground to the point that Jaglan made a deal with the government. The pro-Khomeynist parties, which won the domestic civil war, indulged in local feuds and did not try to confront the Soviets, except for Mohseni' Harakat-i Islami, which has good fighting groups around and inside Kabul (commander Anwari). The Shi'a moved closer to Jamiat and the Persian-speakers. Increasing armed confrontation occurred between Shi'a and Pashtun, on the south-east edges of Hazarajat. These feuds are not politically motivated, but embody a century-old ethnic confrontation, which has a long future.

The change in ethnic balance and identity

We have already mentioned (p. 169) that the war brought a change in the ethnic balance, mainly a decrease in Pashtun influence. The war played also a big role in stressing "macro-ethnic" identities based on purely linguistic and religious (that is Sunni/Shi'a) criteria, pushing local *qawm* to identify themselves with "macro-ethnic" groups, in order to assert themselves politically at the national level, through identification with a stronger group.

We have seen in the pages above that *qawm*, and not ethnic affiliations, are generally enough to explain local politics and feuds among Mujahidin. But participation in a nation-wide political game induces the local *qawm* to express themselves in terms of broader ethnic affiliations. This process had been noticed by ethnologists before the war. For example, some Turkish-speaking groups tended to retain their name and identity (that is, the sense of being a *qawm*), like the Qarluq of Rustaq, but will call themselves Uzbeks in front of other people. Other groups, like the "Tatars" of Doab-i Ruy (Samangan province), although retaining an oral tradition of being of Turkic origin, speak exclusively Persian and were formerly considered as Tajik,[4] like the "Arab" and "Baluch" of Takhar. This ethnic identity can also be bestowed by a dominant group, and not necessarily accepted by the people who are thus "christened". If the Persian-speaking Shi'a are called "Hazara", there are some Sunni Hazara groups which used to call themselves Tajik, but are called Hazara by the Tajik. A good demarcation line, in these cases, is the matrimonial convention: one gives women only to an equal or superior group. It is clear that people try to shape their ethnic identity according to social and political constraints, discarding, when possible, linguistic, racial and historical features.

The war accelerated this process of ethnic crystallisation, and brought about a sort of political awareness of ethnic identity. The Sunni Persian speakers, for instance, did not previously use the word "Tajik", applied to them by both Soviet and Western ethnologists. But today they tend to define themselves as an ethnic group, of which the majority has been attracted by the Jamiat party, the only one headed by a non-Pashtun. Aymaq, Taymani, Timouri etc., who were listed as separate ethnic groups by ethnologists, do not behave differently from the other Sunni Persian speakers in terms of political affiliation: they tend also to be seen as Tajik. Before the war, the non-Pashtun groups had no tradition of handling weapons. The war provided them with opportunities to own and use weapons. Commanders like Massoud are heroes for the Tajik: military efficiency is no more seen as a Pashtun prerogative.

The regime propaganda coined the word *melliat* (a translation for the Soviet concept of "nationality") to give a political expression to the non-Pashtun groups: this policy did not succeed in rallying many people, because the regime is still perceived as mainly Pashtun, but it provides a new ethnic awareness among dominated ethnic groups.

If one looks at politics at the national level, thus discarding the local inter-*qawm* feuds, we can see that five "macro-ethnic" groups are emerging through the war. The "Tajik" (including all Sunni Persian speakers), the Hazara, the Uzbek, and the Pashtun, divided between Durrani on the one hand and the Ghilzay and Eastern Pashtun on the other hand.

Today the main political actors are Ghilzay. Both the Kabul regime and the Peshawar-based aliance are recruiting mainly among Ghilzay. The majority of the seven Peshawar leaders are Ghilzay (Hekmatyar, Sayyaf, Nabi) or Eastern Pashtun (Khales). Among the three other leaders, two have family links with Ghilzay (Gaylani and Mojaddidi); only Rabbani is a non-Pashtun. There is no "pure-bred Durrani" in the Afghan Interim Government established in February 1989.

The opposition between Durrani on one side and Ghilzay and Eastern Pashtun on the other makes improbable the emergence of an "all-Pashtun" party or coalition.

The main military commanders are Tajik, and Jamiat is probably, today, the most numerous party of Peshawar. But Rabbani's policy has been systematically to deny the identification between Jamiat and Tajik, by favouring the Pashtun minority inside the party and refusing Iranian solicitations.

Two ethnic groups, the Hazara Shi'a and the Uzbek, which used to be dominated by the others before the war, became a stake in the regional balance of power. War brought an ethnic reassertion among the formerly despised Shi'a Hazara, who have liberated their own area and benefit from political support, if nothing more, from Iran. Iran, in Afghanistan as in Lebanon, is using the Shi'a minority as a tool for political and diplomatic influence. In February 1989, the *shura*, or council of the Mujahidin, which was gathered in Rawalpindi (Pakistan) to elect a provisional Mujahidin government, rejected the Shi'a claim to hold 20 per cent of the seats: more than a quarrel on percentages of population, this attitude reveals the strong anti-Shi'a bias among Pashtun, this bias being fuelled by the influential Wahhabi.

The Sunni Uzbek tended to be more receptive towards Soviet propaganda than the other ethnic groups: the direct links established through the Soviet border with the Uzbekistan SSR might also have stressed their ethnic particularism. The USSR might therefore use the Uzbek to retain some influence in the north of Afghanistan.

Strangely enough, the Turkmen, closer to the Soviet border, remained fiercely anti-Soviet, perhaps because they had fled from the USSR in the 1920s. Other ethnic groups, like Baluchi, Nuristani and Pash'ay apparently did not develop a particular ethnic awareness during this war, although they have been listed as "nationalities" by Kabul.

Peshawar, the refugees and the social prospects

The lack of a clear-cut Mujahidin victory and the difficult conditions inside Afghanistan will prevent most of the refugees from going back to Afghanistan. The refugee population in Pakistan and Iran is only very superficially controlled by the Peshawar bureaucracy. The rivalry between most of the field commanders and the Peshawar bureaucracy will prevent the latter from controlling the Afghan countryside, in the improbable case of a victory of the Peshawar-based alliance. Thus the contention between Mujahidin field commanders and the Peshawar bureaucracy on the one hand, and between this bureaucracy and the refugees on the other, might become a political issue.

In spite of this contention, almost all field commanders retain their political affiliation to one of the parties. Field commanders have never tried to establish a political entity that would openly challenge Peshawar, and even Massoud asked Rabbani for a green light to create his "supervisory council".

The bureaucracy established, through foreign subsidies, by the Alliance in Peshawar is manned by the new educated middle class, opposed both to the aristocraty and to the field commanders. These young urbanites either left Kabul directly for Peshawar with little or no fighting experience, or were trained in Western-sponsored training programmes organised in Pakistan. They have the same sociological background as the communists. Even in the "moderate" parties, the new bureaucracy consists of young educated people, not of *khan* or *'ulama*. In camps and in Pakistani towns, thousands of young Afghans are now educated either through Western-sponsored programmes or through Wahhabi *madrasa*. Trained as accountants, nurses, teachers, clerks, translators, mullahs or trainers in different fields, they have no future except as state employees. And there is a state in Peshawar: the parties and the Alliance. Naturally enough, most of these educated young tend to join the radical and anti-Western, but nevertheless technocratic, Hekmatyar school of thought. Uprooted people tend to be more extremist than field commanders confronted with the complexity of their society. They also became a good target for Wahhabi proselytism. The lack of real political prospects also encouraged the trend towards the adoption of more fundamentalist, inward-looking and formalist religious practices.

Exile to Pakistan or Iran means urbanisation for a lot of Afghan refugees. First, *stricto sensu*, because hundreds of thousands of Afghans are living or working in cities, but also because life in camps tends to create an urban atmosphere: women are secluded, there are schools, dispensaries and administration; traditional leaders have lost the power in favour of young, educated middle-class men (except perhaps in the

Quetta camps, where tribal leaders remain strong).[5] People are either idle or working outside in non-agricultural activities. A refugee camp is closer to the new suburbs that are mushrooming in Third World big cities than to an Afghan village. A lot of these refugees are unlikely to go back to their former villages and will probably go to Kabul, if they return.

In these conditions, *qawm* affiliations tend to play a lesser role among refugees, at least in their traditional aspects, but political factions are constituted in the same client/patron relationship that is at the core of the *qawm's* function. The same phenomena that we noticed inside Afghanistan are at work. Changes brought by the war altered leadership and traditional segmentation, but not the fact that the segmentation operates on a non-political basis. "Political factions" work along the same rules as a *qawm*. Money, weapons, jobs and women are distributed among the group members in order to enhance the prestige of the leader, but not to achieve a politically motivated strategy. At the same time urbanisation of the Mujahidin refugees might induce a radicalisation of their political and ideological stands.

Internal displacement inside Afghanistan resulted also in urbanisation. If pro-Mujahidin cities like Herat and Kandahar saw a decrease in population, pro-government towns like Mazar, Farah, Jellalabad and even Kabul have swelled up. The question is whether Afghanistan is still a peasant society.

Another problem is that most of the present fighting Mujahidin became professional warriors, do not have education or professional skills, and might be reluctant to abandon the high status they have achieved as warriors to seek jobs in a devastated countryside or in overcrowded cities.

A last problem will be the attitude of peasants towards returning land-owners. If most of the refugees go back to the countryside, there will be not enough land for tenants. Wages and shares of the crops will fall. It should be remembered that the birth-rate is very high, specially among refugees: it is probable that the overall Afghan population has increased in ten years despite all the war casualties. This will reinforce the trend towards urbanisation, which in turn will lessen the political weight of the field commanders and increase political instability, the main agent of stability being precisely the field commanders.

Thus Afghanistan is now divided into urbanites living in Kabul, who are ready for any compromise; urbanites living in Iran and Pakistan, who will probably stay abroad or go back to the cities, even if they are from a rural background; and fighting Mujahidin, who tend to see all urbanites as bad Muslims and spineless people, just able to pay for being left in peace.

Afghanistan is facing considerable social tensions, at a stage where there appears to be no possibility of a stable central government.

Chapter Fifteen

Afghan politics and the outside world

The complexity of the Afghan war is created by the intricacy of all the factors we have discussed in the previous chapters: *qawm*, tribes and ethnic affiliations, combined with ideological and political divisions and exacerbated by the influence of the three neighbouring countries (Pakistan, USSR, Iran), each of them playing both ideological and ethnic cards, in the context of a decade of East–West competition through the numerous "regional conflicts", from Afghanistan to Nicaragua.

From the international point of view, the Afghan war has embodied different levels of conflicts which are inextricably intertwined: an East–West issue, a regional conflict and an ideological confrontation between Islam and Marxism.

The East–West issue

It is the Soviet invasion which turned a local civil war into an East–West issue. For the first time since 1946, Soviet troops invaded a country which was not a member of the Warsaw Pact. Whatever the main reason for the invasion, it was perceived by Washington as a drastic change in the balance of power between East and West, coming after a general setback of the West in the seventies (Ethiopia, Iran, Vietnam, Cambodia etc.). Hence Carter's firmness, followed by Reagan's will to obtain some success in the "roll-back" policy, which consisted of helping "freedom fighters" to topple the recently established pro-Soviet regimes. But in fact, until 1987, most of the American analysts were pessimistic about a Soviet withdrawal from Afghanistan, and thus reluctant to feed a military escalation that could trigger a spill-over into Pakistan. They advocated restraint in arms supplies until 1985, and did not bother about domestic Mujahidin politics, an attitude which would have serious consequences.

It was under Congressional pressure that it was decided to help the Mujahidin "to fight not to die but to win", as stated in the Tsongas Resolution, adopted in October 1984. This firmness of Congress never failed, as shown by the resolution of 1 March 1988, which urged the

Administration to continue to supply weapons to the rebels even if a settlement was agreed in Geneva. The Afghan issue thus became the cornerstone of the American policy in south Asia, overshadowing other issues like nuclear proliferation or US–India rapprochement.

Early 1988, after the Soviet decision to withdraw was known, the American policy makers turned from pessimism to an overwhelming optimism. Two decisions were taken: to favour a short-term military solution and to support exclusively the Peshawar Alliance, instead of a broader coalition. It was also General Zia's choice. In fact, since 1985, the USAID, headed in Pakistan by Larry Crandle, has systematically been trying to upgrade the Peshawar Alliance into an administrative body, by channelling the biggest share of humanitarian help through it and by subsidising the bureaucracy it helped to create. Humanitarian aid was deliberately wasted for the sake of a political scheme, which in the end appeared as counter-productive because it bypassed and neglected the only competent people, the field commanders, and because it enlisted into a relatively well paid bureaucracy thousands of young educated Afghans who were desperately needed inside Afghanistan.

But, at the same time, Washington was still leaving it to Pakistan to choose who, among the Peshawar leaders, would be the main beneficiaries of the aid. Thus Washington was subsidising people it had not itself selected. When General Zia was killed in August 1988, Ambassador Robert Oakley was sent to Pakistan, and played a key role in both the political and military strategy of the Peshawar-based Afghan Interim Government, by imposing on it a policy which in fact had been designed by General Zia.

There was obviously a reverse "Saigon syndrome" among the American officials who were in charge of the Afghan affairs at the time of the Soviet withdrawal. The ill effect was to raise the expectations at such a level that after the failure of the offensive against Jellalabad, the mood began to change among the American public opinion. American policy during 1989 was totally contradictory. On the one hand, the Americans refused in theory to stop providing weapons to the Mujahidin, thus allowing Moscow to pour weapons worth billions of dollars into Kabul. This stance has been called "positive symmetry". But on the other hand, they in practice cut all military supplies to the Mujahidin from December 1988 to July 1989, practising unilaterally what the Soviets had advocated under the name of "negative symmetry". Secondly, the Americans, by giving full support to the Peshawar-based AIG, which has been ineffective and unrepresentative, contributed to undermining the power of the big field commanders, who were the only Mujahidin able to strike any effective military blows against the Kabul regime.

Just as the East–West issue had been brought to the fore by the Soviet invasion, the Soviet withdrawal brought the conflict back to its local and regional dimensions, where Moscow acts as a regional player, not as a superpower. But nobody in Washington seemed to notice it.

The regional conflict

The regional dimension of the war existed before Soviet invasion. It mainly consisted in the protracted conflict born from the partition of the Indian subcontinent. The Iranian revolution added a new aspect: Shi'i versus Sunni, Tehran versus Riyadh.

Pakistan

Pakistan's foreign policy is determined by its relation with India. Afghanistan has been seen as a potential ally for India ever since Kabul, in 1947, challenged the Pakistani sovereignty over "Pashtunistan", that is, the area of the North West Frontier Province, populated by Pashtun, or Pathan, who in 1947 were supporting Gandhi's Congress rather than Jinnah's Muslim League.

Thus all regimes in Pakistan were eager to avoid a Delhi/Kabul axis and to thwart Kabul designs on Pashtunistan. As we have seen (p. 75 above), the decision to support the Islamist opposition was taken by Zulfiqar Ali Bhutto and constantly carried on. But Pakistan had better connections with the Pashtun Islamists than with the groups in the area, for two reasons. Firstly because most of the Pakistani officials from the military secret services (ISI) or workers of the fundamentalist Pakistani Jama'at party who were in charge of dealing with the Mujahidin, were Pashtun, like General Akhtar and Qazi Husseyn Ahmed. Secondly because the strategy of the military was to use the Pashtunistan issue against any central government in Kabul by reverting to the old British colonial policy of dealing directly with the tribes, through bribes and delivery of weapons. But this policy worked better with Ghilzay and Eastern Pashtun than with Durrani. The Pakistanis were suspicious of the former King, Zaher, who could revitalise an Afghan–Pashtun nationalism with the support of the Durrani. Shi'a and Persian-speakers were seen as potential allies of Iran. Thus the Pakistanis chose to support Pashtun Islamists, who happen to be mainly Ghilzay or Eastern Pashtun: Gulbuddin Hekmatyar has been Pakistan's favourite since 1975.

At the same time the ISI had a policy of divide and rule. Pakistan was afraid of a palestinisation of the 3 million or so Afghans living in Pakistan and thus was very reluctant to see the emergence of a single political entity representing the Afghan Mujahidin. In fact it was not very difficult to maintain the Mujahidin in a state of disunity. The problem was to achieve enough unity to challenge the Kabul regime, without the risk of creating an Afghan PLO; for this reason, the Pakistanis did not give Hekmatyar the monopoly of Mujahidin political representation, and allowed traditional parties, like that of Gaylani. More secretly, the Pakistanis encouraged some separatist groups, like the Hazara "Tanzim" and the "Turkic" "Ittihad" of Azad Beg, a great-grandson of the last ruler of Koakand in Soviet Central Asia.

Thus the Pakistani Afghan policy was more determined by geostrategic constraints, as seen from Islamabad, than by ideological commitments. This explains why the policy did not change after General Zia's death in August 1988. Even the replacement of the ISI head, General Hamid Gul, by retired General Kaloo did not bring any change: Kaloo was among Ali Bhutto's trusted officers who established Hekmatyar in Peshawar in 1975.

But when the Soviet withdrawal became inevitable, it was deemed necessary to convert the seven parties' Alliance into an Afghan Interim Government that could fill the political vacuum following the expected collapse of the Kabul regime. The Pakistani policy consisted of favouring the Peshawar bureaucracy against the field commanders, and supporting the fundamentalist parties against both the traditionalists and the Jamiat. After the failure of a first endeavour in April 1988, a big *shura* was convened in Rawalpindi in February 1989. This *shura* was entirely controlled by the ISI, with Wahhabi agents busy behind the scenes. But in fact there was a convergence of interests between the ISI, the Wahhabi and the Peshawar bureaucracy to exclude the field commanders. A Shi'a delegation, which came from Tehran, was rebuked. Ethnically, this *shura* was mainly Ghilzay. Thus the "Afghan Interim Government" that was appointed by this Assembly was no more than the umpteenth combination of the seven Sunni parties, with Mojaddidi, more powerless than ever, elected as Chairman, Sayyaf as Prime Minister, Gulbuddin Hekmatyar as Minister of Foreign Affairs, Nabi for Defence and Rabbani for Reconstruction. Gaylani, openly critical, was in charge of organising elections. Then Washington decided to channel the totality of military and humanitarian help through this government in order to "legitimise" it.

The contradiction in the Pakistani policy was that the only way to topple the Kabul regime was to have a strong united resistance centred around the middle-of-the-road parties (including Jamiat), but Pakistan feared that such an alternative would threaten its own security after a Soviet withdrawal, and trusted Hekmatyar to prevent such a possibility.

The strange thing is that Washington endorsed this policy, although US interests were more threatened by the anti-western stance and dubious attitude of Hekmatyar than by the moderate and neutral approach of the other parties.

But if the Mujahidin did not succeed in taking Kabul, the biggest threat for Pakistan would be the domestic tensions aroused by the presence of disenchanted refugees and frustrated Mujahidin.

Iran

Iran's policy consisted of ensuring its control over the Shi'i minority in order to play a major part in the future of Afghanistan, without being led into a direct confrontation with the USSR during the Gulf War. The end of the war coincided with the Soviet withdrawal. Thus the priority of Iran became to avoid the political vacuum in Afghanistan being filled by Pakistan alone, by the Americans, or, worst of all, by the Saudis. This policy was first developed in the name of the "export of the revolution", which had been achieved among the Shi'i in 1984. The Shi'i parties in Tehran were regrouped, in 1986, under an "Eight Parties Alliance", to which were added some small Sunni splinter groups (like Qazi Amin, of Hezb).

In fact Iran realised that the spread of fundamentalist ideas among the Sunni would not lead to a rapprochement with the Iranian Islamic Revolution, but, on the contrary, was of direct benefit to the Wahhabi, the worst enemy of Iran both on doctrinal grounds (Shi'i are heretics for the Wahhabi) and for strategic reasons (Wahhabism means Saudi Arabia). The Iranian Revolution did not spread outside the Shi'i ghettos. More than that, the growing Wahhabi influence, combined with the traditional Pashtun hatred for Hazara, led to a crystallisation of ethnic and religious antagonisms against the Hazara, who were opposed by the Pashtuns on both ethnic and religious grounds.

For all these reasons, Iran decided early in 1989 to adopt a more balanced policy. References to Islamic revolution were toned down. Tehran attempted a rapprochement with Moscow, where Rafsanjani travelled in June 1989, and ceased to rebuke the royalists or a coalition government with the PDPA. At a seminary in Tehran on 15 January, Velayati, the Iranian Minister of Foreign Affairs called for a "neutral, independent Afghanistan, retaining its Islamic identity": this is far from the Islamic revolution. Iran ceased, from that time, to work towards the lebanonisation of Afghanistan, and urged instead a merger between the two Mujahidin alliances and a political settlement.

Thus for Iran also, geo-strategic constraints weigh more than ideological positions. Iran plays a regional game, where the arch-enemy is not Moscow but Riyadh.

The ideological dimension

The Afghan war is the only case in the contemporary Muslim world of a liberation war waged by peasants in the name of Islam. By contrast, Iran's has been a urban revolution. The Afghan Mujahidin are a part of the fundamentalist wave that has swept the Middle East.

But, in fact, the Afghan war has little impact either among the Iranian revolutionaries, who were more eager to fight the West and the Arabs than to confront the USSR, or among the Arab fundamentalist circles, at least until 1984. Then, as we have seen Arab "Mujahidin" began to arrive in Pakistan. They did not come from the more radical milieu, but instead from conservative Wahhabi and Muslim Brotherhood groups. This Arab influence is the result of a joint venture between Muslim Brotherhood circles and strictly Wahhabi clerics. The Arab teachers, missionaries and fighters sent to Pakistan and Afghanistan were selected, subsidised and channelled through semi-official Saudi organisations, like the Red Crescent, and under the supervision of Abdullah Ezzam in Peshawar. They generally went on the side of Sayyaf *Ittihadia*, of both Hezb, and to a lesser extent of Jamiat.

This move was encouraged by Saudi Arabia, to challenge a possible Iranian influence among fundamentalist groups. Thus the strategic design of Riyadh fitted in well with its religious commitment: to fight "kafir" – that is, communists – but also "heretics" – that is, Shi'i. There is thus a congruence between ethnic, religious and ideological rifts in Afghanistan: Pashtuns were supported by Pakistan for strategic reasons and by Saudis because they were seen as the main bulwark against any Shi'i but also Persian influence. It seems even that Riyadh was more concern to thwart Iranian influence in Afghanistan than to topple the communist regime. Once more the ideological dimension is hiding strategic concerns. Afghanistan provides the stage for the continuation of the Gulf war.

The Geneva Agreements

There have been indirect negotiations between Pakistan and the Kabul regime in Geneva since 1982, through the mediation of the special envoy of the Secretary General of the UN, Diego Cordovez. But the negotiations broke down over the question of the withdrawal of the Soviet troops. Pakistan insisted on a quick withdrawal, in less than twelve months. Kabul and Moscow wanted to obtain a stabilisation of the Kabul regime before the completion of any withdrawal. Thus the negotiations had reached a stalemate, when Gorbachev announced on 8 February the decision to withdraw unilaterally. The decision to leave Afghanistan had probably been taken in the wake of the 27th Plenum of the CPSU, in summer 1986. But when the negotiators met in Geneva in March 1988, new obstacles appeared: Washington refused to stop supplying weapons to the Mujahidin until the completion of the withdrawal, fearing that Moscow could use this period to strike a decisive blow against the Mujahidin.

After a month of negotiations at Geneva, it was decided not to mention any commitment of both sides to stop supplying their allies; Washington made then a unilateral statement pledging "positive symmetry": that is, supplying the Mujahidin as long as the Soviets did the same with the regime. The Geneva agreements were in no way a peace treaty. They merely established the conditions of a Soviet withdrawal, leaving open the key question: who will run Afghanistan? Apparently both sides made a gambit: the Soviets thought that the Kabul regime would hold, the Americans that it would crumble very soon. So the military balance of power remained the ultimate referee. But the Geneva agreements also meant the end of the East–West dimension of the conflict.

The Soviet Union and Islam

As we said in the Introduction, the Afghan resistance movement lies at the intersection of two histories: that of Islam, that of the communist world. These two histories have evolved considerably since the writing of these pages. The USSR is no longer a fortress and the death of Iman Khomeyni was also the death of the dream of an universal Islamic revolution. The Afghan war might have contributed to *perestroika*, in as much as it stressed the stalemate to which Brezhnevian foreign policy was leading the country, but perhaps also to the extent that it has humbled the pride of the Soviet Army, thus reducing its potential opposition to the new policy.

But the Soviet Union is not rid of Islam. Although the messianic dimension of the Islamic revolution is receding, the southern Soviet republics which are striving for more autonomy find in Islam a common identity and in the Afghan war a proof that the Soviet Army can be thwarted by Muslims. Once more, an ideological dimension has turned into a strategic stake. Moscow might wonder whether it would be safer to support at all cost a PDPA regime in Kabul, rather than to see victorious Mujahidin at the Soviet border, or whether it would be more advisable to have a stable regime in Kabul, whatever its ideology. Moscow is now on the defensive, regardless to the political up and downs in Afghanistan.

The resistance parties

Sunni parties

Islamists

Hizb-i islami: radical Islamists, led by Gulbuddin Hekmatyar. Its recruits are amongst those who were educated in the secular government schools and also some *'ulama* from the Kabul region. Mainly Pashtun.

Hizb-i islami (Khalis): moderate Islamists, led by Mawlawi Yunus Khalis. Its recruits come from those educated in the government schools and the *'ulama* of the Khugiani and Jadran tribes as well as in the region of Kabul and Kandahar. Pashtun.

Jam'iyyat-i islami: moderate Islamists, led by Burhanuddin Rabbani. Its recruits come from amongst those educated in the government schools (both religious and secular), the *'ulama* in the north and *naqshbandi* in the north. Mainly Tajik.

Traditionalists

Harakat-i inqilab-i islami: moderate clerical party, led by Muhammad Nabi Muhammadi. It gains recruits from the *'ulama* educated in private *madrasa*. Mainly Pashtun.

Jabha-yi nejat-i milli (National Liberation Front): secular, led by Sebghatullah Mujaddidi. Its recruits come mainly from the tribes, the establishment of the old social order and the *naqshbandi* in the south.

Mahaz-i islami (Islamic Front): Royalist, led by Pir Sayyad Ahmad Gaylani. Its recruits come from the establishment of the old social order, the tribes and the *qadiri* in the south. Mainly Pashtun.

Shi'ite parties

Shura-yi ittifagh-i islami: traditionalist, led by Sayyad Beheshti. Its recruits come from the Hazara peasantry, officered by the *sayyad*.

Nasr: radical Islamists, led by a council. It gains recruits from young Hazara educated in Iran.

Harakat-i islami: moderate Islamists, led by Shaykh Asaf Muhseni. Its recruits are educated Shi'a from all ethnic groups.

Sepah-i Pasdaran (Guardians of the Revolution): radical Islamists who depend very much on Iran. Led by Akbari of Turkman and Saddiqi of Nili.

Glossary

asabiyya: Arabic term which means communal spirit, that is to say allegiance to a communal group

'adat: custom, customary rights, habits

akhundzade: descendant of an important religious figure, very often of a *pir*

'alim (plural: *'ulama*): Doctor of the Law. The term usually refers to someone who has successfully completed a higher degree in a *madrasa*

amir: leader. In the Resistance, someone who has civil and military power

arbab: in the centre and the north, equivalent of *malik*

ash'ari: someone who follows Ash'ari, theologian born in 874, who tried to reconcile traditional faith and rational theology

Aymaq: Persian-speaking Sunni groups, often semi-nomadic, living in the centre of Afghanistan (Ghor province)

'ayyar: swashbuckling brigands in the Persian tradition. The word originally meant "knights", the "Paladins". Here it has the same connotation as Robin Hood

badal: vengeance in the *pashtunwali*

Baluchi: ethnic group living on the frontier between Iran, Afghanistan and Pakistan. They speak an Iranian dialect of the north-west, but include *brahui* groups (Dravidians)

barakat: a sanctity which brings blessing to others and which emanates from certain people or certain objects. People are sanctified by making contact with the person or object

bari: in Nuristan, a caste of slaves owned collectively by the village community and specialising in cutting wood

batin: the esoteric Divine Revelation, which can only be attained by mystical initiation and not through dogmatic theology

bay (or *beg*): in the north, equivalent of *khan*

bid'at: innovation in matters of religion. For the traditionalist, this is a grievous sin *buzkashi*: a rather violent sport played by Afghans in the north. It involves two or more teams of horse riders trying to place a decapitated goat in a circle

cheshtiyya: Sufi brotherhood which has its roots mainly in the Indian subcontinent, but very active in Afghanistan around the town of Chesht-i Sharif (Herat province)

dar al-makhzan (as opposed to *dar as-siba*): the *makhzan* country is part of Morrocan territory under the control of a Sultan, through the intermediary of his army and an embryo administration, mainly composed of influential people integrated into the state structure. The *siba* lands are the tribal zones where the village communities are autonomous, but in which political divisions are rife

da'wat: religious preaching. In modern times the word often has a political connotation

dawlat: state. The sphere of supreme power, as opposed to the state machine (*hukumat*)

dihqan: peasant in general, but usually means "share-cropper". Often applied to groups which have recently adopted Pashtun culture, although sometimes retaining the Persian language, not tribalised and living in the middle of Pashtun tribal zones (Kunar, Urgun)

din-i ilahi: religion made official by the Mogul Emperor Akbar (1556–1605), which sought to achieve a syncretism between Hinduism and Islam

Durrani: Pashtun tribal federation situated in the south-west, from which the Royal family came

faqih: writer on law, specialist in the *fiqh*

faqir: "someone who is poor", a wandering holy man. Sometimes used as a synonym for *pir*

fatwa: legal advice provided on a specific point by a *shaykh ul islam*, that is to say a *qazi* of superior rank

fiqh: Muslim law

futuwwa: brotherhood of young citizens in medieval Islam, especially in Persia and in Iraq. Their reputation fluctuates, according to the period and the commentator, between a kind of knighthood and a Mafia of young thugs

ghausi: Sufi brotherhood which has few members in Afghanistan

ghazi: someone who is victorious in the struggle against the infidel

Ghilzay (*ghilji*): Pashtun tribal federation in the south-east

giraw: an asset which is given to someone who makes a loan. He may derive benefit from it so long as the debt is not repaid

ghund: regiment

Gujar (*gujur*): a nomadic ethnic group of Indian origin which is to be found in the mountains in the north-east of Afghanistan

hadith: words and doctrines preached by the Prophet, handed down by a line of authorities. Its authenticity is the subject of an entire branch of study

Hanafite: school of legal writers who have adopted the style of interpretation of Abu Hanifa (ninth century AD). The most widespread and the most liberal school

harka: a mobile unit of native auxilliary troops in Algeria

hawza: district

Hazara: Shi'a population which has Mongol features, whose origins are not known. They occupy the centre of Afghanistan (Hazarajat: the provinces of Bamyan and part of Ghazni, Oruzgan, Ghor, Jawzjan, Balkh, Samangan, Baghlan, Parwan and Wardak)

hijrat: exodus; Hegira. The exile of Muhammad from Mecca to Medina

hujra: guest room or reception room for strangers, especially in tribal areas

hukumat: state machine, the government

ijaza: certificate. Document with which a student is awarded his qualifications by his teacher

ijma': consensus of believers. A means of interpreting the law in those instances not dealt with by Revelation or the *sunnat*; according to certain schools, this should be interpreted as the consensus of *'ulama* only

ijtihad: personal interpretation, a privilege reserved for the four great historical *mojtahid* (Hanifa, Malik, Shafi'i and Ibn Hanbal) according to Sunni beliefs, or the Doctors of the Law according to the Shi'a

ikhwan: *ikhwan al-muslimin* (Muslim Brothers): the name given to the first Islamist organisation founded in Egypt by Hasan Al-Banna and used in Afghanistan by the enemies of the Islamists to refer to the movements in the same tradition

iqta': the act by which fiscal rights of the state over a certain area of land are transferred to a private individual (usually a soldier), which rights are not inherited by his children

Isma'ili: Shi'a sect which recognises the seventh Imam as the hidden Imam (instead of the twelfth as the orthodox Shi'a would have it). The Isma'ilis have developed a complex mystical gnosis

jabha: "front", in both the military and political senses

jagir: equivalent of the *iqta'* amongst the Mogul emperors and later in Afghanistan. The *jagirdar* is a *khan* or a general to whom the state has granted fiscal rights over an area of land

Jama'at: a Pakistan Islamist political party founded by Mawdudi (1941)

jarib: an area of land just under half an acre

jirga: assembly of men in Pashtun tribal areas. The *jirga* may bring together all those who have been engaged in fighting or only the *malik* and the revered elders

kafir: infidel

kalam: speculative theology; philosophy applied to Revelation

Khad: initials of *Khadamat-i ittila'at-i dawlati*, secret political police of the Kabul government, set up by the KGB

khalifa: successor, lieutenant; the one who succeeds a *pir*

Khalq: "the people". A faction of the Democratic Party of the Afghan People (communist) after the split of 1967. It provided the first two leaders of the revolution (Taraki and Amin) before being ousted by the pro-Soviet Parcham

khan: generally a landowner at the head of a large family and with a large circle of dependents, for whom he provides food and loans. The leader of a tribal faction (clan or tribal sub-group)

khanaqah: place where the Sufis carry out their spiritual devotion

khayl: clan; sub-division of a segment of a Pashtun tribe, whatever the level of this sub-division may be

khilafat: caliphate, function of the *khalifa*; incarnation of the spiritual and temporal succession of the Prophet (in particular in the Ottoman Emperors). Movement for the restoration of the caliphate, very active in India around 1920

Khurasan: province in the east of Persia, which included Herat; cradle of Persian classical culture

khutba: the Friday sermon, traditionally preached in the name of the reigning sovereign, whose authority is thereby asserted

khwaja: descendant of one of the first caliphs; "master"

koka: gang of thugs at Kabul

lashkar: armed body formed by a mass uprising of the tribes

madrasa: higher religious school

mahalli: locals

mahr: dowry. Legally, a sum of money provided for the woman which will support her if she is repudiated by her husband

Mahratte: Hindu confederation which fought against the Mogul Empire in the eighteenth century and which was defeated by Ahmed Shah at Panipat

maktab: either primary religious school (in opposition to *madrasa*), or school in general (thus a government school)

malang: wandering mystics, who live by begging and selling amulets *malik*: village leader, elected by the revered elders

ma'mur: official

markaz: "centre", place where a resistance base has been set up

masjid: mosque

maslahat: general welfare. Concept of Muslim law which authorises the sovereign to lay down laws where the *shari'at* gives no positive indications on a given matter

maslaki: professional soldier

mawlawi: in Afghanistan this means an *'alim*

millat: the nation as opposed to the state. Religious group defined as a community which obeys its own laws (Muslims, Christians)

mirab: someone elected and entrusted with the responsibility of ensuring that water rights are respected, for which he receives remuneration

mlatar: in Pashtu the dependents of a *khan*

modarres: a teacher in a *madrasa*

moghol: Muslim dynasty founded by Babur, of Turkish origin. It conquered India beginning with Kabul; it reigned in India from the sixteenth to the nineteenth centuries

mojtahid: someone who is authorised to practice *ijtihad*. The Sunni no longer have any; amongst the Shi'a, the term refers to the great Ayatullahs

monism: any theory which affirms the identity of the Creator and the created, and between the self and God

moqi: amongst the Isma'ilis, the equivalent of the *pir*. A master of thought, a leader both in the temporal and the spiritual sense

mu'allem: someone who teaches in a government school

mu'avin: assistant, second in command

Mujahidin: one who is fighting for *jihad*, holy war

mukhles: "disciple" of a *pir*, although not involving personal initiation. In a social rather than a spiritual sense, a follower, servant, client

mullah: a low-level Muslim priest

munjani: a small ethnic group in Badakhshan, converted to Isma'ilism

murid: disciple of a *pir* from whom he receives personal initiation

murshid: spiritual leader

mutaharek: mobile, a mobile group

myan: in tribal areas, a religious figure whose status is below that of the *sayyad* (for the *myan* is not a descendant of the Prophet). He plays the same role as an intermediary in conflicts

naqshbandiyya: Sufi brotherhood founded in the fourteenth century by Baha'uddin Naqshband ("the dyer")

nihzat: movement of Islamic Renaissance

nizam: order, organisation, political programme

Nuristani: ethnic group living in the mountains in north-east Afghanistan; only converted at the end of the nineteenth century

padshahgardi: the "stratagems of kings", succession of Amirs to the throne

Parcham: "the flag". Faction of the Democratic Party of the Afghan People (Communist Party) which split in 1967. Led by Babrak Karmal, it was opposed to the Khalq

Pashtu: language spoken by the Pashtun (Iranian branch from the east)

Pashtun: dominant ethnic group in Afghanistan, living in the south of the country

pashtunwali: both an ideology and a system of traditional rights amongst the Pashtun tribes

Patriotic Front: *jabaha-yi padarwatan*, organisation set up by the Khad to work outside the framework of the Communist Party in order to win support for the government from families of influence

paygah: base.

payluch: "urchins", gang of thugs at Kandahar

pir: "the old one". Sufi spiritual master, whose authority derives from the fact that he is a link in a chain of people who have been spiritually initiated (*silsila*)

potlatch (American Indian term): gift symbolic of status through which a man of influence asserts his authority over those who are unable to rival his largesse

qabila: "tribe", as opposed to *khayl*. It always refers to a large, established tribe

qadiriyya: Sufi order founded by Abdul Qadir Gaylani in the thirteenth century

qalandar: a wandering mystic, often belonging to a Sufi order

qanum: state law in opposition to religious law

qarargah: military base (in Panjshir)

qawm: communal group, whose sociological basis may vary. It may be a clan (in tribal zones), a village, an ethnic group, an extended family, a professional group

qazi: a religious judge who applies the *shari'at*

qesher: the junior clan in the Pashtun tribes. It originated in a junior lineage as opposed to the older clans (*masher*), which have more status and are generally more richly endowed with men and goods

qisas: "the law of retaliation" allowed by the *shari'at* to meet out private vengeance. The injured party may ask for financial compensation rather than proceeding with the strict application of the law

qiyas: method of arguing by analogy from previous examples, which

makes it possible to come to a judgement in cases not encompassed by
the *fiqh*

qizilbash: "red head". Shi'a in Afghan towns, whose language is Persian
and who are descendants of the Turk contingent left behind by Iran in
the eighteenth century

rish safed (*aqsaqal* in Turkish): "revered elders" of the village, whom
form the council in which real power resides (except in those instances
when there is a *khan* in the village). They elect the *malik*

riwaj: local custom, customary rights (as opposed to the *shari'at* and
qanun)

roshanfikr: a neologism which translates as "intellectual" (cf. Arabic
munawwar ul fikr). Literally "enlightened thought"

ruhani: in Iranian Persian and amongst the Shi'a this means a member of
the clergy. Amongst the tribes it means a Sufi *pir* who is not an *'alim*
(Maraboutic Sufism)

rushani: unorthodox sect founded in the sixteenth century by Bayazid
Ansari, which was at the centre of the uprising of the eastern Pashtun
against the Mogul state

salafiyya: movement of reform in Islam during the nineteenth century,
with Jamaluddin Afghani and Muhammad 'Abduh canvassing for a
return to the ancient doctrine the better to meet the challenge posed by
the West

SAMA (sazman-e azadibakhsh-e mardum-i Afghanistan: Liberation
Organisation of the Afghan People): a left-wing movement which
developed from the Maoist movement and which was established in
1980 to oppose the Russians. Founded by 'Abdul Majid Kalakani

sangar: "entrenchment"; takes the same metaphorical sense as "trenches" or "barricades" in English

sar-e grup: head of a fighting group

sayyad: someone who is believed to have descended from the Prophet
(through his daughter Fatima)

shahid: "martyr", someone who has fallen in combat

shari'at: the totality of the Muslim religious law

shaykh: "ancient". It sometimes refers to a *pir* but it is also used by the
Afghan Shi'a to refer to the *'ulama* who have studied in Iran or Iraq

shaykh ul-islam: *qazi* whose authority extends over a region or a territory
and who has authority to set up *fatwa*

shol'e-yi jawid: Maoist organisation founded in the sixties

shura: council, consultative assembly

Sikhism: Indian religion founded in the fifteenth century which recruits
members from amongst the Punjabi. They have long been enemies of
Muslims

silsila: a chain formed of those who have been directly endowed with the authority of the *pir* of a Sufi order; genealogy

sitam-i milli; "National oppression", left-wing organisation founded by Taher Badakhshi in 1979, to oppose the Soviet Union, the Khalq, and the domination of the Pashtun

siyasat: "policy"

sohrawardiyya: Sufi brotherhood founded in the twelfth century by 'Abdul Qahir Sohrawardi

Sufism: Islamic mystical doctrine

sunnat: "tradition", more especially tradition of the Prophet: accounts of his deeds and actions and his "sayings" (*hadith*)

tafsir: commentary on the Qur'an

tahrik: movement (in the political sense)

Tajik: refers not so much to an ethnic group as to the Persian-speaking Sunni of Afghanistan

takfir: the action of declaring a Muslim to be an infidel

talib (plural *tulaba*): student of religion in a *madrasa*

ta'mir: "building", government post

tanzim; a nationalist and leftist Hazara group

taqlid: imitation. Amongst the Shi'a, the imitation of a moral instructor chosen by the believer

tariqat: the way. Sufi brotherhood

ta'zir: discretionary punishment provided for by the law of the prince, in those cases when the offence is not provided for by the religious law

tulaba: see *talib*

Turkmen: a Turkish-speaking ethnic group in the north of Afghanistan

'ulama: see *'alim*

ulus: tribal federation

uluswal: district in Afghanistan (there are about 350 of them)

umma: the Islamic community, the totality of Muslims in the world

'ushr: tithe, an Islamic tax on income which goes to the state

Uzbek: a Turkish-speaking ethnic group in the north of Afghanistan and the south of the USSR

Wahhabism: a strict puritan sect founded in Saudi Arabia in the eighteenth century, and dominant in that country. By extension, and incorrectly, it refers to the fundamentalists in the Indian subcontinent

wahdat al wujud: unity of Being, opposed to *wahdat al shuhud*, unity of phenomena. The first theory identifies the creature with God, the second, which characterises orthodox Sufism, maintains that there is an ontological difference between the two

wali: governor

wesh: periodical redistribution of individually owned land between two or three Pashtun clans

zahir: appearance, the exoteric, the external message of revelation

zakat: legalised alms. An Islamic tax on capital, reserved for a very carefully selected group of beneficiaries (the poor, the clergy, etc.)

zikr: litany of the names of God, which characterises one of the ecstatic rites of the Sufi orders

ziyarat: tomb of a "saint" which has become a place of pilgrimage

Chronological table

1747: victoryof the Durrani tribal federation led by Ahmad Shah of the Saddozay clan of the Popalzay tribe. He founded a Durrani empire which stretched as far as India

1761: victory of Panipat against the Marathes

1773–1793: reign of Timur Shah

1793–1799: reign of Zaman Shah

1803–1809: reign of Shah Shuja'

1809: British delegation to Peshawar led by Mountstuart Elphinstone

1809–1818: reign of Mahmud

1818–1835: civil war

1835–1863: reign of Dost Muhammad

1839–1842: first Anglo-Afghan war, the interregnum of Shah Shuja'

1856: the Persians take Herat

1863–1879: the reign of Shir 'Ali

1878: the second Anglo-Afghan war

1879: Treaty of Gandamak signed by Yaqub Khan, which included the agreement that a British representative should be installed at Kabul

1880: the British recognise Abdurrahman as Amir

1880: British defeat at Maywand

1885: occupation of the Panjdih oasis by the Russians

1887: Russo-Afghan agreement on the northern frontier of Afghanistan

1893: Durand agreement on the eastern frontier of Afghanistan

1901: death of Abdurrahman. His son Habibullah becomes Amir

1911: the founding of the modernist journal *Siraj ul-Akhbar* by Mahmud Tarzi

1919: the assassination of Habibullah. Amanullah becomes Amir

1919: the third Anglo-Afghan war

1921: the Amir of Bukhara takes refuge in Afghanistan

1921: 21 February, treaty of friendship with the USSR

1924: tribal uprising at Khost

1927: visit of the King to Europe

1928: a series of reforms followed by an uprising by the Shinwari and the Bacha-yi Saqqao

1929: abdication of Amanullah, defeat of Bacha and victory of Nadir Khan supported by a tribal federation

1933: assassination of Nadir Khan; Zahir becomes King

1946: the founding of the University of Kabul

1947: partition of India and the independence of Pakistan; Afghanistan first makes claim to Pashtunistan

1953–63: Daoud, cousin of the King becomes Prime Minister

1955: in December official visit of Kruschev and Bulganin

1961: crisis between Afghanistan and Pakistan

1963: Daoud removed from power, the beginning of the constitutional era

1963–1965: the Yusuf ministry

1965: General Election (August), student riots and the dismissal of Yusuf's cabinet (October)

1965: the founding of the Democratic Party of the Afghan People (communist)

1969: elections for parliament's second term

1973: 17 July, *coup d'état* by Prince Daoud, who establishes a republic

1978: 27 April, communist *coup d'état*

1979: 27 December, Soviet invasion

Notes

Introduction

1 See *Esprit* "Le Proche Orient dans la guerre" (May–June 1983); G. Michaud "Terrorisme d'Etat, Terrorisme contre l'Etat" in *Esprit*, October–November 1984; M. Seurat "Les Populations, l'Etat, la Société" in *La Syrie d'Aujourd'hui*, Centre National de la Recherche Scientifique 1980.

2 For a critical discussion see Barry 1984 (pp. 8off and 276ff).

3 See Shayegan 1982.

4 Mitchell 1969, Mortimer 1982, Carre and Michaud 1983, Kepel 1984.

5 I have borrowed this term from J.F. Clément "Pour une compréhension des mouvements islamistes" *Esprit* January 1980, who says that he first heard this used by Habib Boulares. The term seems to have appeared in Muslim circles in the Maghreb around 1970 in order to distinguish between *muslim* and *islami*, the latter being those who see Islam as a political ideology.

6 See on this point the article of Souhayr Belhassen "Femmes islamistes tunisiennes" in CNRS 1981.

7 See Jean-Pierre Charnay, *Technique et géosociologie*, Anthropos, 1984, for a very illuminating comparison.

1 State and society in Afghanistan

1 On the opposition of state and society, see Roy 1981, and especially P. and M. Centlivres 1981.

2 See Azoy 1982 and Anderson 1983.

3 For a typology of social strata linked to the state see Daoud 1982.

4 Ahmed 1982, pp. 168ff; Centlivres 1976, pp. 8ff.

5 Ahmed 1982, pp. 8ff; Steul 1981.

6 Elphinstone explains that there is an ideal type of tribalism of which an example may be found amongst the eastern Pashtun. Other forms amongst the Durrani may be explained on this basis, even if they differ from the ideal type (Elphinstone 1972, vol. 2, p. 2). For tribalism amongst groups other than the Pashtun, the term can be used in the strict sense for the Nuristani and the Baluchi, but not for the Tajik or Uzbek. For the Hazara, tribalism has largely disappeared following the Pashtun conquest. The Aymaq are the most interesting, for they call themselves "tribespeople", but nobody has ever been

able to map out their territory and the names that they use are often contradictory. There may have been a rebirth of tribalism (more imaginary than real) when their area was infiltrated by the Pashtun at the end of the nineteenth century. At that time a tribal mythology was created so they could feel that their pedigree was as good as that of their rivals (some of the Aymaq, adopted names borrowed from Pashtun clans). In any case, in none of these four groups is there any survival or memory of tribal codes of conduct or institutions, even though people's membership of a communal group shows a regular pattern: *qawm* has a broader sense than "tribe".

7 Newell 1981, p. 34; Gregorian 1969, p. 48. Not very much is known about the ethnic origins of the Pashtun; it is clear that they embrace a range of peoples of diverse origins. They are not often mentioned before the eighteenth century although Babur describes them as a community given to plundering who live to the south of Kabul. The growth in their political influence was certainly due, in part, to a sudden increase in their numbers and was also assisted by their role as mercenaries in the Persian and Mogul armies. In all there are three different groups of tribes: the Durrani in the west, the Ghilzay between Kandahar and Kabul, and the eastern Pashtun on either side of the present-day frontier between Afghanistan and Pakistan (the Durand line).

8 The best description to be found in the first book written on the Pashtun, by the first British ambassador (Scottish, as were the majority of the British who served in Afghanistan), Mountstuart Elphinstone, *An account of the Kingdom of Caubul* (1st edition 1815, republished in 1972). See in particular vol. 1, pp. 211, 218, 330; and vol. 2, p. 283: "For the consolidation of his power at home he [the king] relied, in great measure, on the effects of his foreign wars. If these were successful, his victories would raise his reputation, and his conquests would supply him with the means of maintaining an army and of attaching the Afghan chiefs by favours and rewards: the hope of plunder would induce many tribes to join him whom he could not easily have compelled to submit."

9 See Ahmed 1980, pp. 181 and 193.

10 Daoud 1982, p. 101; Dupree 1980, p. 754; Etienne 1972, p. 172; Bernardin 1972; Grassmuck *et al.* 1969, p. 171; Daoud 1982, p. 101.

11 Hostility between cousins is quite traditional amongst the *pashtunwali* (*tarbor* means both cousin and the enemy). From Abdurrahman to Zahir Shah, conflicts between cousins are commonplace.

12 For a (confused) description of this establishment see Adamec 1975.

13 The best book (but too descriptive on the process of modernisation) is Gregorian 1969. For Abdurrahman see Kakar 1979.

14 It is quite wrong to see the *shari'at* as a vestige of medieval life. At the beginning of the twentieth century it was not unusual to see the return to the *shari'at* being made by people whose viewpoint was that of modernism. The *shari'at* introduces a principle of universality into law and thus takes justice out of the hands of local communities (the Afghan *qawm* or the Arab *asabiyya*). The modern state could only be established by breaking down the

communities which existed upon a subordinate level. For an interesting example, see the way in which 'Abdul Krim used the *shari'at* to override common law during the Rif war: Youssofi, in *Abdel Krim et la Republique du Rif* ('Abdul Krim and the Rif Republic), pp. 81 and 89ff.

15 Kakar 1969, pp. 156, 157, 178.
16 See the speech made by Amanullah on his return from Europe: Gregorian 1969, p. 259.
17 Research into which European authors (or books introducing these authors) were being read by Asian intellectuals at this period would be useful; they were in general those writers steeped in positivism and scientism.
18 Etienne 1972, p. 239.
19 Davies 1975, p. 16.
20 Elphinstone 1972, vol. I, p. 125.
21 Gregorian 1969, p. 200; Schinasi 1979, p. 133.
22 Kakar 1979, p. 10; Gregorian 1969, p. 151.
23 P. and M. Centlivres 1981; this provides the most acute analysis of relations between the state and the peasants.
24 Canfield describes (with admiration) the case of a *uluswali* who arrested and condemned a Hazara murderer for a crime which was carried out to even the score between two warring families, under the direction of the elders: Canfield n.d.
25 Tapper 1983, p. 245.
26 Etienne quotes the commonplace examples of officials demanding bicycles in order to get around, as these are symbols of modern living, and refusing horses, although the latter are more practical. Etienne 1972, p. 109.
27 M. and R. Poulton 1979, vol. III, p. 137.
28 There is a vast literature on the dialectic of power amongst the *khan*, especially in the tribal zones; see all the writings of Ahmed and Anderson (in particular 1978 and 1983).
29 Elphinstone 1972, vol. I, p. 328.
30 There are instances amongst the Nuristani tribe where what a *khan* must do to maintain his status is codified to a remarkable extent; for example, at Waygal how often a *khan* provides collective meals for the village and the size of each individual meal determines in a very precise fashion what his status is: see Jones 1974.
31 A recent example has been provided by the colonisation of the Helmand valley between 1953 and 1973: the state installed *qawm* in the newly developed land by negotiating with their *malik*; see Scott [n.d.], p. 3.
32 Rubinstein 1982, p. 134; Daoud 1982, pp. 296ff; Grassmuck 1969, pp. 172ff.
33 S. Kushkaki's newspaper *Karawan* complained that the 216 deputies represented 216 different political platforms (21 May 1973).
34 Etienne (1972, pp. 22 and 82) denies that there is such a thing as a real village community.
35 Ferdinand 1962, pp. 152ff.
36 A good example is the village militia, which are *elected* and given the responsibility of ensuring that community decisions are respected; Elphin-

stone provides a description of how this practice used to operate amongst the Ghilzay in the past (1972, vol. 2, pp. 153ff) and Edelberg gives an account of how it operates amongst the Nuristani of Waygal in the present (Edelberg and Jones 1979, p. 57).

37 On this theme see the interview with P. and M. Centlivres conducted by P. Bourdieu, *Actes de la Recherche en Sciences Sociales*, No. 34, September 1980.

38 A good example, in the field of agriculture, is provided by Gentelle (1979): the introduction by the state of artificial fertiliser, crops intended for industrial purposes (such as cotton) and mechanisation, have removed the control over farming out of the hands of the peasant; the expert, the mechanic and the planner all know more about it now than he does.

2 Islam in Afghanistan

1 Newell 1972, p. 26; Grevemeyer 1980, p. 163; Dupree 1980, p. 107.
2 For an example in the Kunar, see Christensen 1980, p. 82.
3 Elphinstone 1972, vol. 2, p. 108.
4 Shayegan 1982, p. 144.
5 Ahmed, in Ahmed and Hart 1984, pp. 314ff.
6 Rives 1963, pp. 76 and 84.
7 Ahmed 1976, p. 54; 1980, p. 88; Steul 1981.
8 Kakar 1979, p. 36.
9 For inheritance, Gregorian 1969, p. 41, Ahmed 1980, p. 295; for dowry and divorce, *ibid.*, p. 250; for vengeance, Dupree 1973, p. 104; on the *wesh*, Elphinstone 1972, vol. 2, pp. 14ff.
10 For a recent case, see Ahmed 1982, p. 318.
11 Einzmann, 1977, p. 7.
12 Ahmed 1980, pp. 161ff.
13 Ahmed 1982, p. 185; for the connection between the charismatic mullah and tribal uprisings, see pp. 62ff.
14 The best overall book if Schimmel 1975; for Sufism see pp. 364ff.
15 Centlivres 1972, pp. 165ff.
16 See p. 55.
17 These associations are like the *futuwwa* described by Cahen (1970, pp. 124ff). It is interesting to find a medieval tradition, thought to have died out, still in existence: "in the most distant times, the fityan seemed to have practised initiatory rights . . . each group invoked its own patron who had lived in ancient times, who was connected with the present master through a long chain of intermediaries" (p. 126). Cahen identifies these groups of young people with the *ayyar* (p. 125), a tradition which is still very much alive in the collective memory of the Afghan people (but in the countryside, in particular in Shamali).
18 See Schimmel 1975, p. 365.
19 See the following chapter.
20 Poullada 1973, pp. 126 and 198.
21 Centlivres 1972, p. 60.

22 Peshawar was already an important educational centre at the beginning of the nineteenth century; Elphinstone 1972, vol. 2, pp. 249ff.
23 On the difference between intellectuals and *literati* see Centlivres P. and M. 1980, p. 5.
24 On the question of the growing inflexibility of the tradition of learning, the stereotyped manuals, the legalism and the lack of any personal intellectual research, accompanied by a failure to renew an outdated schema, see Gardet 1977, p. 305.
25 Gregorian 1969, p. 135.
26 A great number of studies have been carried out, principally by English-speaking authors, on the question of competition for political power amongst the *khan*. Only P. and M. Centlivres (1972, 1980) and M. and R. Poulton (1979, vol. 3, pp. 64ff) have noted the way in which the *mawlawi* continue to assert their influence.
27 Kakar 1979, p. 153.

3 The origins of Afghan fundamentalism and popular movements

1 The writer Khallilulah Khallili refers to the tradition of the *ayyar* (outlaws who fight injustice) in his account of the revolt of Bacha-yi Saqqao (Khallili 1983). See also chapter 2, n. 18.
2 The Soviets sometimes depict Shah Waliullah as a feudal thinker, sometimes an enlightened member of the bourgeoisie (see the review of the book by Gordon-Polonskaya and the critique by Y. Payevskaya, quoted in *Central Asian Review*, 13, no. 2, 1965). For Maudi, Shah Waliullah is a forerunner of twentieth-century Islamism (Maudi 1981, pp. 82ff). See also Mortimer (1982, pp. 64–8) and Ahmad (1970, pp. 201ff), who see him rather as a modernist. Ahmad's expression, "reformist orthodox revival" (p. 211) seems to be near the mark.
3 The best book on the subject is that of Aziz Ahmad (1970). The link between Mujaddid Alf-e Thani, Shah Waliullah, Barelvi and Maudi is quite clear and insisted upon by each of them; see Maudi 1981.
4 *Ibid.*, pp. 182ff.
5 This movement is, nevertheless, described as Wahhabite by the British, as it is also by Muslim authors (Q. Ahmad 1979). This is because the term "Wahhabite", used in a pejorative sense, included all the fundamentalist "agitators" who had returned from Mecca, at the beginning of the nineteenth century, when Wahhabism was most influential. Sayyad Barelvi, like the Algerian Al-Sanussi, founder of the order of the same name, retained close links with the Sufi orders which the Wahhabites condemned, in spite of the influence exercised by the latter. There is not even any proof that there was a direct link between the two fundamentalists and the Wahhabi. For an excellent critique of the merging of Sanussi/Wahhabism see Evans-Pritchard 1949, pp. 6–11, where the reader will find a clear analogy with Afghan fundamentalist Sufism.

6 See chapter 2.

7 For an account of the theory of the caliphate in the Sunni world, see Laoust 1977, pp. 430ff. For the position of Waliullah, see Ahmad 1970, p. 206.

8 See amongst others Maleek 1980, ch. 6.

9 See Ahmad 1967, pp. 104ff and Minault 1983, pp. 25ff.

10 Adamec 1975, p. 107; see also Maleek 1980, ch. 8.

11 See Caroe 1973, ch. 13 and pp. 226ff; Elphinstone 1972, vol. 1, pp. 274ff; Ghobar 1980, pp. 313ff; Vercellin 1979, p. 70; Kakar 1979, p. xix; Aslanov (Académie . . .1981), pp. 32ff. We shall not discuss here the very individual and somewhat irrelevant interpretation which makes of the *rushani* movement the first example of the Afghan struggle for national liberation (confused with the Pashtun of the east, the very ones who had never established any institutional relations with the Afghan state). It seems that the heretical character of the *rushani* movement attracted certain thinkers who were inclined towards Marxism and wished to found an Afghan nation-state on secular grounds. The fact that the *rushani* insisted on using the everyday Pashtun language is not of any significance, since their fundamentalist adversaries (Mullah Darwaza) did the same.

12 Caroe 1973, p. 199.

13 Ahmed 1976, p. 93. This book is the best study of the charismatic mullah in the Pashtun tribes.

14 The clearest expression of this is to be found in Poullada 1973, p. 152, with regard to the uprising against Amanullah: "the rebellion was primarily political in nature and was merely an aggravated recurrence of tribal separatism". The same idea may be found in Dupree and Barth (criticized in Ahmed 1976, p. 14 and *passim*).

15 See Maleek 1980, pp. 170ff.

16 One finds cases during the war of resistance of groups who are united in a single party, but who refuse quite firmly to engage in any tactical cooperation for fear that a rival group from another tribe may gain some advantage by capturing the enemy's weapons.

17 The *shari'at* was opposed to the tribal code by the *akhund* of Swat (Ahmed 1976, p. 97). In Kunar, a *jirga* from Salarzay and Mamund called into session by the mullahs at Palangati in 1953 insisted that the *wesh* should be renounced because it was held to be contrary to the *shari'at* (oral communication). During the Rif war, 'Abdel Krim also attempted to replace tribal customs by the *shari'at*: Charnay 1984, p. 24.

18 Ahmed provides the example of a *malik* supporting the British to strengthen his local power (Ahmed 1980, p. 189). He also comes to the conclusion that the British always supported the *malik* against the charismatic religious leaders (*ibid.*, p. 70). Another example of a refusal on the part of the *khan* to wage war against the British: Ahmed 1976, p. 109.

19 For a study of a contemporary case where the two elements are interlocked, see Ahmed 1982, n. 2.

20 Caroe 1973, p. 264.

21 On the relations between Abdurrahman and some of the *'ulama* and on relations with the British see Kakar 1979, pp. 153ff.

22 On the alliance between the conservative *'ulama*, modernists and members of the Afghan establishment with regard to pan-Islamism and the support for Turkey, see Gregorian 1969, pp. 213–23, and 234–9.

23 This coalition soon split on the question of a choice of successor. The fundamentalists chose Nasrullah, brother of Habibullah (he was crowned by Mir Sayyad Jan Padshah, the successor of Hadda Mullah); while the modernists and the tribal aristocracy supported Amanullah. Upon the death of Nasrullah, Inayatullah, brother of Amanullah, was the candidate supported by the fundamentalists; his maternal grandfather was the *khan* of the Safi of Tagao, where the *naqshbandi* influence was very strong; while the maternal grandfather of Amanullah was a Barakzay (therefore a member of the Durrani aristocracy); one can see the complexity and the importance of these networks in Afghan political life (see chapter 9).

24 Gregorian 1969, p. 234.

25 See Minault 1983, p. 38. To my knowledge, this book is the only one to deal generally with the Khilafat movement.

26 The best book on the reforms carried out by Amanullah, although written from the point of view of the court, is Poullada 1973.

27 Gregorian 1969, p. 208.

28 See Bennigsen and Wimbush 1980.

29 I. Reissner, Soviet specialist on Afghanistan (Reissner 1929) described the movement of Bacha-yi Saqqao as being a peasant, revolutionary and anti-feudal movement, while the tribal revolt was presented as being more reactionary. In 1954, he described Bacha as a reactionary instrument of English imperialism (quoted in *Central Asian Review*, 4, 2, 1956, p. 198, n. 23).

30 Source: seminar "Lokale Tradition und Staatliche Reformpolitik in Mittelasien", chaired by Hölzwarth, summer 1982; review in *Bibliotheca Afghanica*.

31 This is a reference to Ghulam Mohammad Safi, one of the in-laws of Inayatullah, Amanullah's brother. Later appointed the commandant of the Safi regiment based at Mazar-i Sharif, he was involved in a revolt in favour of Inayatullah. He supported Bacha-yi Saqqao (Adamec 1975, p. 148).

32 *Ibid.*, p. 164.

33 Jakel 1977, although Poullada writes that he was self-appointed (Poullada 1973, p. 178).

34 Ghobar 1980, Poullada 1973 amongst others. Gregorian (1969) is more subtle. Stewart's book (1973) is totally absorbing.

35 Gregorian 1969, p. 276; Jakel 1977.

36 Jakel 1977.

37 It is interesting to see that the historian Ghobar, who likes to celebrate the Afghan progressive cause and who presented Bacha as the last word in obscurantism and reaction, has not been disavowed by the Islamists with regard to his general view of the march towards "enlightenment", even though they disagree with him on the subject of the revolt led by Bacha. This is

further evidence of the complexity of the relations between modernism and tradition, and thus of the falsity of the view that we are dealing with two clearly opposed camps.

38 Maududi 1981, pp. 108ff.

4 The Islamist movement up to 1978

1 Dupree 1980, p. 605; Tapper 1983, p. 41; Halliday 1980, p. 47; many others have written on the same subject (see the BIA journals).

2 The Frenchwoman Andrée Viollis, a militant of the Popular Front, was fulsome in her praise of Nadir, the new King of Afghanistan, who had triumphed both over the peasants of Shamali and the reforming King Amanullah. (Viollis 1930).

3 See Habiburrahman's speech at the demonstration of 25 February 1972 (Habiburrahman 1972).

4 Communiqué of Muslim Youth, *Karawan* (journal), 19 May 1973, Kabul.

5 R. and M. Poulton, 1979, vol. 3, pp. 64, 317ff.

6 It seems that a number of movements opposed to the Afghan regime (Islamists, but also separatist) were encouraged at that time by the Pakistanis to counter the subversion which Kabul was encouraging in Pashtun areas (in particular Hazara autonomous movements like the *tanzim*).

7 Rouinsard and Soulard 1979, p. 60.

8 Sivan 1983.

9 Maududi 1980, p. 207.

10 Bahadur 1978, p. 45.

11 Maududi 1980, p. 206.

12 See, for example, a small manual of political philosophy written by Massud's deputy at Panjshir, 'Abdul Hayy Panjshiri, *Islam, mektab-e etedal* ("Islam, school of the *juste milieu*"), which begins with a paragraph on the Hegelian dialectic.

13 Rosenthal 1971, p. 74; Bahadur 1978, p. 207.

14 CRESM 1981B, p. 230, where M. Tozy studies this problem in Morocco.

15 Significantly, one of the rare allusions of an Islamist to the Gospels has to do with the coming of the kingdom of God on earth. Quoting Matthew 6.10: "Thy Kingdom come, thy will be done on Earth *as* in Heaven", Maududi underlines the "as" (Maududi 1980, p. 177).

16 References to a political programme are scattered through the publications of *Hizb-i islami* and in the Jamiat. For an introduction to Islamist political theories in the Muslim world in general, see Fleury in CRESM 1981A, p. 183.

5 The Communist reforms and the repression, 1978–9

1 The best accounts of the communist coup are those by Arnold 1981 and 1983, Broxup 1983 and Newell 1981.

2 The ideological gap between Amin and the Tartar Sultan Galiev, president of the Muslim Military College at the time of the October revolution, was not very great. Sultan Galiev also saw the army as providing a substitute for a non-existent working class; he dreamt of an independent way to socialism that could be taken by Muslims, while at the same time he was an intransigent atheist. See Bennigsen and Lemercier-Quelquejay, 1968, pp. 98ff.

3 Speech to students on 1 February 1979 (government brochure: *Bibliotheca Afghanica*).

4 Speech of 1 January 1979 on the 14th anniversary of the 1st PDPA Congress.

5 See interview with Khalq militants in the film *Afghanistan, visa pour l'ennui* by Christophe de Pontfilly (January 1984).

6 Vercellin 1979, pp. 105ff lists the decrees.

7 The figures for the size of the various properties vary but the threshold of 20 *jerib* seems to be a general one. See *Area Handbook of Afghanistan* 1973, p. 36, quoted by Chaliand 1981; Davydov quoted by Vercellin 1979, p. 81; Etienne 1972, p. 83; see also Grevemeyer 1980, pp. 140ff.

8 Grevemeyer 1980, p. 167.

9 Ch. 1, Art. 2, par. A of Decree 8 in Vercellin 1979, p. 107.

10 Art. 5 of Decree 6; see also Etienne 1972, p. 154.

11 Olesen 1982.

12 Newell 1981, p. 81.

13 Ch. 2, Art. 7 of Decree 8 in Vercellin 1979, p. 109.

14 Grevemeyer 1980, p. 167.

15 Etienne 1982, p. 58.

16 Anderson 1978.

17 Shahrani 1980.

18 *Alifba*, course manual for the first year, Ministry of Instruction and Education, Kabul 1358 (1979).

19 Bernardin 1972.

20 For a collection of eye-witness accounts of the repressions see Barry 1980.

6 The uprisings, 1978–9

1 The best account is to be found in Schneiter 1980, pp. 237ff.

2 Another atypical conflict took place in March 1979 in Badakhshan, with the uprising of a violently anti-Pashtun Maoist organisation, the *Sitam-i milli*, led by a friend of Babrak Karmal, Taher Badakhshi, and centred on Jurm. They attacked Baharak in April. Because they met with no support from the peasants, the *sitami* were soon crushed by both the Khalq and the members of the Jamiat resistance movement. The survivors rallied to the government in 1980 (Shahrani 1980).

3 Information provided by Michel Verron, an experienced member of UNESCO at Kabul during this period.

4 As we have seen, this thesis is prominent in Marxist commentaries, as also in the writings of many Western authors with the reference to English bribes

deleted (Poullada 1973); the role of the Tajik in these events has been underestimated.

5 Shalinsky (1982) examines the way in which the Uzbek of the north feel that they belong to an ethnic group, a feeling which is found nowhere else except amongst the Hazara.

6 See Moos and Huwyler 1983.

7 Vercellin 1979, pp. 63–4.

7 The establishment of political parties

1 See Bennigsen and Lemercier-Quelquejay 1981, pp. 231ff.

2 See Adamec 1975.

3 Arnold 1981.

4 Report of P. Blanchet, in le Nouvel Observateur.

5 The *Harakat-i inqilab* was described as a "leftist" party in many works published in 1980. See amongst others "Mouvement de Soutien a la Resistance Afghane", June 1980, p. 18.

6 See appendix 1.

7 Published in *Le Monde*, 22 June 1983.

8 The development of the parties between 1980 and 1984

1 The best analysis is to be found in the unpublished report of Jean-Jose Puig (1981), the Centre for Forecast and Analysis, Ministry of Foreign Affairs, Paris.

2 On the *jam'iyyat-i 'ulama* see P. Metge, p. 12.

3 Wiegandt 1980.

4 Centlivres 1976.

5 All the literature on support movements in 1980 and 1981 expressed a belief in the reality of the independent fronts, thought to be formed into a federation by "progressive organisations" which had developed from the Maoist movement; this came either from ideological conviction or misunderstanding. In the first category we have *Afghanistan en Lutte* published by MSRA (especially the first numbers), Khalid (1980), Metge (1982), Flandrin (1981); in the second, Tapper (1983), p. 41; Francis Clerc in *Afghanistan en Lutte*, o, p. 29.

6 See No. 11, April 1984, of the review *Seda-ye Afghanistan* (in Persian), edited at Karlsruhe, by the Federation of Afghan Students Abroad.

9 The role of the Shi'a in the resistance

1 See Bacon 1951.

2 Kakar 1973.

3 According to local sources, the first president of the *shura* was Abdul Wahid Sarabi, a former minister and native of Ghazni. He seems to have gone over to Amin's government one month after his election. I have not been able to assess the truth of this.

4 Temirkhanov 1972.
5 A. Stepanov: "Springtime in Herat", in *Temps Nouveaux*, April 1983.

10 Society and the war

1 Before the war there was no uncontrolled growth around the capital city, resulting in urban sprawl. Premonitory signs appeared in the sixties, but Afghanistan does not have the characteristics of an underdeveloped country; the birth rate has not exceeded the growth rate, the level of economic activity is low and the economy is only in part a money-based one. See Lacoste 1967.
2 There are numerous specific studies on the refugee problem, in particular Viguie 1982.
3 Pickthall 1930: VIII /74 and IV /97.
4 Ferdinand 1962.
5 See the somewhat theoretical but very interesting study by Allan and Stahel (1983).

11 From freedom fighter to guerilla

1 For a recent case, see Ahmed 1980, pp. 155–9.
2 *Ibid.*, pp. 67ff.

12 Military operations

1 See A. Davlekanov in *Izvestia*, 3 August 1983. The government in Kabul has also accused Iran of having provided aerial support for the Mujahidin in Nimruz, but an accusation of this kind has never been levelled against Pakistan. (See, as one example amongst many, *Kabul New Times*, 12 October 1983.)

14 Cultural patterns and changes in society: an assessment

1 The psychological motivation for such local commanders is the personal ideal of a traditional notable; it has been well described by Whitney Azoy, *Buzkashi: Game and Power in Afghanistan*, University of Pennsylvania Press, 1982, ch. 2.
2 For a similar process of transformation of a political group into a network of people united by familial links forged after the establishing of the group as a political entity, see the case of *parcham*: Olivier Roy, "Le double code afghan, Marxisme et tribalisme", *Revue Française de Science Politique*, December 1986. For ethnic identity as a dynamic process, see Pierre Centlivres and Micheline Centlivres-Demont, *Et si on parlait de l'Afghanistan?*, Maison des Sciences de l'Homme, Paris 1989, pp. 9–77; Jean-Pierre Digard (ed.), *Le Fait ethnique en Iran et Afghanistan*, CNRS, Paris, 1988; Azoy, *Buzkashi*, p. 32.
3 See Pierre Centlivres, "Les Ouzbek du Qataghan", *Afghanistan Journal*, 2 (1), 1975; this paper is one of the most informative on Uzbek ethnic identity in Afghanistan.

4 Personal observation, August 1987.
5 See Pierre Centlivres and Micheline Centlivres-Demont "Hommes d'influence et hommes de partis: L'organisation politique dans les villages de réfugiés afghans au Pakistan", in Grötzbach (ed.) *Neue Beiträge zur Afghanistanforschung*, Bibliotheca Afghanica, Liestal, 1988.

Bibliography

Abd el-Krim et la République du Rif, 1976: group authorship, Maspero.

Abdurrahman, 1980: *The Life of Abdurrahman* (1st edn, 1900), Oxford University Press, Karachi.

Academie des Sciences de l'URSS, 1981: *L'Afghanistan: le passé et le présent*, Moscow.

Adamec, Ludwig, 1967: *Afghanistan 1900–1923*, University of California Press, Berkeley.

1975: *Who's Who in Afghanistan*, Akademische Druck und Verlagsanstalt, Graz.

Afghanistan Journal, 1976–1982, appears four times per year, Graz.

AFRANE, from 1980: *Les Nouvelles d'Afghanistan*, periodical, Paris.

Ahmad, Aziz, 1967: *Islamic modernism in India and Pakistan*, Oxford University Press.

1970: *Studies in Islamic Culture in the Indian Environment*, Oxford University Press, Pakistan (st edn 1964, Oxford).

Ahmad, Qeyamuddin, 1979: *The Wahabi movement in India*, National Book Foundation, Islamabad.

Ahmed, Akbar, 1976: *Millennium and Charisma among Pathans*, Routledge and Kegan Paul, London.

1980: *Pukhtun Economy and Society*, Routledge and Kegan Paul, London.

1982: "Order and conflict in Muslim Society: a case study from Pakistan", *Middle East Journal*, 36, 2.

Ahmed A. and Hart D., 1984: *Islam in Tribal Societies*, Routledge and Kegan Paul, London.

Algar, Hamid, 1976: "The Naqshbandi Order", *Studia Islamica*, 44.

Allan P. and Stahel A., 1983: "Tribal guerilla warfare against a Colonial power", *Journal of Conflict Resolution*, 27, 4, pp. 590ff.

Allworth, E., ed., 1967: *Central Asia: a Century of Russian Rule*, Columbia University Press, New York.

Anderson, Jon, 1975: "Tribe and community among the Ghilzay Pashtun", *Anthropos*, 70.

1978: "'There are no *khans* anymore'", *Middle East Journal*, 32.

1983: "Khan and Kheyl: dialectics of Pushtun tribalism", in Tapper 1983.

Arnold, Anthony, 1981: *Afghanistan, the Soviet Invasion in Perspective*, Hoover Institution.
   1983: *Afghanistan's Two-Party Communism*, Hoover Press.
Azoy, Whitney, 1982: *Buzkashi*, University of Pennsylvania Press.
Babur, 1980: *Le Livre de Babur* (*c.* 1589), Publications Orientalistes de France, Paris.
Bacon, Elizabeth, 1951: "The inquiry into the history of the Hazara Mongols of Afghanistan", *Southwestern Journal of Anthropology*, 7.
Bahadur, Kalim, 1978: *The Jama'at-i-islami of Pakistan*, Progressive Books, Lahore.
Balland, Daniel, 1982: "Contraintes écologiques et fluctuations historiques dans l'organisation territoriale des nomades d'Afghanistan", *Production pastorale et société*, 11.
Barfield, Thomas, 1981: *The Central Asian Arabs of Afghanistan*, University of Texas Press.
Barry, Mike, 1971: *Afghanistan*, Editions du Seuil, Paris.
   1980: "Repression et guerre soviétiques", *Temps modernes*, July/August.
   1984: *Le Royaume de l'Insolence*, Flammarion, Paris.
Bibliotheca Afghanica
Bennigsen, Alexandre and Lemercier-Quelquejay, Chantal, 1968: *L'Islam en Union Soviétique*, Payot, Paris.
   1980: "L'expérience soviétique en pays musulman: les leçons du passé et l'Afghanistan", *Politique etrangère*, 4.
   1981: *Les Musulmans oubliés*, Maspero, Paris.
Bennigsen, A. and Wimbush, Enders, 1980: *Muslim National Communism in the Soviet Union* (1st ed. 1979), The University of Chicago Press, Chicago and London.
Bernardin, 1972 (?): "Enseignement et aide internationale en Afghanistan", *Coopération technique*, 68.
BIA (Bureau International Afghanistan), from February 1981: *La Lettre du BIA*, Paris.
Blanc, Jean-Charles, 1976: *L'Afghanistan et ses populations*, PUF, Paris.
Bradsher, Henry, 1983: *Afghanistan and the Soviet Union*, Duke University Press.
Broxup, Marie, 1983: "The Soviets in Afghanistan: the anatomy of a takeover", *Central Asian Survey*, 1, 4.
Cahen, Claude, 1970: *L'Islam, des origines jusqu'à l'Empire Ottoman*, Bordas, Paris.
Canfield, Robert, undated: *Hazara Integration into the Afghan Nation*, Occasional Paper 3, Asian Society, New York.
   1973: *Faction and Conversion in a Plural Society*, Anthropological Papers, 50, Ann Arbor, Michigan.
Caroe, Olaf, 1973: *The Pathans* (1st edn. 1958), Oxford University Press, Karachi.
Carre, O. and Michaud, G., 1983: *Les Frères musulmans*, Julliard, Paris.

Bibliography

Carrère d'Encausse, Hélène, 1966: *Réforme et révolution chez les Musulmans de l'empire russe*, Presses de la Fondation nationale des sciences politiques, Paris.

Castagne, Joseph, 1925: *Les Basmatchis,* Leroux, Paris.

Centlivres, Pierre, 1972: *Un Bazar d'Asie Centrale*, Ludwig Reichert, Wiesbaden.

    1976: "Problèmes d'identité ethnique dans le Nord de l.Afghanistan", *Iran moderne*, l'Asiathèque, Paris.

Centlivres, P. and Micheline, 1980: "Et si on parlait de l'Afghanistan?", *Actes de la recherche en sciences sociales*, 34, Paris.

    1981: "Village en Afghanistan", *Commentaire*, 16, Julliard, Paris.

Central Asian Review, 1953–1968, Vols. 1–16.

Central Asian Survey, from July 1982, Oxford.

CEROAC, 1980: *La Syrie d'aujourd'hui*, Éditions du CNRS, Paris.

Chaliand, Gérard, 1981: *Rapport sur la résistance afghane*, Berger-Levrault, Paris.

Charnay, J.P., 1984: *Technique et Géosociologie*, Anthropos, Paris.

Christensen, Asger, 1980: "The Pashtuns of Kunar", *Afghanistan Journal*, 3.

Cockburn, Andrew, 1983: *The Threat: Inside the Soviet Military Machine*, Random House, New York.

CRESM, 1981A: *Islam et Politique au Maghreb*, Éditions du CNRS, Paris.

    1981B: *Le Maghreb musulman en 1979*, Éditions du CNRS, Paris.

Daoud, Zemaray, 1982: *L'Etat monarchique dans la formation sociale afghane*, Peter Lang, Berne and Frankfurt.

Davies, Collin, 1975: *The Problem of the North-West Frontier* (1st ed. 1932), Curzon Press, London.

Delloye, Isabelle, 1980: *Des femmes d'Afghanistan*, Éditions des Femmes, Paris.

Dupree, Louis, 1964–79: a number of articles in the *Reports* of the American Universities Field Staff, New York.

    1980: *Afghanistan* (1st ed. 1973), Princeton University Press.

Edelberg, L., and Jones, S., 1979: *Nuristan*, Akademische Druck-und Verlaganstalt, Graz.

Einzmann, Harald, 1977: *Religioses Volksbrauchtum in Afghanistan*, Franz Steiner, Wiesbaden.

Elias, N., 1886: *Report of a Mission to Chinese Turkestan and Badakhshan*, Calcutta.

Elphinstone Mountstuart, 1972: *An Account of the Kingdom of Caubul* (1st ed. 1815), Oxford University Press.

Esposito, John *et al.*, 1980: *Islam and Development*, Syracuse University Press.

Etienne, Gilbert, 1965: "L'Economie de l'Afghanistan", *Tiers-Monde*, 24.

    1972: *L'Afghanistan ou les aléas de la Coopération*, PUF, Paris.

    1982: *Développement rural en Asie*, PUF, Paris.

Evans-Pritchard, E.E., 1949: *The Sanusi of Cyrenaica*, Oxford University Press.

Expedit, Bernard, 1981: "Géographie et histoire militaire: la crise afghane", *Stratégique*, December.

Ferdinand, Klaus, 1962: "Nomad expansion and commerce in Central Afghanistan", *Folk*, 4, Copenhagen.

Flandrin, Philippe, 1981: "La Guerre du peuple afghan", *La Croix*, 27/28 November, 1/2 December.

Franceschi, Patrice, 1980: *Ils ont choisi la liberté*, Artaud, Paris.

Fullerton, John, 1983: "The Soviet occupation of Afghanistan", *Far Eastern Economic Review*, Hong Kong.

Gafourov, B. *et al.*, 1975: *L'Asie Centrale des temps modernes*, Novosti, Moscow.

Gardet, Louis, 1977: *Les Hommes de l'Islam*, Hachette, Paris.

Gentelle, Pierre, 1979: "L'Afghanistan et l'aide internationale", *Tiers-Monde*, 80.

Ghobar, Mir Gholam, 1980: *Afghanistan dar masir-é târikh* (1st ed. 1958), Tehran.

Glaubitt, Klaus, 1979: *Effekte staatlicher Aktivitat in Entwiklungslandern*, Erdmann, Tubingen and Basle.

Grassmuck, G. *et al.*, 1969: *Afghanistan, Some New Approaches*, University of Michigan.

Gregorian, Vartan, 1969: *The Emergence of Modern Afghanistan*, Stanford University Press.

Grevemeyer, Jan-Heeren, 1980:"'Afghanistan: das 'Neue Modell einer revolution' und der dorfliche Widerstand", *Mardomnameh*, Frankfurt-am-Main.

Guillo A., Puig J.J. and Roy O., 1983: "La guerre en Afghanistan: modifications des déplacements traditionnels de populations et émergence de nouveaux types de circulation", *Ethnologica Helvetica*, 7, Berne.

Habiburrahman (Engineer), 1972: *Afshâ-ye dasâyes-é estema'r dar manteqe*, Jamiat-é islami, Tehran.

Halliday, Fred, 1978: "Revolution in Afghanistan", *New Left Review*, 112.

1980: "Guerre et révolution en Afghanistan", *Critique communiste*, 32.

Hammond, Thomas, 1984: *Red Flag over Afghanistan*, Westview Press, Colorado.

Harrison, Selig, 1981: *In Afghanistan's Shadow*, Carnegie Endowment for International Peace.

Ibrahim, Amr, 1983: "Laicité, religiosité et politiques islamistes", *Esprit*, 5/6.

Institut Francais de Polemologie, 1984: *La guerre d'Afghanistan*, Symposium (publication forthcoming), Documentation Française.

Jakel, 1977: "Reform und Reaktion im Afghanistan", *Mardomnameh*, 3.

Jentsch, Christoph, 1973: *Das Nomadentum in Afghanistan*, Anton Hain, Meisenheim-am-Glan.

Jones, Schuyler, 1984: *Men of Influence in Nuristan*, London.

Kakar, Hasan, 1973: "The pacification of the Hazaras of Afghanistan", Afghanistan Council, Occasional Paper, 4.

1979: *Government and Society in Afghanistan*, University of Texas Press.

Kepel, Gilles, 1984: *Le Prophète et Pharaon*, La Découverte, Paris.

Khalid, Detlev, 1980A: "Afghanistan's struggle for national liberation", *Internationales Asienforum*, 11, Munich.

1980B: "Antiparlementarische und antidemokratischen Positionen in der politischen Philosophie des Islam", in Steul 1980.

Khallili, Khallilulah, 1983: *Ayyar az Khorasan*, Pakistan.

Kolzwarth (seminar led by), 1982: "Lokale Tradition und Staatliche Reformpolitik im Mittel Asien", Berlin, unpublished.

Lacoste, Yves, 1967: "Kaboul", *Bulletin de l'Association des géographes français*, 355/56.

Laoust, Henri, 1977: *Les schismes dans l'islam*, Payot, Paris.

Leca, Jean, 1984: "L'hypothèse totalitaire dans les pays du Tiers-Monde: les pays arabo-islamiques", *Totalitarismes*, Economica, Paris.

Maleek, Hafeez, 1980: *Moslem Nationalism in India and Pakistan*, People's Publishing House, Lahore.

Mardomnameh *et al.*, 1980: *Revolution in Iran und Afghanistan*, Syndikat, Frankfurt.

Maududi, S.A., 1980: *Islamic Law and Constitution*, Islamic Publications, Lahore.

1981: *A Short History of the Revivalist Movement in Islam*, (1st ed. 1955), Islamic Publications, Lahore.

Metge, P., 1981–2: "La Resistance dans le Nimruz", *Afghanistan en Lutte*, 6.

1983: "Quand l'aide étrangére fait obstacle à l'unite", *Le Monde diplomatique*, April.

Minault, Gail, 1983: *The Khilafat Movement*, Columbia University Press.

Mitchell, R.P., 1969: *The Society of the Muslim Brotherhood*, Oxford University Press.

Moos, Iren von and Huwyler, E., 1983: "Entvolkerung eines Bergtales in Nordostafghanistan", *Ethnologica Helvetia*, 7, Zürich.

Mortimer, Edward, 1982: *Faith and Power*, Faber and Faber, London.

MSRA, from 1980: *Afghanistan en lutte*, Paris.

Newell, Richard, 1972: *The Politics of Afghanistan*, Cornell University Press.

1981: *The Struggle for Afghanistan*, Cornell University Press.

Olesen, A., 1982: "The Musallis: the graincleaners of east Afghanistan", *Afghanistan Journal*, 1, p. 28.

Panjshiri, Abdul Hayy, undated: *Islam, mektab-é e'tedâl*, Jamiat-é islami, Tehran.

Pickthall, Marmaduke, 1930: *The Glorious Koran*, Allen and Unwin, London.

Poullada, Leon, 1973: *Reform and Rebellion in Afghanistan, 1919–1929*, Cornell University Press.

Poulton, M. and R., 1979: "Ri-Jang, un village tadjik dans le Nord de l'Afghanistan", thesis, EHESS.

Puig, Jean-José, 1980: "Genèse d'une résistance", *Les Temps modernes*, July/August.

1984: IFP Symposium papers (forthcoming).

Reissner, I., 1929: "Die Lehren der Bauernbewegung in Afghanistan", *Agrar Problem*, Munich.

Rives, Georges, 1963: "Les problèmes fondamentaux du droit rural afghan", *Revue internationale de droit comparé*.

Robertson, George, 1975: *The Kafir of the Hindu-Kush* (1st ed. 1896), Oxford University Press.

Rosenthal, E., 1971: *Studia semitica: Islamic Themes*, Cambridge University Press.

Rossignol, Gilles, 1974: "Les institutions afghanes et le droit musulman traditionnel", thesis, University of Paris I.

Rouinsard and Soulard, 1979: "Les premiers pas du socialisme en Afghanistan", *Le Monde diplomatique*, January.

Roy, Olivier, 1981: "Afghanistan, la guerre des paysans", *Révoltes logiques*, 13.
    1982: "Intellectuels et *ulemâ* dans la résistance afghane", *Peuples méditerranéens*, 21.
    1984: "Les techniques de pacification soviétique", IFP symposium, Documentation française (publication forthcoming).

Rubinstein, Alvin, 1982: *Soviet Policy toward Turkey, Iran and Afghanistan*, Praeger, New York.

Schimmel, Annemarie, 1975: *Mystical Dimensions of Islam*, University of North Carolina Press.

Schinasi, May, 1979: *Afghanistan at the Beginning of the Twentieth Century*, Istituto Universitario Orientale, Naples.

Schneiter, Vincent, 1980: "La guerre de libération nationale au Nouristan", *Les Temps modernes*, July/August.

Scott, R. (n.d.) "Tribal and ethnic groups in the Helmand Valley", Occasional paper, Afghanistan Council.

Shahrani, Nazif, 1980: "Causes and context of differential reactions in Badakhshan to the Saur Revolution", *Revolutions and Rebellions in Afghanistan*, symposium of the American Anthropological Association, Washington.

Shalinksy, Audrey, 1982: "Islam and ethnicity: the Northern Afghanistan perspective", *Central Asian Survey*, 1, 2/3.

Shayegan, Daryush, 1982: *Qu'est-ce qu'une révolution religieuse?*, Les Presses d'Aujourd'hui, Paris.

Sivan, E., 1983: "Ibn Taymiyya: father of the Islamic Revolution", *Encounter*, May.

Stepanov, A. 1983: "Springtime in Herat", *Temps nouveaux*, April.

Steul, Willi, 1981: *Pashtunwali*, Franz Steiner, Wiesbaden.
    1980: *Im Namen's Allah*, Ullstein Buch, Frankfurt.

Stewart, Rhea Talley, 1973: *Fire in Afghanistan 1914–1929*, Doubleday, New York.

Tapper, Richard, ed., 1983: *The Conflict of Tribe and State in Iran and Afghanistan*, Croom Helm.

Temirkhanov, L. 1972: *Khazarejtsi*, Nauka, Moscow.

Temps modernes, 1980: Afghanistan, special number July/August.

Velter, Delloye and Lamothe, 1979: *Les Bazars de Kaboul*, Hier et Demain, Paris.

Vercellin, Giorgio, 1979: *Afghanistan 1973–1978: dalla republica presidenziale alla republica democratica*, Universita degli Studi di Venezia, Venice.

Victor, Jean-Christophe, 1983: *La cité des murmures*, Lattès, Paris.

Bibliography

Viguie, Gérard, 1982: "Le problème des réfugiés afghans", MS. report, Ministry of Agriculture, Paris.

Viollis, Andrée, 1930: *Tourmente sur l'Afghanistan*, Librairie Valois, Paris.

Wiegandt, W.F., 1980: *Nicht aus heiterem Himmel*, Orell Füssli, Zürich.

Index

Index

LaVergne, TN USA
16 November 2009
164237LV00002B/29/A